THE PLASTIC BANKNOTE

FROM CONCEPT TO REALITY

DAVID SOLOMON AND TOM SPURLING

PUBLISHING

National Library of Australia Cataloguing-in-Publication entry

Solomon, David, author.

The plastic banknote: from concept to reality/David Solomon and Tom Spurling.

9780643094277 (paperback)
9781486300327 (epdf)
9781486300334 (epub)

Includes bibliographical references and index.

Bank notes.
Polymers.
Inventions – Australia.

Spurling, Tom, author.

769.559

Published by

CSIRO Publishing
36 Gardiner Road, Clayton VIC 3168
Private Bag 10, Clayton South VIC 3169
Australia

Telephone: [+613] 9545 8555
Local call: 1300 788 000 (Australia only)
Fax: +61 3 9662 7555
Email: csiropublishing@csiro.au
Website: www.publishing.csiro.au

Front cover (from top): A representation of a current $10 Australian banknote; Australian currency notes (Jan Hopgood/Shutterstock.com)
Back cover: $7 banknote courtesy of David Solomon

Set in Adobe Garamond Pro 10.5/13.5
Edited by Adrienne de Kretser, Righting Writing
Cover design by Andrew Weatherill
Typeset by Desktop Concepts Pty Ltd, Melbourne
Index by Indexicana
Printed by Ingram Lightning Source

Feb26_RP_ILS

Foreword

It is an honour to have the opportunity to commend Dr Solomon and Dr Spurling for this account of the evolution of the plastic banknote – a technology now accepted virtually worldwide and one to which Dr Solomon has made such a scientific and practical contribution.

I myself was present during the development of the polymer banknote on two important occasions.

First, in 1968 I accompanied Dr H.C. Coombs, then Governor of the Reserve Bank of Australia – the note-issuing authority for Australia – to a meeting he had convened of 'all the talents' involved at the time in banknote production and issue. The meeting was called due to the discovery of a high-quality counterfeit of a very recent banknote issue by the Reserve Bank.

What to do? Discussion produced many suggestions but, as this book records, all had to be rejected, including some promising ones, because they could not be incorporated in the paper substrate of the notes. There was a dejected silence around the table. This silence was broken by Dr Solomon's comment that 'paper was not the only possible substrate'. He instanced polymer. The meeting broke up with great relief and hope for the future. Thus began the polymer period!

My other involvement was in 1986 when, as Reserve Bank Governor, I had the privilege of authorising the issue of the polymer note. Even after several years of development of the new technology, Australia was the only country in the world to try it and therefore would have faced a very public embarrassment if the note proved to be a failure!

The first public issue in 1988 coincided with the 200th anniversary of the arrival of the First Fleet and the note was given commemorative status, which led to substantial sales. Fears of failure proved unfounded. The banknotes were well received by the public! International usage of the new process followed quickly.

This was a very happy outcome for the CSIRO and the Reserve Bank who had worked together throughout. It would be un-Australian to suggest that there were no occasions when there were differences of opinion along the path which led to the ultimately resounding success of the polymer note. But there was no difference of opinion about the major contribution of Dr Solomon.

I wish the authors great success with this book.

Robert A. Johnston AC

Dr Solomon and Mr Johnston at the opening of the RBA Museum of Australian Currency Notes, March 2005. Reproduced courtesy of the Reserve Bank of Australia.

Contents

Preface

This is the story of the Reserve Bank of Australia and CSIRO working together to produce the world's most secure and durable banknotes. It was known within CSIRO as 'the Bank project', and was one of the organisation's longest and most successful projects. It is the story as told by the CSIRO leader of the project and its principal scientist and by one of the scientists involved in the project who has a deep interest in the history of Australian science and innovation.

The project to develop more secure banknotes commenced in 1968 following the 1966 discovery of forgeries of the new Australian decimal currency. Our story ends in 1988 with the release of the $10 bicentennial commemorative banknote. Of course the search for more secure banknote technology never ends.

Our account draws upon personal recollections of events and the archived CSIRO records of the project. It is therefore very much the story of the project not only from a CSIRO point of view but from the point of view of two people intimately involved in the project.

We hope that our account will do two things. The first is to convey not only the fun and excitement of doing highly applicable science but also the frustration and hard work involved in bringing ideas to the market place.

The second is to show how CSIRO contributes to the nation's economic and social well-being by conducting 'market pull' projects. Such projects were rare at Fishermens Bend in the 1960s and 1970s. Indeed, the Bank project was one of the first genuine 'market pull' projects in CSIRO. In 1968 there were no scientists in CSIRO working on projects to make more secure banknotes with the idea of contacting a banknote producer to see if they were interested in such an invention. CSIRO was given the problem by the Bank and had to assemble all the skills and disciplines needed to solve the problem. This meant that, in addition to having to enlist his chemists to work on the project, one of the authors had to recruit physicists and engineers to his Division of Applied Organic Chemistry. In those days there was little incentive for other parts of the Organisation to lend their skills to the project. This is not the case in the modern CSIRO. Neither is the flexibility that the 1970s Chief had to muster resources. CSIRO knows that it needs to constantly review and modify its approach to the users of its research. There is no answer to this perennial question. We hope that our book will allow the modern organisation to learn from its illustrious past.

We wish to acknowledge the assistance of Dr Emma Prime in producing many of the diagrams in the book and for her helpful suggestions for improving the manuscript.

We thank Adam Shand for giving us the image of the counterfeit banknote in Plate 2.

Plates 7 and 12 are from: Prime EL and Solomon DH (2010) Australia's plastic banknotes: fighting counterfeit Currency. *Angewandte Chemie International Edition* **49**, 3726–3736. Copyright Wiley-VCH Verlag GmbH & Co. KGaA. Reproduced with permission.

We are very grateful to John Manger and the staff of CSIRO Publishing for their patience with us during the writing of the book and for the great contributions of the editorial staff.

David Solomon and Tom Spurling

About the authors

Dave Solomon joined CSIRO in 1963 with a unique background for those times; he had 17 years industrial experience. This was obtained at BALM Paints, now Dulux, where he worked in all aspects of paint production including quality control, development and research. Work on paint sparked his interest in polymers and he has been recognised both nationally (Prime Minister's Prize in 2011) and internationally (Fellow of Royal Society 2004) for his work in this area. While at BALM Paints he invented a new polymer system and was seconded to ICI Paints Division in England to further develop that work. His industrial experience had taught him the importance of intellectual property protection and about the restrictive licence agreements that local companies had with their overseas licensors. These generally prohibited local inventions from being commercialised in Australia. At CSIRO Solomon had patented an invention and spent 12 months at a US company introducing that invention.

The Bank project provided a unique opportunity to fulfil Solomon's desire for a local industry founded on Australian science and exporting to the world. His work in developing the world's first plastic banknote has been recognised by a number of national and international awards including the Australian Bicentennial Science

Dr Solomon receiving the Australian Bicentennial Achievement Award. Left to right: W.T. Mulligan, General Manager, Crown Corning Science Products Division, Dr D.H. Solomon and Dr C.M. Adam, Director, CSIRO Institute of Industrial Technologies.

Achievement Award, the Ian Wark Medal of the Australian Academy of Science (1989) and the Sellafield Ltd Award for Engineering Excellence (2007) of the Institute of Chemical Engineering in the UK. He shared the 1987 CSIRO Chairman's Medal with Don Addison of the Bank.

Tom Spurling joined CSIRO at Fishermens Bend in November 1969 and heard about a secret project soon after. He was involved in some of the diffraction grating work, in psycho-physical testing for the 'feel' of a banknote and in the sale of the project to the Reserve Bank. He succeeded Dave Solomon as Chief of the CSIRO Division of Chemicals and Polymers in 1989 and was then involved in the CSIRO interactions with Note Printing Australia. In 1991 he commissioned the Australian Science Archives to collect and archive all records of the project still in the possession of CSIRO officers. His ambition was to write a history of the project from the point of view of a CSIRO observer. He retired from CSIRO in 2003 to join Swinburne University of Technology and is now the Director of the Centre for Transformative Innovation at Swinburne. He has been a CSIRO Board Member since 2008.

Timeline of major events and meetings

14 February 1966: Decimal currency introduced.

8 April 1968: Dr H.C. Coombs' meeting with selected scientists in Melbourne to discuss banknote security issues.

16 June 1968: Dr H.C. Coombs' second meeting at Thredbo.

10 December 1968: The Bank agrees to support CSIRO research on producing a more secure banknote.

9 June 1971: CSIRO sent report to the Bank including Dr D.H. Solomon's 'Sample 8'.

21 February 1972: Meeting to discuss the Bank's response to the CSIRO's report; M.F.W. Brown produces his plastic note.

27 July 1973: Dr S.D. Hamann and Dr D.H. Solomon invited to an informal luncheon with the Governor of the Bank to discuss aspects of the polymer note project.

16 September 1974: Major presentation of the project to the Governor, at which the Bank accepted responsibility for the project. It became the Currency Notes Research and Development (CNRD) project.

2 October 1974: Dr D.H. Solomon takes the CSIRO project team to a three-day planning workshop at Mornington. This became known as the 'Mornington think tank'.

13 August 1976: The CNRD Committee agrees to the specifications of a prototype banknote. This is known as the 'design freeze'.

26 February 1979: The Bank establishes the Forward Planning Group chaired by Professor Tom Fink.

1 August 1982: R.A. Johnston appointed Governor of the Reserve Bank of Australia.

26 January 1988: The $10 commemorative polymer banknote is released.

Chapter 1
Introduction

Contact

'Have you got any ideas on how to make a better banknote?' asked Dr J.R. (Jerry) Price as he walked into the office of Dr Dave Solomon in the CSIRO research laboratories at Fishermens Bend on 25 March 1968.[1] Dr Price was the Chairman of CSIRO and Dr Solomon a polymer scientist in the CSIRO Division of Applied Mineralogy, recently recruited from BALM Paints Pty Ltd (now Dulux Pty Ltd).

'The budget can't be that bad' would have been the smart reply. What Solomon actually said was 'What about plastic paper?' to which Price replied, 'That sounds all right. Why don't you get some samples?' The occasion was the defining moment in Solomon's career, the careers of many CSIRO scientists, the history of banknote technology and the commercialisation practices of CSIRO.

Professor Ken McCracken reports a more dramatic incident.[2]

> The phone rang.
> 'Professor McCracken?'
> 'Yes.'
> 'Professor Ken McCracken?'
> 'Yes, that's right.'
> 'You are in the Physics Department of the University of Adelaide, and have worked for NASA in the USA?'

McCracken began to wonder what the man was up to. It didn't get any clearer.

> 'Could I come and discuss something with you?'
> 'What will it be about?'
> 'Oh, I'm sorry, I can't tell you that.'
> 'Well, whom do you represent?'
> 'I can't tell you that either.'

Professor McCracken eventually agreed to the meeting.

Price and McCracken's visitor explained that the Reserve Bank of Australia ('the Bank'), in particular its Governor, Dr H.C. (Nugget) Coombs, was very concerned about the quality of the recent $10 forgeries and was seeking ideas from some of Australia's leading scientists on how to produce a more secure banknote. This book is the story of the project that emerged from those discussions, that eventually led to the introduction of plastic banknotes in Australia and subsequently many other countries. We refer to this as the 'Bank project'.

The introduction of decimal currency

The 1966 decimal currency, both banknotes and coins, was important in the development of a more independent Australia. In his policy speech for the December 1958 election Prime Minister Robert Menzies announced on behalf of the government that 'We accept the principle of decimal coinage. We will set up an independent committee to advise how and when and on what terms to effect this reform.'[3] The committee was formed in February 1959 and reported in August 1960, recommending firmly in favour of decimal currency. The government took until April 1963 to announce that it had accepted the committee's recommendations in full and February 1966 was tentatively set as the date for the introduction of the new currency. The government set up a public competition to find a name 'with an Australian flavour' for the new currency. Nearly 1000 names were suggested including 'austral', 'boomer', 'kwid' and 'ming' (the nickname of the Prime Minister). No consensus emerged and in June 1963 the government announced that it had decided to name the new currency the 'royal'. This proved most unpopular. In July 1963 the Treasurer, Harold Holt, stated to Cabinet:

> There can be no doubt that we made a very unpopular choice of name ... We selected 'royal' because it was distinctive, euphonious, met the technical considerations and had an interesting historical association with the British currency ... Of the choices open to us the least unsatisfactory – uncomfortable and embarrassing though it might be – is to admit that we have misjudged the public acceptability of 'royal', that we recognise the controversy surrounding it has greatly strengthened public support for 'dollar', and that in a matter where members of the public are so directly and personally involved, we should meet what we have gathered to be a wish for a change to 'dollar'.[4]

Cabinet agreed and on 19 September 1963 the government announced that 'dollar' would be the name of the new currency.[5]

The Bank decided to attempt the ambitious task of designing a new series of banknotes and producing and distributing them by Decimal-Day, 14 February 1966. It acted quickly and decisively. It appointed Russell Drysdale as artistic adviser and commissioned four artists (Gordon Andrews, Richard Beck, Max Forbes and George Hamori) to prepare preliminary designs. The designs by Gordon Andrews were accepted and in April 1964 detailed designs were commenced in Milan by the specialist banknote printing firm Organisation Giori. New banknote printing machinery was obtained from Thomas De La Rue of the UK and the first banknotes were produced in June 1965.[6] The changeover to the new currency was well planned and executed, including a very effective public education campaign. By April 1966 most of the imperial banknotes had been withdrawn from circulation. The public acceptance of the change from pounds, shillings and pence to dollars and cents, the bold new banknotes, was better than the Bank had expected.

The new banknotes were state of the art in terms of security and resistance to forgery attempts. The $10 banknote of 1966 is shown in Plate 1. It was made with quality paper (a so-called rag paper made out of cotton and linen fibres). Security features included a watermark ~25 mm square and a metallised plastic thread which ran through the banknote, both introduced during manufacture of the paper, and quality printing called intaglio, which gives a raised print profile and contributes to the characteristic feel of a quality entity such as a banknote. Intaglio printing requires expensive equipment not readily available to small forgery groups.

Forgeries!

It took less than a year for forgers to pass a fake $10 banknote. Forgers don't have to reproduce a banknote accurately; they only need to produce a simulation that is good enough for at least one transaction. The 1966 forgery involved ordinary paper purchased at a regular office supply outlet, and no intaglio printing. The forged notes had no watermark and no metal thread, although both were simulated during the printing process, the latter via a printing ink that contained aluminium flakes. The forgers used simple office equipment which they had modified in quite an ingenious manner, but nevertheless they had been able to forge the banknotes with readily available raw materials and equipment.

The forged banknotes resulted from a plan conceived in the south-east suburbs of Melbourne.[7] Francis Papworth, an artist from Bentleigh, got to know Jeffrey Mutton when Mutton owned a milk bar in Moorabbin and Papworth worked at a printing plant nearby. They met occasionally at the Boundary Hotel in East Bentleigh. On one of these occasions in January 1966 they discussed whether Papworth and his friends in the printing business could forge a 10 shilling banknote if Mutton could provide some finance.[8] The choice of the 10 shilling note (Fig. 1.1) was curious as forgers generally choose a higher-denomination note. They decided that it was feasible; Mutton agreed to be in the scheme and enlisted Dale Code, described in newspaper reports as either a sales representative or a tailor, with whom Mutton had business dealings. On 14 February 1966 decimal currency was introduced into Australia and they agreed that it would be easier to forge the new $10 note. They weren't daunted by the state of the art security. One of Papworth's friends, Ronald Adam, a photographer from Ferntree

Fig. 1.1: A 10 shilling banknote.

Gully, needed about $800 to buy a lens to photograph the genuine notes in order to make the printing plates. Neither Mutton nor Code had that amount of cash so, without informing Papworth, they approached a 'safe-breaker' known to Mutton to finance the scheme. Mutton gave evidence to a court hearing in 1969 that the person was Robert 'Bert' Kidd.[9] The safe-breaker agreed on the condition that he had complete control of the distribution of the forged notes. Mutton and Code agreed to that condition but never intended to honour the agreement. However, if they had followed the professional criminal's plan the outcome could well have been much more successful for the forgers. Kidd's plan was to buy opals from the opal fields with the forged notes and then sell the opals for cash. The rest of the forged notes would be sent to moneychangers in Hong Kong, who would not be familiar with the new Australian notes.

When Papworth's printer pulled out of the scheme Code decided that he could learn enough about printing to do it himself. With the underworld figure's cash, Code and Mutton purchased a Gestetner 201 four-colour offset printer and had it installed in Code's sister's garage in Beaumaris.[10] Code had one week's training from Gestetner and spent some time in the State Library studying books about printing. During this time Adam was preparing the printing plates. Papworth's only contributions were drawing the watermark on paper for Adam to photograph and touching up the printing plates. Adam was aghast when he discovered that Mutton and Code were going to do the printing themselves but gave them some advice on colours and on the technical limitations of the Gestetner machine. Mutton and Code devised ingenious modifications which reduced the number of passes needed to produce a multi-coloured banknote. They tried various types of papers before settling on Original Charter Mill paper, burning their failures in an incinerator in the backyard of Code's sister's house. By early December 1966 they had worked out how to produce a passable banknote; they classified the quality as 'A', 'B' and 'C'. It is difficult to know exactly how many banknotes they produced. There were probably about $200 000 worth of A notes, about $400 000 worth of B notes and possibly about $200 000 worth of C notes (see Plate 2). Mutton and Code thought that the notes did not 'feel' right, so at the last minute coated them with wax. Mutton and Code dismantled the printing machine after they finished the production runs. Kidd collected the dismantled parts and disposed of them.

After the notes had been printed, instead of giving them all to Kidd, the notes were divided five ways between Papworth, Mutton, Code, Adam and Kidd. Mutton buried two containers with about $170 000 in his back yard. Mutton went with the underworld figure for a drink after the distribution of the notes and saw him hand a paper bag containing six bundles of notes to three men in a car outside the hotel where they were drinking. Mutton claimed that the three men were detectives from the Malvern police. Mutton distributed his share of the notes to his friends and relations, including his brother Desmond, on Thursday 22 December. He gave his brother strict instructions not to use the notes until Friday night after the banks had closed. Desmond gave two of the notes to his wife Moira to pay for Christmas shopping but forgot to tell her not to use them until late on Friday. Moira Mutton purchased some items from a milk bar in Ashburton on the Friday afternoon. The owner thought that the notes felt different, noted Mrs Mutton's car number and notified the police. Mutton and his collaborators were charged on 30 December. If the distribution had been carried out in the more professional manner planned by Kidd the forgeries may not have been discovered so quickly.

Adam, Code and Mutton were tried and found guilty of forgery but Papworth, who had been a source of information to the police, was found not guilty. Kidd was not arrested in 1967 but was arrested in 1969 after Mutton, who was in gaol at the time, gave evidence against Kidd. In the subsequent trial Kidd was found not guilty.

There was some debate at the time as to the quality of the forged notes. On 26 December 1966 Inspector Cox of the Malvern CID declared them to be the 'best forgeries that I have ever seen' and the General Manager of the Note Issue Department (W.H. Wilcock) said 'These are pretty good forgeries by comparison with any'.[11] On 30 December an article in *The Age* commented 'The approach to Interpol seems to indicate that the expertly produced forgeries found in the past few days were produced overseas.'[12] But in the 1967 trial Montague (Monty) Frank Brown, Works Manager at the Bank's Note Printing Branch, gave evidence that there were some faults, that the notes varied in size due to poor guillotining and that they had a waxy feeling unlike genuine notes.[13] In discussions between Solomon and Brown during the Bank project to develop polymer notes Brown recalled meeting one of the forgers and quizzing him on how he modified the office printer. Brown was very impressed with the ingenuity of the modification. However, whatever the opinion of the Bank's printer on the quality of the notes, it is the public's opinion that counts. The forged notes were good enough for many to be passed into circulation from December 1966 and for Kidd's share to be passed into circulation until his arrest in 1969. Indeed, they were good enough for the Bank's Governor to call the meetings of scientists that started the long project described in this book.

Despite the early detection of the forged notes, by the middle of January 1967 more than $140 000 worth of notes had been seized by detectives and more than 1500 had been successfully passed by the 'distributors' or 'retailers'.[14] There was a period of unrest during which many people refused to accept $10 notes in normal cash transactions. In 1967 $10 was a considerable amount of money and the main method that the Bank recommended to the public to distinguish a genuine from a forged note was to look at the number. Numbering each forged note differently presents significant difficulties, as at that time forgers rarely had access to an automatic printer for the numbering. The forgers were aware of the need to have as many serial numbers as possible and used a combination of eight letter prefixes and eight numbers. The Bank recommendation to check the serial number highlights the limited value of the sophisticated security devices such as the watermark, metal thread and intaglio print. The 1966 forgeries had none of these but were nevertheless accepted by the public. Not surprisingly many, if not most, people checked the number with the intention of refusing to accept a possible forgery – anyone who handed a forged note to authorities would not receive a genuine note in return. Some members of the Amalgamated Engineering Union decided not to accept $10 notes in their pay packets, a decision supported by the union secretary, Laurie Carmichael. Carmichael argued that the workers should not have to carry the loss if they handed the notes to the authorities.[15]

Dr Coombs' response

Coombs was understandably concerned that the latest banknote security (which was the best available worldwide) had been so easily and so quickly simulated. His vision was that science should be able to put a bigger distance between what forgers could so easily simulate and what the Bank could produce. As a first step in realising this vision he visited the Head Office of the CSIRO in Melbourne with the proposal that the problem of banknote structure be investigated. Dr Fred White, Chairman of CSIRO, suggested that the Bank arrange for a group of senior scientists from CSIRO and the universities to meet the Bank's senior officers to brainstorm possible new directions for a more secure banknote technology.[16]

Coombs' response to the forgeries should be seen in the context of his overall leadership approach. In his history of the Reserve Bank, Boris Schedvin commented, 'He took a broad approach, constantly searching for ways that the system could be improved. His central theme was the possibility of social progress by the use of reason and cooperation under the leadership of gifted individuals.' Faced with the forgery,

Schedvin said that 'Typically, in one of his last initiatives as Governor, Coombs responded by seeking the assistance of leading scientists.'[17]

Schedvin's summary of the project delineates the themes of this book. He claimed:[18]

> Both the timescale of the project and the degree of technical difficulty were hopelessly underestimated, and the mood of optimism prevailing in 1974 soon evaporated. Effective relations between CSIRO and the note printing branch were not established, and it was not until the early 1980s that the development was transferred to the Bank. With the benefit of hindsight, it can now be said that the development of such complex new technology was an over-reaction to the problem of counterfeiting ... It is probably true, too, that the Bank was not particularly skilled at managing state-of-the-art product development, and for a time senior management allowed the project to drift.

With the benefit of hindsight, we can say that Coombs did not overreact to the problem of counterfeiting. International note printing authorities and associated companies all recognised the problems that colour photocopiers and technological advances would pose, and commenced research programs on new security devices. The difference between those efforts and the Bank project was the aim to both introduce new security devices and to replace paper with a polymer substrate. The technology incorporated in the plastic banknotes, while different from that incorporated in paper notes, is no more complex but is considerably more secure. In addition to having more secure banknotes, Australia now has a thriving note manufacturing industry exporting to more than 30 countries.

This book tells the story of a revolutionary change in the production of banknotes. It is a contemporary illustration of an old observation:

> Nothing is more difficult than the introduction of a new order because all who have done well under the old are enemies and those who may do well under the new, are lukewarm.
>
> *The Prince*, Niccolo Machiavelli (1469–1527)

Endnotes

1 In 1990 the CSIRO Division of Chemicals and Polymers commissioned the Australian Science Archives Project to collect, arrange, list and index the records of the Bank project that were available in CSIRO. The collection is deposited at the Australia Archives Victorian Branch, series number B5609. The collection will not be open to public access until 2019. The authors were given access to the collection by CSIRO. Documents quoted from this collection will be referenced as NAA: B5609, and the

appropriate item number. This account uses the archived documents and documents in the authors' personal possession.

2 Personal communication Spurling.

3 R.G. Menzies, federal election 1958: policy speech of the Prime Minister (the Right Hon. R.G. Menzies, CH, QC, MP) delivered in the Canterbury Memorial Hall, Victoria, on 29 October 1958. Liberal Party of Australia, Canberra, 1958, p. 30.

4 NAA: A5819 Vol. 21, Agendum 843.

5 *Canberra Times*, 19 September 1963, p. 1.

6 C.B. Schedvin (1992) *In Reserve: Central Banking in Australia, 1945–1975*. Allen & Unwin, Sydney, p. 415.

7 *The Age*, 15 March 1967, p. 8.

8 Adam Shand, 'The money changers', *The Australian*, 8 June 2012. Adam Shand has a copy of an unpublished manuscript by Jeffrey Mutton, '10 years for $10', written while Mutton was in prison. He gave the current authors access to the manuscript and some of the detail in these paragraphs comes from reading Mutton's manuscript and newspaper accounts of the trial. He also provided us with the image in Plate 2. Reports of the trial can be found in *The Age*, 31 December 1966, p. 3; 12 January 1967; p. 3; 8 March 1967, p. 3; 9 March 1967, p. 2; 10 March 1967, p. 3;15 March 1967, p. 8; 16 March 1967, p. 7; 17 March 1967, p. 3; 7 June 1967, p. 11; 9 June 1967, p. 6; 15 June 1967, p. 3; 27 June 1967, p. 8; 20 September 1967, p. 8; 25 October 1967, p. 7; 26 October 1967, p. 10; 3 November 1967, p. 6; 4 November 1967, p. 6; 10 November 1967, p. 3.

9 *The Age*, 28 February 1969, p. 10; 3 June 1969, p. 10.

10 *The Age*, 9 March 1967, p. 2.

11 *The Age*, 26 December 1966, p. 1.

12 *The Age*, 30 December 1966, p. 1.

13 *The Age*, 17 March 1967, p. 3.

14 *The Age*, 11 January 1967, p. 1.

15 *The Age*, 4 January 1967, p. 3.

16 Letter from Sir Frederick White to D.H. Solomon dated 26 April 1987 in the possession of the authors.

17 C.B. Schedvin (1992) *In Reserve: Central Banking in Australia, 1945–1975*. Allen & Unwin, Sydney, p. 416.

18 C.B. Schedvin (1992) *In Reserve: Central Banking in Australia, 1945–1975*. Allen & Unwin, Sydney, p. 417.

Chapter 2
From rum to plastic banknotes

Currency and Australian history

Currency, whether coins, banknotes or rum, has played a large role in Australia's history.[1]

When Captain Arthur Phillip landed at Sydney Cove in 1788 he had 11 ships, more than 1300 convicts, officials, crew and marines, and enough provisions to last for two years. He had very little currency, either coins or paper. He had been supplied with Netherlands' ducats to pay the Dutch officers at the ports of call and was authorised to purchase provisions at Rio de Janeiro and Cape Town with bills on the English Treasury. The colony was a gaol and it was thought that the needs of the inhabitants would be supplied by the Government Store. However, free settlers arrived, freed convicts stayed and trading ships called into the new settlement so a need for money soon emerged.

For the first decade of the colony, survival in the unfamiliar environment was the major task of the population. They soon bartered for goods and services, particularly with food and drink. Governor Phillip departed in 1792 but his successor, Captain John Hunter, did not arrive until 1795. The Lieutenant-Governors, first Francis Grose then William Paterson, used the intervening years to benefit themselves and their fellow officers in the New South Wales Corps. In particular, they used their ability to raise capital by borrowing against their regimental pay to purchase 7500 gallons (~2830 L) of rum in 1793 from the American trading ship, the *Hope*. They sold it at inflated prices and rum became a means of exchange. The trade in rum was not controlled by Governors Hunter and King and Governor William Bligh's attempt to do so resulted in his downfall in 1808. It wasn't until the arrival of Governor Lachlan Macquarie in 1810 that trade in rum was gradually brought under control.

During this time the official currency was pounds, shillings and pence but there was little of it in circulation. There were private promissory notes and IOUs, various coins and rum. In 1800 Governor King issued a proclamation defining the value of all coins (or specie) circulating in the colony. These included the Dutch guilder and ducat, the Bombay rupee, the Portuguese johannes and the English copper coin.

A variety of paper money also circulated, including store receipts (from His Majesty's Stores), banknotes and bills from England and Ireland, police fund notes and various private notes. Soon after his arrival in 1810 Governor Macquarie saw the need for a bank in the colony. The Bank of New South Wales was eventually established in 1817 (even in those days banks were slow to act) and from April 1817 it issued 5 shilling, 10 shilling, £1 and £5 banknotes. Banks were later established in Hobart and they also issued notes.

Governor Brisbane tried to establish a 'dollar system' based on the Spanish dollar but this came to an end in 1825 when the government in London proclaimed a standard sterling value in all English colonies. This could not take full effect in the colonies until a sufficient volume of the currency actually arrived in the colony. It took full effect on 7 August 1829 when Governor Darling issued a General Order which proclaimed 'that none of the Departments of Government will receive payments in Foreign Coins after 15th of the present month.'

The currency of England thus became the sole legal currency until the Commonwealth of Australia issued its own currency in 1913 (see Plate 3).[2]

The scientist, science journalist and publisher A.R. Michaelis wrote that 'Replacing the heavy and cumbersome coins with paper money of equal face value must be considered as one of man's most ingenious inventions during the last 1000 years.'[3] The Chinese invented paper, printing and paper money. The first use of paper in transactions was at the beginning of the ninth century. It was called 'flying money' but was a draft rather than real money. A merchant could deposit cash in one city and receive a paper certificate which could be exchanged for coins in a distant city. During the period of the Five Dynasties (907–979) iron coin was in circulation but its clumsiness led people to deposit it into 'deposit houses' and use their receipts in financial transactions. Under the first Emperor of the Northern Song Dynasty, 16 merchants were given permission to issue promissory notes which were printed in red and black from blocks bearing various patterns. The merchants did not always reimburse their clients and widespread protests resulted. In response the government established a Bureau of Exchange Medium in 1023 and issued the first banknotes in 1024. They involved a special 'paper' made from mulberry bark. Their printing was very elaborate and consisted of six wooden blocks, each with a unique design. Blue dyes were used to produce a distinct effect.[4] Banknotes were so readily accepted by the Chinese,that 100 years later over 70 million were in circulation. In the ensuing years various Chinese governments issued banknotes but they were often not backed by any deposits, causing inflation. Paper notes ceased circulation in China by the 15th century and did not reappear until the 18th century.

The use of banknotes in western society did not become widespread until the 16th century when goldsmiths, who had extensive vaults for the safekeeping of their precious metals, gold and silver, began to accept deposits and gave 'receipts' in exchange. With time, the receipts became tradeable. The evolution of those receipts to banknotes is described on the Bank of England website.

Today the study of banknotes is 'the most recent branch of numismatics, a scholarly subject embracing coins and medals'.[5]

Counterfeiting and forgery

Counterfeiting, whose beginnings go back centuries before banknotes, has been called the 'second-oldest profession'. Indeed it would seem that in some individuals the desire to 'beat the system' is so strong that it appears part of their genetic code. For example, one banknote forger gave as his reason the 'intellectual challenge' of producing a good forgery.

The advent of banknotes was welcomed by counterfeiters; it was a far more profitable business than reproducing coins or works of art and had a wider population or 'market' for the products. Indeed, since most banknotes cost little to produce, the successful passing of a forgery is virtually all profit. We even have an expression, 'a licence to print money', which reflects this.

The central bank's first line of defence against forgery is the general public. In each transaction the receiver of the banknote is expected to examine it carefully and be satisfied that it is genuine. This 'person in the street' recognition is a vital plank in the Reserve Bank's (the Bank) and other central banks' strategy to beat forgers. If you accept a forgery, you are the loser.

The US uses a different strategy to achieve person in the street recognition; all its banknotes are the same size and colours and it is essential to peruse the note to see the denomination. One enterprising forger used the one-size-fits-all policy and stripped the ink from a $1 and converted it to $100! Other countries rely on a policy whereby the size of the note increases with denomination. In Australia, up to and including the 1966 decimal currency, both width and length increased with the value of the banknote. This was changed in the plastic series – all have the same width but increase in length with denomination. One virtue of the variation in size is that it assists the visually impaired to identify the denomination; also, lower denominations cannot be 'converted' to higher as was done with the US banknotes.

Penalty for forgery

All societies regard forgery as a most serious crime and in past eras the penalty for it was similar to that for murder. Indeed, the earliest surviving banknote, issued by the Chinese Emperor Hung-Wu (1368–1398), carried the warning 'Whoever counterfeits notes and circulates them will be beheaded.'[6] Some countries still have the death penalty for counterfeiting.[7] There are several reasons why we consider forgery such a serious crime. Historically, banknotes carried an image of an emperor or head of state, and it was considered an insult or treason for a commoner to forge their portrait. More importantly, the state suffers a financial loss (seigniorage), which is the difference between the face value of the banknote and the production cost. For example, a $100 banknote costs only a few cents to produce so the state, in effect, suffers a $100 loss for each forgery it pays out on. Of even greater importance is that modern society needs confidence in the authenticity of currency for day-to-day living. For example, in Australia the forging of the $10 banknote in 1966 resulted in many people refusing to use or accept $10 banknotes in transactions. Finally, forgery has been and still is used as a weapon of war or conflict between nations. The most famous (or notorious) example was Nazi Germany's forgery of the Allies' currency during World War II. This massive forgery was code-named Operation Bernhard by the German SS, who aimed to flood the British and US economies with quality forgeries to disrupt their day-to-day operations and hence their war effort. The Germans used the skills of concentration camp inmates to produce printing plates and excellent forgeries which could be detected only by 'scrupulous inspection under magnification'.[8] Towards the end of the war, the Germans were producing 500 000 British notes a month. Fortunately the war ended before Operation Bernhard was fully implemented but the SS did use some forged notes to buy war equipment from neutral countries and to pay British spies. With defeat imminent, the SS dumped the forged notes and printing plates in sealed waterproof bags, along with the printing equipment, in Lake Toplitz. This lake is one of the deepest known and the SS considered the forgeries and equipment would not be recovered. However, the Allies recovered many of the notes. The lake is still a challenge and some consider that other treasures may also have been deposited in its deep waters. After the war Britain had to re-issue its currency because of the few circulating Operation Bernhard banknotes.[9]

It is a crime to buy or sell counterfeit currency. But even so, it is possible to buy Operation Bernhard notes on the internet. Interestingly, they will cost you more than the genuine notes. There's a moral in that story somewhere. Operation Bernhard was apparently Adolf Hitler's own idea but he was not the first to use forgery as a weapon of war. Milan in 1470–76 sought to undermine the Venetians by forgery and Frederick the Great used counterfeit notes during the Seven Years War. The British, during the American War of Independence, counterfeited Continental currency to such an extent that our modern language still retains the expression, 'not worth a Continental'. There are numerous other examples where governments used counterfeiting in attempts to destabilise the enemy; only selected examples are mentioned here. Napoleon forged Austrian and Russian notes to buy food and equipment during his European campaign. In modern times it has been suggested that certain countries use the threat of forging US currency when negotiating foreign aid. The US is alleged to have used counterfeiting in the war on Cuba and in Vietnam. In 2008 North Korea was accused of producing high-quality US forgeries and laundering them through the gambling houses of Macau. This was a serious threat to the US and added to the tension between the countries.[10] It has been suggested that the CIA forges currency for covert operations.[11]

Forgeries by governments use massive technical resources and are difficult to counter. Given sufficient technical resources it's possible to make quality forgeries, which are difficult to detect, of most, if not all, banknotes. Fortunately most forgeries are done by small groups with limited resources.

The US currency seems to be a target for many forgers because of its wide acceptance. Counterfeiting of the US $100 banknote had become so widespread that in 1984 the US set up a Far East Counterfeiting taskforce.[12]

Simulation not reproduction

The perfect forgery has never been detected! The forger does not need to reproduce the actual banknote, only a simulation that can be passed at least once. The forger does not need to worry about durability but must make several compromises dictated by the resources and skills available.

Banknotes have always challenged the forger in two technical areas: the printing and design and the material on which it is printed (the substrate). Forgers usually find it difficult or impractical to produce a simulation of banknote paper substrate, which has evolved considerably over the years. These days it is made of cotton fibres and is referred to as rag paper. It contains various security features which are introduced during the manufacturing process. These features include watermarks, metallic threads or particles and other unique features, all of which are introduced during the formation of the paper from a water slurry. Even plastic stripes have been incorporated in recent times.

One recorded forgery where a simulated paper was produced was in France in 1951–64. The French were then using a very thin paper and the forger, a Polish engineer living in Paris, used cigarette paper, rainwater and a bidet to make a substitute paper.[13] The early experiments at CSIRO made paper from plastic fibres on a Buchner funnel; they did not use a bidet! The French forger was slow to be apprehended; he produced over 50 000 notes in his 13-year project.

Ink and printing processes have also made significant progress over the years. Perhaps the most significant improvement is intaglio printing. This requires expensive equipment which is rarely available to the forger; it gives the raised print and hence the characteristic feel to traditional banknotes. On the other hand, the making of printing plates is now relatively simple and not restricted, as in the past, to a few skilled tradesmen.

Forgery rings range from a single individual up to syndicated crime groups and even government-organised operations. The quality, as judged by ease of detection, also varies. Given sufficient resources and with modern technology it should be possible to produce quality forgeries of even the latest banknotes, but such detailed reverse engineering is costly and usually not available or worthwhile. The general principle is that there is a direct correlation between the size of a gang and its likelihood of being caught.

Small-time forgers are often ingenious but do something stupid which leads to their detection. During the course of our project, the Bank related numerous stories on how forgers were caught. A few will be repeated here to provide background on what was to be the 'enemy' or opponent in this story.

In a European country, a printer employed by the country's approved banknote printing factory decided to work some unofficial overtime. He returned one evening and set about printing sheet after sheet of notes for himself. For the purposes of this story, and to protect the country concerned, we will assume the notes were $20. In normal operation, as each sheet of banknotes is printed the numbering mechanism automatically advances: so that the numbering sequence would not betray the would-be crook he locked the mechanism on the number of the last genuine (authentic) production. Hence, after unlocking the mechanism when he finished printing his unofficial notes, the numbers would continue in sequence the next morning. However, this meant that all the illegal notes had the same number.

To convert forged or illegal notes to genuine currency, various laundering techniques are employed. These range from gambling transactions down to the man in the street operations where a cheap article, for example a $2 chocolate bar, is purchased with an illegal note, say $20. Our European gentleman got tired of multiple small transactions – he may also have got sick of chocolate bars – so he went to the local bank with a pile of mint-condition notes. The teller became suspicious and found that all the notes had the same number. The near-perfect crime was discovered! The story also illustrates the value of the number on each note; in fact, the number is what distinguishes one banknote from another.[14]

A similar, and even more bizarre, example of the importance of the number on a banknote comes from a brazen counterfeiting of the Portuguese currency in the late 1920s. Banco de Portugal, the Portuguese central bank, used a London firm of printers to produce its banknotes. Alves dos Reis decided to get his own notes with minimum physical effort by forging a Banco de Portugal contract and placing an order for Portuguese notes with the London printers. Eventually up to 1% of Portugal's gross domestic product had been laundered. The crime was detected by an alert bank teller (again) who noticed duplicate numbers. The notes were not forged but were not legitimate. This crime seems incredible. How did a security printer issue duplicate numbers? Didn't it have records?[15]

Everyone working on the Bank project was conscious of the need to outsmart the counterfeiter. Sometimes, however, the criminal mind works in strange ways. A group in England produced Bank of England 'special issue' banknotes with a face value of £500 000 and tried to convince the Bank to pay out on them. This proved impossible; the Bank of England had never issued such banknotes.[16] The criminals spent time in gaol.

In a northern Victorian (Australian) town two mates, one a printer and the other a printing plate maker, entered into partnership to forge Australian banknotes, e.g. the $50. The plate maker was progressing well and in a prototype, as a joke, included his friend's signature instead of the usual one, i.e. the Governor of the Bank. He took the plates around to show his friend, the printer, who was out at the local hotel, so he left the plates at the friend's house. The printer returned home and, having had a few beers, didn't notice the wrong signature, thought the plates were the real thing and used them to print forged notes, which he then passed out. The police had no trouble locating those forgers![17]

Forgery still occurs in most countries and even if the percentage of such notes in circulation is low, e.g. 0.01%, the value of forged notes can be high. For example, in 2006 the US Treasury estimated that of US$760 billion in circulation US$76 million was counterfeit.[18]

Philosophies on producing 'difficult to forge' banknotes

Lessons from the past, including the experience of the Australian 1966 forgery, give some guidance on how to proceed with the development of a new banknote. The simple last-minute doubts of the 1966 Australian forgers led to their early downfall. Forgery gangs often operate with 'wholesalers', who produce the forgeries, and 'retailers' who buy the forgeries then 'pass' them. The act of changing a note in a quiet suburban milk bar in 1966 was a stupid move but it illustrates that the greater the number of people in the forgery chain the greater the chance of detection; someone will make a mistake. Hence complex technology, which requires the wholesalers in the forgery chain to have a wide range of skills, is desirable. Also, since genuine banknote production is high-volume it is possible to use expensive operations.

In effect, the advances in technologies have reduced the size of the forgery rings and hence reduced the likelihood of detection when notes are printed on paper. Colour copiers were a major concern when the plastic banknote project commenced in 1968.

The technology incorporated in the plastic banknotes from the Bank project requires would-be forgers to have a knowledge of plastic properties (preparation, processing, printing), an understanding of replication techniques, and some insight into the chemistry/physics behind the security devices included in the banknotes. These include devices like the Captain Cook diffraction grating (see Ch. 3) on the $10 commemorative banknote, the colours of which vary depending on the angle of viewing (an optically variable device) or the clear area made possible by the use of plastic. Thus the project would force the forger away from the usual combination of rag paper, printing plates and a printer and the chance of detection would increase with such a wide diversity of required skills. Added to this, of course, was the much higher level of science we were to use in the plastic banknotes. However, smart science is of little value if the public can't recognise or see what it does.

Endnotes

1 W.J.D. Mira (1981) *Coinage and Currency in New South Wales, 1788–1829; and, An Index of Currency References in the Sydney Gazette 1803–1811.* Metropolitan Coin Club of Sydney.

2 <http://www.australianstamp.com/coin-web/aust/earlyaus.htm>.

3 A.R. Michaelis (1988) *Interdisciplinary Science Reviews* **13**, 251.

4 A.R. Michaelis (1988) *Interdisciplinary Science Reviews* **13**, 251.

5 A.R. Michaelis (1988) *Interdisciplinary Science Reviews* **13**, 251.

6 A.R. Michaelis (1993) *IBNS Journal* **32 (3)**, 5.

7 Amnesty International. <http://www.amnesty.org/en/death-penalty>.

8 A.R. Michaelis (1993) *IBNS Journal* **32 (3)**, 6.

9 A.R. Michaelis (1993) *IBNS Journal* **32 (3)**, 6.

10 T. Johnson, McClatchy Newspapers, 10 January 2008. <http://www.mcclatchydc/com/2008/01/10/24524>.

11 K.G. Hall, McClatchy Newspapers, 10 January 2008. <http://www.mcclatchydc/com/2008/01/10/24521>.

12 A.R. Michaelis (1993) *IBNS Journal* **32 (3)**, 5.

13 A.R. Michaelis (1993) *IBNS Journal* **32 (3)**, 5.

14 Personal communication to Solomon from Brown.

15 M.T. Bloom (1962) *The Man Who Stole Portugal.* Charles Scribner's Sons, New York. See also <http://www.businesspundit.com/10-most-notorious-counterfeiting-operations-of-the-last-100-years/>.

16 <http://www.dailymail.co.uk/news/article-489190/>.

17 Personal communication to Solomon by Brown.

18 *The Use and Counterfeiting of United States Currency Abroad, Part 3.* Final report to Congress by the Secretary of the Treasury, September 2006.

Plate 1: Security features of the 1966 $10 banknote.

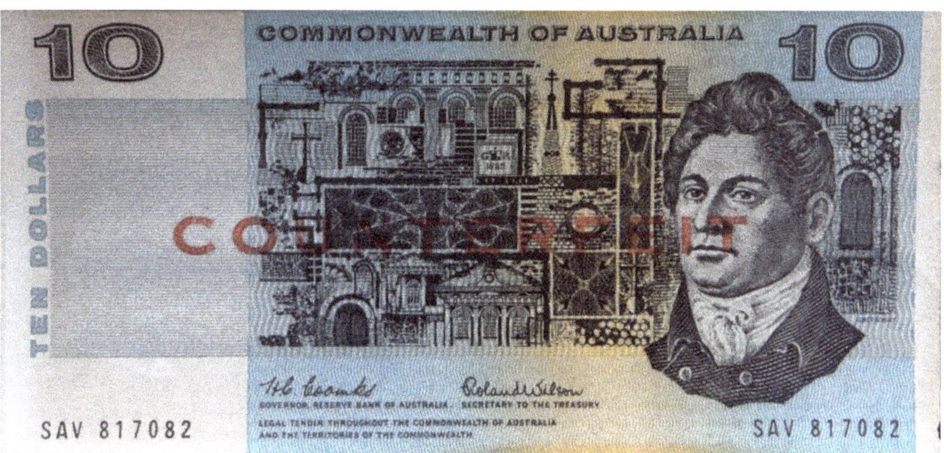

Plate 2: A counterfeit 1966 $10 note.

Plate 3: 1913 Australian banknotes.

Plate 4: A $7 banknote printed on a paper laminate substrate.

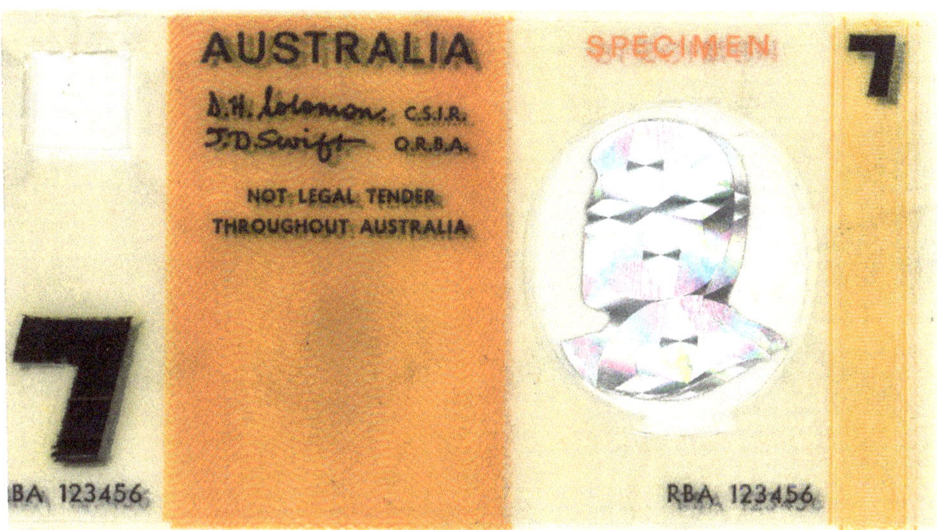

Plate 5: A composite grating incorporated into a CSIRO $7 banknote.

Plate 6: A banknote incorporating a CSIRO pattern.

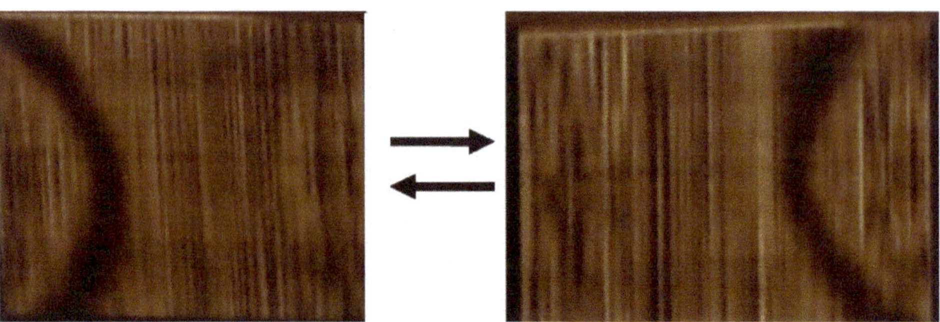

Plate 7: A moiré device that could be incorporated into a banknote only by hand alignment. Source: *Angew. Chem. Int. Ed.* **49**, 3726–3736.

Plate 8: A $50 banknote incorporating a 'winking' moiré device. The winking device invented by Dr Hawthorne could be incorporated into the banknote on the production line.

Plate 9: Some test specimens.

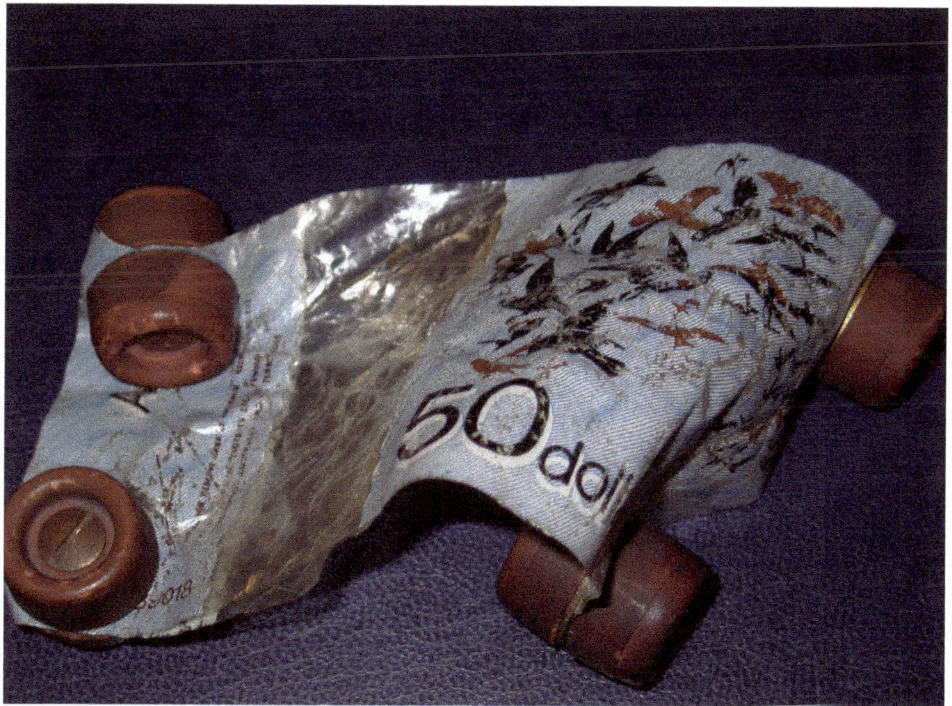

Plate 10: A $50 CSIRO banknote after the Turbula test.

Plate 11: The banknote shown by Monty Brown at the February 1972 meeting.

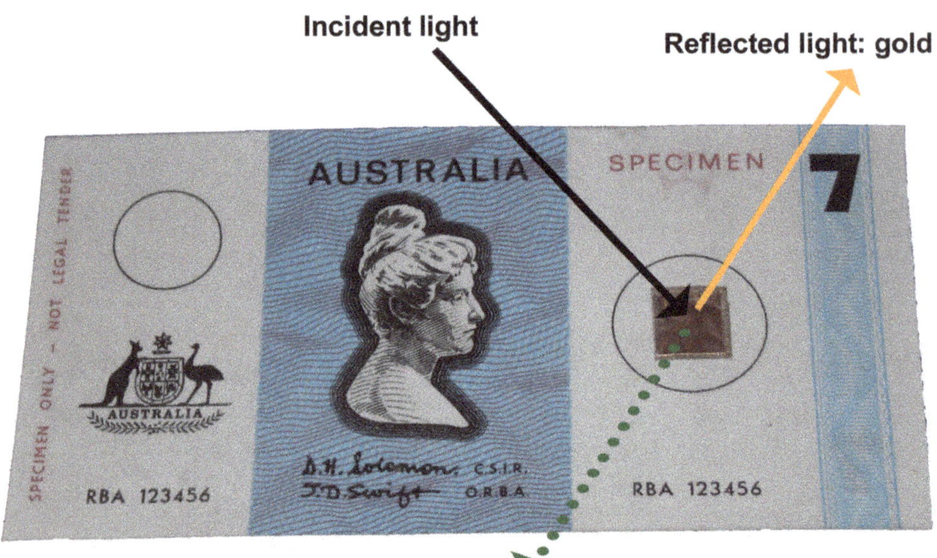

Plate 12: The $7 banknote produced as a trial using gold film as a security device. Source: *Angew. Chem. Int. Ed.* **49**, 3726–3736.

Plate 13: Grating based on a portrait of the Queen.

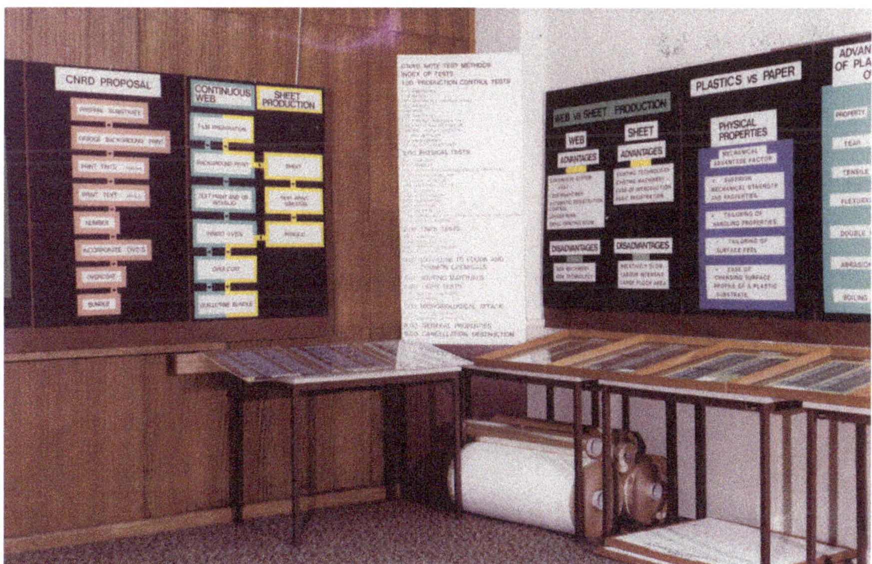

Plate 14: Four-Nation presentation. The display showed that more than 50 million banknotes had been produced, incorporating more than 2 million optically variable devices, that intaglio print on plastic was superior to that on paper and that extensive tests had been carried out.

Plate 15: The 1988 $10 commemorative banknote, the first use of the polymer substrate.

Chapter 3
Producing Australian banknotes

In this chapter we discuss technical aspects of banknotes in general, the 1966 Australian paper banknotes, the various plastic banknotes proposed by CSIRO and the plastic banknotes now in circulation in Australia. Many people were involved in the project and their individual contributions are discussed in subsequent chapters. Two CSIRO scientists who were present at one or both of the meetings called in 1968 by the Reserve Bank Governor Dr H.C. Coombs were Dr S.D. Hamann and Dr D.H. Solomon; some of their technical contributions to the project are discussed in this chapter.

The technical aspects do not include the artistic design of the note. This was always known to be the responsibility of the Bank. However, from the outset of the project CSIRO was aware that any technical development that restricted the freedom of the designer would be counterproductive. Similarly, CSIRO was quick to understand that any new note must have mechanical and handling characteristics compatible with the existing notes. This became more important as the Bank and retail banks began to introduce machines to count, authenticate and distribute notes. As we document later, newcomers to the project often started discussing matters such as the size and thickness of the notes and the denomination of the first new note to be issued, not understanding that these were matters secondary to the development of the new technology.

Banknotes in general

Banknotes are printed on a substrate and have built in security devices. The most commonly used substrate is a special paper made from cotton fibres with linen fibres sometimes included. Common paper is made from wood fibre.

The first plastic banknote substrate was the DuPont product Tyvek®. This is a non-woven fibre product made from high-density polyethylene. It was developed for use as a durable banknote substrate by the American Bank Note Co., which used it to produce banknotes for Haiti (issued 1980 and 1982) and Costa Rica (issued 1983). A former UK engraving and printing company developed a version of Tyvek® called Bradvek® and used it to produce banknotes for the Isle of Man (issued between 1983 and 1988).[1] The Tyvek® substrate had problems with ink adhesion and fragility and banknotes using this substrate are no longer produced. These banknotes were designed to be more durable, not more secure, than paper banknotes.

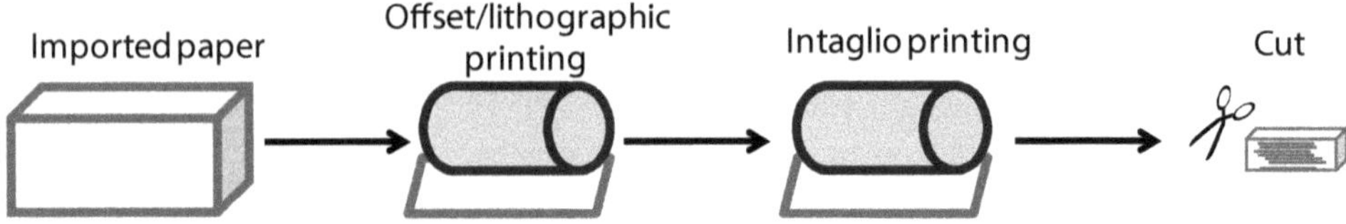

Fig. 3.1: Process for printing paper notes.

The first banknotes using a plastic film as the substrate were the Australian 1988 commemorative notes. Further technical details of the development of that substrate are given below.

Banknotes typically go through two printing processes (see Fig. 3.1). Background printing is applied by what is termed offset printing. In this process the design image is etched into a printing plate by well-established methods and the ink is applied using specialised printing machines. These machines can apply several different colours simultaneously, print both sides of the paper simultaneously and keep the images in perfect registration. This printing process is referred to as Simultan® printing after the brand of the most commonly used machine.

The second printing process is called intaglio printing and this gives the banknotes their distinctive raised printing. Intaglio printing is quite different from the offset process. In this process ink is carried in recessed graves (grooves). This ink is transferred to paper under high pressures, up to 140 000 kPa. These inks often take up to 14 days to dry (because they need to oxidise) and to avoid smudging each banknote sheet is separated from the next by interleaved sheets of paper. This is very inefficient in production terms. Some banknotes have a second intaglio print on the other side of the note. After drying the notes are inspected, guillotined to size and stacked ready for distribution.

All banknotes incorporate security devices to assist in preventing forgeries. There are three levels of security devices. Primary security devices can be recognised by the consumer and include intaglio printing, metal strips and the clear area of the plastic banknote. Secondary security devices are those that require a machine to detect them. Australian banknotes, both the past paper notes and the current plastic notes, do not have secondary security devices. Tertiary security devices are those that can only be detected by the issuing authority when the banknote has been returned. The presence or absence of such devices is rarely documented by the issuing authority. The Bank project was mainly concerned with developing the new substrate, which was itself a primary security device, and other primary devices. There was some work on tertiary devices, which were referred to as 'taggants'.

Plastics and polymers

Plastic materials are those that can be shaped or moulded. In this book we are dealing with the class of plastic materials that are synthesised from petrochemicals. These materials are called polymers because they are made from many units (poly) of a chemical or monomer (mer). When the new notes were released in 1988 the Bank described them as 'polymer' notes rather than 'plastic' notes. This was because of the perception that 'plastics' were 'cheap and nasty' and therefore not suitable for banknotes. Like many such marketing ploys, many members of the public ignore it and continue to refer to the notes as plastic.

Some of the first synthetic polymers to appear on the market were synthetic fibres designed to replace natural fibres such as cotton, silk and wool. Nylon and Terylene® are familiar trade names of such polymers. Nylon is a polyamide and Terylene® is polyester.

Synthetic polymers are used extensively as packaging materials. Polyethylene, sometimes marketed as polythene, was one of the first to appear on the market in 1933. It is the main component of GLAD® Wrap. GLAD® Wrap was invented in Australia by Dr Doug Ford, then a research scientist at Union Carbide in Sydney and later a member of the CSIRO Executive during the time of the Bank project. As noted earlier, a nonwoven form of polyethylene, Tyvek®, was used in banknotes in the early 1980s. Polyethylene terephthalate (PET) is used extensively as a packaging material, most commonly in soft drink bottles.

Polypropylene is a tough and flexible polymeric material that was introduced to the market in 1957. It is widely used in packaging, textiles and automotive components. It is the polymer substrate used in the Australian banknote.

The 1966 Australian banknote

The 1966 Australian banknote was a conventional paper banknote that included the most advanced security devices then available (see Plate 1).

The substrate was the cotton/linen paper supplied by Portals, the same supplier used by the Bank for the pre-decimal currency. It came to the Bank with two security devices included. One, a watermark, was also in the pre-decimal currency. The new security device was a thin metal strip; this was difficult for a forger to replicate but was not difficult to simulate. Intaglio printing was used as a third primary security device. The notes had no secondary or tertiary security devices.

Initial thoughts on plastic banknotes

Between 1968 and 1972 Solomon and Hamann both thought about and carried out preliminary experiments on novel substrates and security devices, in addition to contracted work with the Division of Forest Products (see Ch. 4). They always understood that printing was the business of the Bank. Both thought that they needed to consider security devices that could not be photographed and Hamann commenced some experiments on moiré patterns, which we will describe in more detail later in this chapter. Hamann initially thought that it might be possible to improve the security of conventional

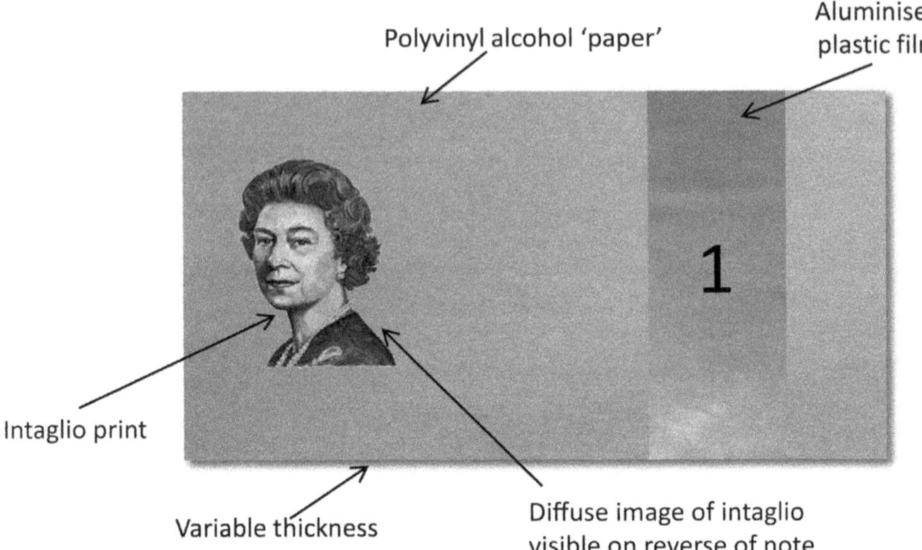

Fig. 3.2: Essential features of Solomon's Sample 8. Sample 8 used a polyvinyl alcohol substrate with variable thickness, intaglio printing and a metallised plastic film.

paper banknotes. Solomon was always of the view that the future lay in developing a novel plastic substrate that could more easily incorporate novel security devices.

Solomon's early experiments used polyvinyl alcohol fibres to make synthetic papers where the thickness varied within the sheet. The idea was that a dye or ink applied on one side of the substrate would have variable colours on the other side due to the variable lengths of the diffusion path. Nothing came of that idea. In one experiment Solomon incorporated an aluminised plastic film into the polyvinyl alcohol 'paper', thinking that the optical properties of the thin metal film could be developed into a security device (Sample 8 in the report submitted to the Bank; see Fig. 3.2). As outlined in Chapter 5, this was a crucial experiment because it alerted the Bank to the possibility of including metallised diffraction gratings into a banknote.

The first prototype banknotes

Substrates

Following a 1972 meeting at the Bank when Brown produced a mock plastic $1 note made from two layers of PET film with a diffraction grating between them, Solomon turned his attention to producing plastic laminates as the substrate.

Despite Brown having printed on his plastic banknote, and all the evidence available from the packaging industry, there was some scepticism within the Bank about the ability to do quality printing on plastic. So the first substrate that Solomon

Fig. 3.3: The structure of a five-layer paper laminate, with printing on a tissue paper inner layer and two plastic outer layers.

produced consisted of five layers: an inner layer of printed tissue paper, two layers of low-density polyethylene (LDPE) to protect the printing then outside layers of high-density polyethylene (HDPE) making the note the right thickness and improving its mechanical properties (see Fig. 3.3). CSIRO chose $7 and occasionally $3 for the denominations of trial banknotes, initially as a joke but actually to avoid any possibility of being accused of forgery (see Plate 4). This initial substrate was soon abandoned because of its inferior mechanical and tear properties. A version of the substrate, with a PET outer layer, is now marketed by the company Louisenthal as 'Hybrid' (see Ch. 13).

In order to improve the tear and mechanical properties of the substrate, the inner tissue layer was replaced by a thin layer of woven PET. The printing was now done on the surface of the LDPE and protected by the outer layer of HDPE. This change meant that the inner LDPE layers could be made opaque by the inclusion of white pigment titanium dioxide (TiO_2). This substrate was the basis of Strand 75 (see Fig. 3.4; discussed in later chapters).

Security devices

Developing new security devices was the second aspect of the project.

The group at Fishermens Bend had a wide-ranging approach to developing security devices that had the potential to thwart the forger. It included devices based on both chemistry and physics.

The chemical devices included liquid crystals, photochromic inks and spectroscopically detected taggants.

Liquid crystals are partly ordered materials in a state somewhere between their liquid and solid phases. They were discovered in 1888 by Austrian chemist Friedrich

Fig. 3.4: The structure of Strand 75.

Reinitzer when he was trying to determine the melting point of cholesterol. He found that the compound seemed to have two melting points: the first occurred when the solid crystal melted to a cloudy liquid and the second when the cloudy liquid became a clear liquid. In 'nematic' liquid crystals the molecules move around as in a liquid but are still ordered in their orientation. If the molecules are 'chiral' they are arranged in structures that can reflect visible light in different colours depending on the temperature. This property is now being used in thermometers. In 1972 there were limited commercial uses for liquid crystals but now liquid crystal displays dominate the electronic display market. CSIRO did extensive testing on the use of cholesterol ester liquid crystals as banknote security devices. In one example displayed at the March 1973 meeting numbers become visible when the colour of the liquid crystal is changed by the heat of the body. Liquid crystals were quite stable in the laboratory but seemed to fade in a few days when incorporated into the ink used on the note.

Photochromic inks are inks that contain chemicals that change colour when exposed to light of a certain wavelength. These inks are colourless in the dark of a wallet or purse but turn blue when exposed to light. Such devices were incorporated into the early CSIRO banknotes but none was considered stable enough to be in the final note.

CSIRO did some preliminary thinking on tertiary security devices. The most promising early device was a chemical additive to an ink that could be rapidly detected by an infrared spectrometer.

Three different physical security devices – diffraction gratings, moiré patterns and embossed patterns – featured in the early work.

For either a diffraction grating or a moiré pattern to be a successful security device in a banknote three barriers need to be overcome. There needs to be a design that is easily recognised by the person in the street and yet not easily simulated by the forger, there has to be a method of manufacturing the device and there needs to be a method of incorporating the device into the banknote production line.

Diffraction gratings

Diffraction gratings are formed from line patterns in a substrate. Usually these line patterns, typically 12 000 lines per mm, are coated with a very thin film of a reflecting metal (e.g. aluminium). Light is diffracted from these lines and gives various colours which change as the grating is moved. The directions of the beams depend on the spacing of the grating and the wavelength of the light, so the grating acts as the dispersive element. Because of this, gratings are commonly used in monochromators and spectrometers. Dr Alan Walsh, and his group in the CSIRO Division of Chemical Physics, was expert in the production of diffraction gratings for use in spectrophotometers. As mentioned in Chapter 4, Walsh wore a tiepin made from a straight line diffraction grating to the first meeting convened by Dr Coombs.

Designing a diffraction grating that is easily recognised by the person in the street but is not easily simulated or reproduced by the forger was one of the Bank project's most difficult tasks.

When CSIRO began work on this problem in the early 1970s, commercially available diffraction gratings were either the straight line gratings used mainly in scientific instruments or the spiral gratings used in novelty packaging. In both cases the spacing between the lines was constant and the gratings were produced on mechanical ruling machines or in a lathe. Such gratings were not unique, did not have particularly spectacular diffraction patterns and could be easily simulated or replicated by a forger. In addition, they did not have the artistic quality that is usually associated with banknote design.

So CSIRO decided to attempt to design diffraction gratings that were not commercially available and that would give the banknote artist complete freedom in design. Banknotes generally feature a portrait of an important individual, either the head of state or a historical figure. CSIRO thought that it would be desirable if a diffraction pattern could be incorporated in some way into a portrait. The team recognised that they needed to consider design and manufacture of the grating together. They had to produce a 'master grating' which, as described below, could be used to incorporate a grating into the banknote.

CSIRO had three approaches to producing a unique master grating: a montage, photographic reduction and electron beam lithography.

The first grating prepared by CSIRO was a portrait-like composite grating made by a cut and paste technique using segments cut from commercially available gratings. As can be seen in Plate 5 it illustrated the concept remarkably well when incorporated in one of the very early banknotes. This grating was unique and would force the forger to use replication techniques to simulate it, but it was only an interim step since it used commercially available gratings.

The CSIRO team realised that to satisfy the requirements of uniqueness and freedom of design they would need to have the science and technology that would allow the production of diffraction gratings with any line pattern and with variable spacing between the lines. Hamann worked out the mathematics of such a pattern; this became known as the 'butterfly grating' (see Fig. 3.5). CSIRO understood that if they could make this grating they could make any other mathematically devised pattern.

Solomon settled on two approaches to making the butterfly grating – photographic reduction and electron beam lithography (EBX).

The photographic reduction technique required the cooperation of two laboratories of what is now known as the Defence Science and Technology Organisation. The Defence Standards Laboratory at Maribyrnong had a large printer (supplied by the US company, Gerber) which was able to make a 640 × 640 mm print of the butterfly pattern. This print would then be reduced to 25 × 25 mm by using state of the art

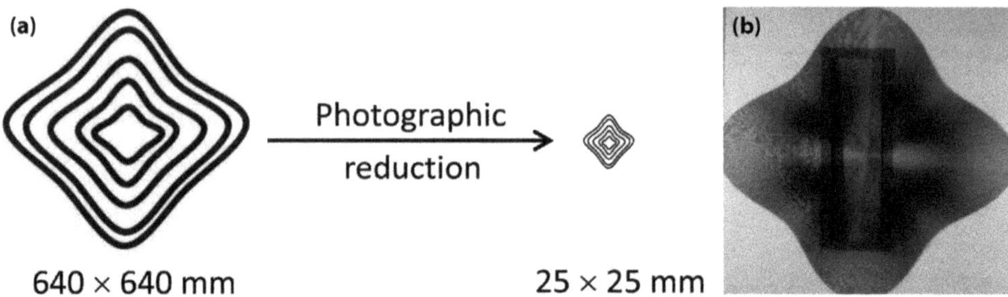

Fig. 3.5: (a) Butterfly grating. The diagram shows the the non-linear line pattern and the variable spacing between the lines. (b) Photograph of butterfly grating.

photographic reduction equipment at the Weapons Research Establishment (WRE) at Salisbury in South Australia. CSIRO had to negotiate confidentiality agreements with the two defence laboratories and confirm the secret nature of the project.

The group at Salisbury had indicated that to get the 25:1 reduction they would need a special lens, but since its purchase had not been included in the current year's budget CSIRO would have to wait at least a year for the work to be done. Solomon could not wait that long and used the much more flexible purchasing arrangements of CSIRO to buy the lens for about $5000. He then 'gave' it to WRE in exchange for their in-kind support. To assuage any doubts in the minds of the Salisbury group, Solomon had Price write a letter confirming the permanency of the 'gift'.[2]

This was a very effective collaboration and resulted in a master butterfly with 1200 lines/mm. This was the diffraction grating used in 1976 in the first pilot plant production of polypropylene banknotes. These were known as 'design freeze' banknotes. At this low line intensity the diffraction effect is not striking or brilliant. It demonstrated to the Bank that it was possible to have a complete process for a diffraction grating from design to incorporation in the banknote.

When Solomon joined the CSIRO Division of Applied Mineralogy in 1963 he formed a friendship with Alan Wilson, who was in charge of the division's electron microscope (see Fig. 3.6). Solomon and Wilson had published a novel method of examining the microstructure of a polymer and Solomon knew that Wilson was always interested in using his instrument in novel ways. It was known that the electron beams at the centre of electron microscope technology could be used to produce straight line gratings and the circuits on silicon chips. The question was whether it was possible to 'write' lines of any shape with an electron beam. Wilson showed that it could be done, producing some primitive gratings on the electron microscope at Fishermens Bend. The line density of these gratings was not high enough to use in a banknote but the experiment did serve to demonstrate the feasibility of the method.

Fortuitously, at about this time Solomon had a visit (through his RACI connections) from Dr Murrae Bowden, an Australian scientist working at the Bell

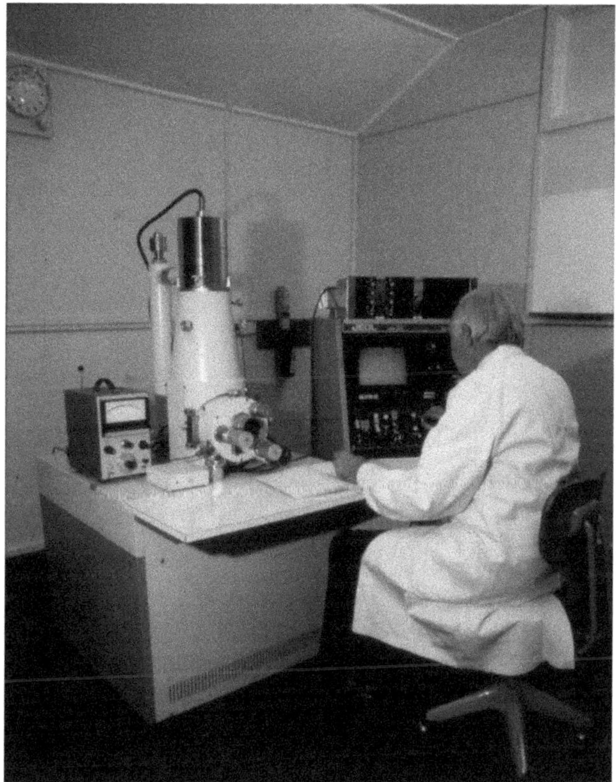

Fig. 3.6: Alan Wilson at his electron microscope at Fishermens Bend.

Telephone Laboratories in the US. Solomon and Bowden shared a common interest in polymer science and during the visit discussed Bowden's work on the electron beam resists used for microcircuitry. Solomon immediately saw the relevance of this to the diffraction grating problem. Without divulging the reason for his interest, Solomon asked, as a matter of urgency, for Bowden to send a sample microcircuit to Fishermens Bend. This sample was used to demonstrate the feasibility of the technique to the chief executives at the 1974 meeting.

Technically, the challenge was that the computer-controlled electron beam at that time could only focus over an area of ~2 × 2 mm. Since a grating of 25 × 25 mm was needed, this required a method of moving the stage and in effect drawing ~144 small areas. The major challenge was 'butting' the lines each time the stage was moved (see Fig. 3.7).

None of the commercially available EBX machines could do this, but since Wilson had demonstrated it on his electron microscope, CSIRO was confident that it could be done. Wilson conducted a survey of the available instruments and their suitability to be modified for the project and recommended that a JEOL instrument would be

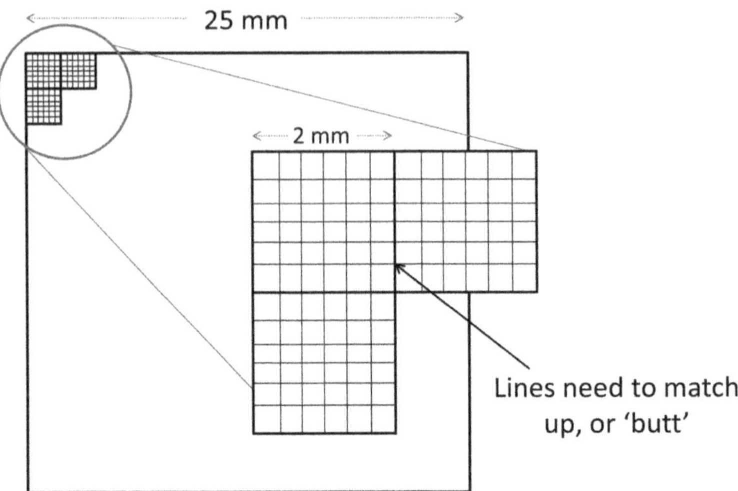

Fig. 3.7: Butted grating, showing the difficulty of building up a 25 × 25 mm grating from smaller gratings.

suitable. Through Wilson's contacts with the company's Australian representatives CSIRO was given access to a machine for a two-week period before its delivery to the customer who had purchased it. Wilson and Solomon made the visit to the JEOL factory in Japan in 1976, taking tape produced at Fishermens Bend by Graham Quint containing the algorithm needed to drive the machine.

There were some problems. In some areas the diffraction grating was excellent, but large sections had no grating at all. This was caused by minor coding problems that were discovered at Fishermens Bend by a team consisting of Quint, Dr John Lane and Dr Tom Spurling. Solomon was having difficulty explaining the precise problem over the phone to the Fishermens Bend group. The Scientific Liaison Officer at the Australian Embassy in Japan, Dr Bert Anderson, was helping with the visit and knew of a method of sending a picture by phone, but the service was available at only a few post offices. He arranged for this and as a result the problem was solved by the group back at Fishermens Bend (see Fig. 3.8). Today these 'pictures' are called faxes.

At the end of the visit Wilson had produced a small section of a 25 × 25 mm butterfly diffraction grating, and demonstrated the feasibility of the concept.

Having produced a master grating either by photographic reduction or by electron beam writing and metallised it using standard vacuum metallising technology, a method had to be developed to incorporate a copy into the banknote.

The first step was to replicate the valuable master diffraction grating by forming a series of submasters. This can be done using a number of techniques. CSIRO used three methods:

Fig. 3.8: The computer room at Fishermens Bend in 1976. Left to right: Jean Swift, Tom Spurling and Graham Quint.

1. embossing the master into a polymer that has a lower softening point than the polymer the master is made from. This pattern is then metallised in the vacuum metalliser;
2. making replicas in epoxy resins. The master is coated with epoxy resin and after the resin has hardened it is separated from the master and metallised;
3. electroplating.

CSIRO developed these methods before they had their own master gratings using the straight line gratings from the Division of Chemical Physics and commercially available spiral gratings.

Having produced the submasters, the next step is to make sufficient copies of the grating to transfer to each banknote. CSIRO developed and patented a novel transfer foil technology.[3]

A transfer foil line in effect uses a carrier on which a very thin parcel of three films is built up. This parcel is then transferred to the desired object by applying heat through either a hot stamp or a hot roller (see Fig. 3.9).

Initially CSIRO evaluated commercially available foils and embossed the submasters into the thin metallised layer of the commercial product, but this approach revealed two major problems.

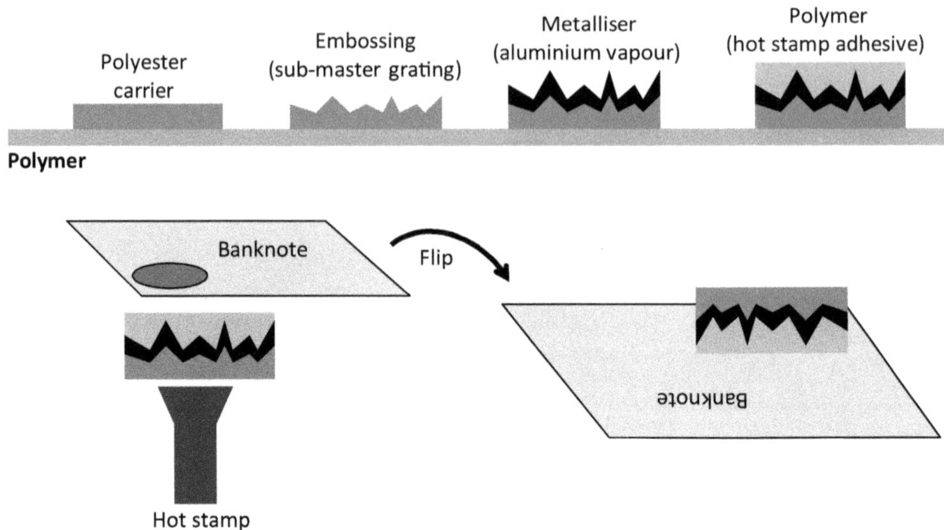

Fig. 3.9: Transfer of foil line.[4]

The first was that for the foil to release from the carrier, a release agent was needed. This release agent is a substance that causes poor adhesion between the carrier and the foil package and so assists in the transfer operation. Inevitably, some of the release agent is carried with the transferred foil. In most commercial operations this is not a problem, but it becomes a problem if the object transferred is to be further coated. This was the case for the banknote.

The second problem was that when the smooth aluminium layer was embossed some cracking of the aluminium resulted, leading to poor diffraction efficiency. CSIRO evaluated 39 commercial foils and a wide variety of adhesives before deciding to develop novel foils. The problem was addressed by carrying out the embossing step before the metal was applied. As a consequence CSIRO had to purchase and commission its own continuous metalliser. Figure 3.10 shows the metalliser being used at Fishermens Bend.

To avoid the poor adhesion which results from transfer of some release agent, none were used. CSIRO was able to avoid their use by careful selection of the polymers, particularly in the first layer.

The hot-stamp or transfer step also offered the opportunity to transfer complex patterns. Solomon understood that this would further complicate any attempt by a forger to simulate the grating since it would force them to use transfer foil technology. Gordon Andrews, the Bank's artist, saw the security potential of this idea and provided a variety of designs to the Forward Planning Group (see Ch. 10). One of the CSIRO patterns incorporated into a banknote is shown in Plate 6.

Fig. 3.10: Ian Marwick at the metalliser at Fishermens Bend.

In the 1988 bicentennial $10 banknote the foil package is barely detectable when fingers are passed over the grating, since it is only a few microns thick.

Apart from the very thin package which constitutes the diffraction grating, careful attention was paid to the composition of the polymers used in the diffraction grating package. Solomon was aware that a possible method of forging gratings from a banknote could involve a technique to selectively remove one of the layers. An obvious one would be to use a solvent which, although difficult, was a possibility. Hence, polymers that could be lightly cross-linked were used. This makes the polymer layer insoluble. It also means that the grating will swell and distort.[5]

This novel diffraction grating transfer foil offered security by virtue of:

- very thin film, total thickness a few microns;
- difficulty of gaining access to it;
- complex patterns that would force a forger to hot-stamp techniques.

Moiré patterns

Moiré patterns are produced when two line patterns are superimposed on a flat or curved surface and slightly displaced from each other. A predictable moiré pattern can also appear if two mathematically conceived line patterns are superimposed at a fixed predetermined displacement and the device is moved with respect to a light source. Moiré is the French word for a textile with a 'watered' appearance. A common example is the pattern observed when light passes through sheer overlaps on window coverings.

In 1968 Hamann commenced investigations of moiré patterns with the assistance of the CSIRO mathematician Charles Johnson. Late in 1972 Hamann discovered striking moiré patterns formed by superimposing screens of randomly spaced lines or dots on similar, but modulated, screens. They were described in a series of reports to the Currency Notes Research and Development (CNRD) Committee, entitled *Moiré Gratings with Modulated Random Spacings*, and the invention was covered by an Australian patent application.[6] These were demonstrated on A4 transparencies but never successfully incorporated into a banknote.

The suggestion by Solomon's team of the use of polypropylene as a transparent substrate offered the possibility of placing a randomly spaced moiré screen on one side of a transparent note and its modulated counterpart on the other side, to give the distinctive effects in transmission. The optical performance of such a transmission moiré is determined by a relationship between the line intensity and the distance between the two screens. In practice it proved impossible to achieve, by conventional printing, the line intensity and the accuracy of registration needed between the two screens. Plate 7 shows such a moiré, which could be incorporated into a note only by hand alignment.

The need for accurate registration was eliminated by a reflecting moiré device which used a single screen on one side of the banknote and a mirror to reflect its image on the other side. The ruling selected was a Fresnel zone-plate which is a set of concentric circular zones. A moiré device of this type was incorporated into the 1976 'design freeze'. There were two problems with this device. The first was that it became badly degraded when the notes were crumpled. The second was that when incorporated into a note containing a diffraction grating it looked too similar to the grating. So this approach was also abandoned.

Another type of moiré device was suggested by Dr Geoff Hawthorne. He pointed out that both the problem of registration and the crumpling problem could be eliminated if a zone-plate ruling on one side of the transparent film was matched with a straight line ruling on the other side. The device 'winked' when the banknote was tilted about an axis parallel to the straight lines (see Plate 8).

The polypropylene story (a clear plastic laminate)

While there are many plastic films available on the market none have the mechanical properties required for use as a banknote. To be acceptable as a banknote substrate, a polymer film needs to have properties similar to the existing notes. In some ways this was fortunate since if CSIRO needed to develop a unique substrate then so would the forger.

As outlined in Chapter 7, at the Mornington conference, CSIRO came to the conclusion that, while Strand 75 had many desirable properties, the need to punch a hole in order to form a clear area limited the number of security devices that could be incorporated. After a survey of the mechanical properties of plastic films available commercially CSIRO decided that the one with the most potential was polypropylene (PP).

PP was available as a biaxially oriented film (BOPP), i.e. during manufacture it is stretched (oriented) in both the machine and tranverse directions. This is achieved using either a bubble or an extruder technique. The latter is known as the Tenter process.

There are two properties of PP that need to be taken into account when it is used as packaging material and as a banknote substrate. The first is that, before it softens, the biaxial orientation relaxes and the film shrinks and loses its mechanical properties. When the $10 commemorative banknote was introduced there were complaints that the note shrunk when ironed or heated in a microwave oven. Why people were ironing or cooking banknotes is not clear!

Second, PP has a high softening temperature, making heat-sealing of packages difficult. To overcome this commercial PP films usually have outer layers of other polymers, at least one of which heat-seals at a lower temperature.

The films of interest to CSIRO were supplied by ICI ANZ and by British Cellophane through its Australian affiliate Wrightcel Pty Ltd. CSIRO experimented with:

- ICI Propafilm® M, a PP with outer layers of polyethylene (lower softening temperature);
- ICI Propafilm® C, where one of the outer layers was polyvinylidene chloride (PVDC);
- SCX and SCC, similar Wrightcel products.

None of the commercial films was thick enough to have the mechanical properties for a banknote. They were typically 25–30 microns and a banknote substrate needed to be ~70–80 microns. A banknote substrate could comprise either two 35 micron films or two 25 micron films and one 30 micron film. CSIRO concentrated its efforts on the polyethylene-coated films and Wrightcel was contacted to investigate the use of PVDC. While it was easier to print on PVDC, it was later shown that on external exposure it liberated hydrochloric acid. The laminating equipment CSIRO used for this work was the same as that used to manufacture Strand 75 (see Fig. 3.11).

There are two methods of laminating plastic films of this type – adhesive lamination and heat lamination. Adhesion lamination was contracted out to Wrightcel and CSIRO did the heat lamination in-house, because at this time industry had no experience with heat lamination of PP. Both the two- and three-layer laminates were experimented with, and the two-layer laminates proved to be the most useful.

Fig. 3.11: The laminator at Fishermens Bend.

In the early experiments with these laminates the 'feel' was modified by embossing the surface as had been done on Strand 75 but this step was eliminated by the use of a varnish. Feel is a complex property which is influenced by the 'oiliness' of the surface and by the physical profile. The oiliness was controlled by the chemical composition of the varnish and the physical profile by the addition of silica particles to the varnish. The varnish was applied over the entire banknote and so served to protect the security devices and the printing. The varnish applied over the grating did not contain silica.

Testing without a field trial

Testing a revolutionary new banknote poses problems rarely encountered in other products. It is not possible to field trial a new banknote, so the challenge was how to use laboratory tests as a guide to performance. Great confidence is needed in the tests since the general failure of a banknote would have dire economic consequences. Traditional paper-based notes have a long history of practical experience which has been correlated with laboratory testing. In particular, great reliance has been placed on a double-fold test and on tensile measurements. Thus small incremental changes to paper notes could be made with confidence and the release of an improved paper note is a relatively easy process. A copy of the test specifications is given in Fig. 3.12. CSIRO developed a series of tests which were a valuable part of the intellectual property of the

SPECIFICATION OF AUSTRALIAN DECIMAL CURRENCY NOTES PAPER, AS SET OUT IN THE MEMORANDUM ACCOMPANYING MESSRS PORTALS LETTER OF 28 AUGUST 1964.

	Size of Sheet	Ream Weight (500's)
1 Dollar	$28\frac{1}{2}$" x $22\frac{1}{8}$"	37lbs. 4oz.
2 Dollar	$23\frac{25}{32}$" x $19\frac{31}{32}$"	28lbs.
5 Dollar	$24\frac{9}{16}$" x $20\frac{9}{16}$"	29lbs. 13oz.
10 Dollar	$25\frac{3}{8}$" x $21\frac{1}{8}$"	31lbs. 10oz.
20 Dollar	$26\frac{5}{32}$" x $21\frac{3}{4}$"	33lbs. 9oz.

(The fibres making up the paper are all rag).

<u>Strength:</u> The paper will have a strength of 2,500 minimum Mean Double Folds.

<u>Substance:</u> 83 grammes per square metre, with a tolerance of plus or minus 5%.

<u>Quality:</u> The paper will contain Melamine and will have the same gelatine and glycerine content as the last deliveries of your 10/-d. and £1 papers.

<u>Watermark:</u> This will be in accordance with the approved specimen number 3, sample of which we received with your letter of the 18 August. Tolerance for position of Watermark – 3mm. in any direction from the correct position in each note.

<u>Security Thread:</u> The paper will contain continuous bands of Metal Security Thread as included in the 50 sheets supplied to you in May last. The tolerance for the position of the Thread will be 6mm. on either side of the standard position.

Fig. 3.12: Specifications for paper for the 1966 decimal banknote.

project. As noted in Chapter 13, the Bank (and other note printing authorities around the world) partially solved the problem of the new type of banknote by issuing a commemorative note before changing all the currency. A commemorative note can be withdrawn from circulation without disrupting the economy and its issue can be saturated in one or two areas.

In devising the range of tests needed for polymer notes, Solomon recalled the 1951 movie *The Man in the White Suit*, starring Alec Guinness, who played a chemist working as a cleaner at a textile mill and who invented an incredibly strong fibre that never got dirty and was indestructible. He was lauded by all until both management

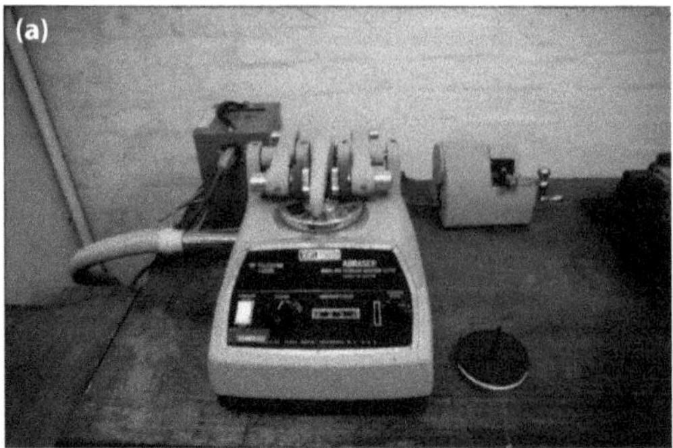

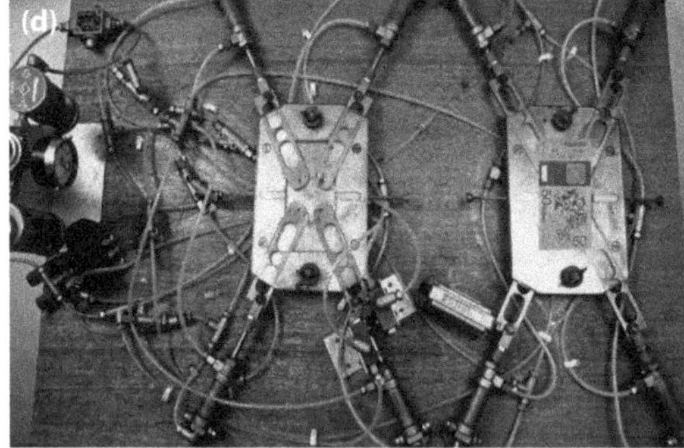

Fig. 3.13: (a) Test for abrasion. (b) Test for double-fold. (c) Test for UV exposure. (d) Crumple test.[7]

and labour realised that such an invention would put them all out of business. The invention eventually failed because the chemist had not adequately tested the long-term stability of the new fibre. Solomon did not want the new banknote to fail because CSIRO had not thought of an important property to test! Solomon's concern was reinforced by many 'what if' questions from Bank staff, such as 'What if the note is subjected to lipstick? To nail lacquer? To beer or tomato sauce?'

Solomon was concerned that the new banknotes might be affected by some obscure situation that hadn't been tested for. As a result CSIRO carried out hundreds of tests, many obvious, some not. Many possible foods, liquors, detergents, nail lacquers and beauty treatments were tested. The team developed tests to simulate air

Fig. 3.14: Solomon with some of the test booklets.

travel, deep sea diving and other leisure pursuits. Many of the staff carried notes in their wallets and 'bought' morning tea in the security of the production building. Plate 9 shows some of the test specimens. The obvious tests included abrasion resistance, double-fold tests, a test for UV exposure and a test for crumpling (see Fig. 3.13).

CSIRO documented standard operating procedures for all tests in a series of booklets (see Fig. 3.14).

The Turbula or tumble test

Of particular significance was the Turbula or tumble test developed by Jack Ross. Spurling assisted with the statistical analysis of the results. This test was critical in providing data for both the release of the notes to the public and the prediction of their lifetime (necessary to assess the economics of the new notes). The US expert employed to evaluate the total package (see Ch. 11) held the view that the test regimes were of significant value because they correlated laboratory testing with field performance.

The test was based on the most common reasons why paper banknotes were withdrawn by bank tellers – the notes were either dirty or torn. Hence a test to simulate dirt pick-up and tearing was needed.

The test used weights placed in the corners of the note which was then tumbled in a kerosene tin with controlled amounts of synthetic dirt, an abrasive and artificial sweat (see Fig. 3.15, Plate 10). The test was calibrated by first using mint-condition paper notes. The time in the Turbula test to reach a given level of dirt pick-up or tear was compared to the paper notes withdrawn from circulation by bank tellers. From the number printed on the paper note withdrawn from circulation, we could estimate the time it had been in circulation and hence, using statistical methods, the Turbula test was calibrated using paper notes. Then the plastic notes could be tested and an estimate

Fig. 3.15: (a) Components of the Turbula test, showing the weights attached to the corners of each banknote, the abrasive pellets and synthetic dirt.[8] The weighted banknotes were placed in the kerosene tin. (b) Alf Desira operating the Turbula test in a lathe at Fishermens Bend.

of their expected lifetime arrived at. This test was crucial in deciding to release the note and proved remarkably accurate, maybe slightly conservative, in predicting the field performance of the notes.

Endnotes

1 A.R. Michaelis (1993) *IBNS Journal* **32 (3)**, 9.
2 NAA: B5609, 6/2.
3 D.H. Solomon, M. Girolamo and J.B. Ross, *Production of Embossed Transfer Foils and the Like.* International Patent Application PCT/AU82/00136.
4 Prime EL and Solomon DH (2010) Australia's Plastic Banknotes: Fighting Counterfeit Currency. *Angewandte Chemie International Edition* **49**, 3726–3736. Copyright Wiley-VCH Verlag GmbH & Co. KGaA. Reproduced with permission.
5 D.H. Solomon, M. Girolamo and J.B. Ross, *Production of Embossed Transfer Foils and the Like.* International Patent Application PCT/AU82/00136.
6 S.D. Hamann, *Improved Novelty or Security Device.* Australian Patent 503862 (7 September 1979).
7 Fig. 3.13d is from: Prime EL and Solomon DH (2010) Australia's Plastic Banknotes: Fighting Counterfeit Currency. *Angewandte Chemie International Edition* **49**, 3726–3736. Copyright Wiley-VCH Verlag GmbH & Co. KGaA. Reproduced with permission.
8 Prime EL and Solomon DH (2010) Australia's Plastic Banknotes: Fighting Counterfeit Currency. *Angewandte Chemie International Edition* **49**, 3726–3736. Copyright Wiley-VCH Verlag GmbH & Co. KGaA. Reproduced with permission.

Chapter 4
The first two meetings

The scientist 'guests'

The first meeting of the group of selected scientists and the chosen Bank officials was held at the Melbourne office of the Reserve Bank on 8 April 1968 and the second at Thredbo, an Australian Snowy Mountains resort town, on 16 June 1968.

The guests[1] (as they were described in the minutes of the meeting) were Dr J.R. Price (an organic chemist but there as a member of the CSIRO Executive), Dr S.D. Hamann (a physical chemist, Chief of the CSIRO Division of Applied Chemistry) and five physicists: Dr A.K. Head, Dr J.P. Wild and Dr A. Walsh from CSIRO, Professor K.G. McCracken from the University of Adelaide and Professor J.C. Ward from Macquarie University. The Bank had a high-level contingent (discussed in more detail below). It was represented by the Governor, Dr H.C. (Nugget) Coombs, H.M. Knight (Deputy Governor Designate), R.A. Johnston (Manager, Investment Department), J.G. Menzies (Manager, Victoria), W.H. Wilcock (General Manager, Note Issue Department), M.F.W. Brown (Works Manager, Note Printing Branch), L.P. Kearney (Superintendent, Note Issue Section) and R.W. Prunster (Science Liaison Officer, who had organised the meeting). Knight and Johnston became Governors during the course of the project; Governor Johnston was the visionary who made the final momentous decision to go to the market with the world's first plastic banknote.

The Bank had assembled a formidable group of Australian scientists for the first meeting.

Dr J.R. (Jerry) Price (aged 56) was a member of the CSIRO Executive and a distinguished organic chemist.[2] He had been appointed to the Executive on 27 January 1966 from his role as Chief of the Division of Organic Chemistry. One of his first initiatives was to combine his former Division of Organic Chemistry with the Division of Physical Chemistry to form the Division of Applied Chemistry. He wanted these two branches of chemistry to be applied to provide solutions to industrial, economic and environmental problems. From his point of view, the request from the Governor of the Reserve Bank was an opportunity to show how CSIRO could contribute to a national problem. Price was appointed the Chairman of CSIRO on 26 May 1970 and maintained a great interest in the project while Chairman and after he retired from CSIRO in 1977. He was elected a Fellow of the Australian Academy of Science in 1959 and was awarded a KBE in 1976 for his services to science and government. He died in 1999.

Dr Alan K. Head (aged 43) was a Chief Research Scientist in the CSIRO Division of Tribophysics.[3] He was a mathematical physicist 'who was so widely read that he could turn his hand to anything that had a scientific basis'. He had joined CSIR as a Research Officer in the Division of Aeronautics (which became the Aeronautical Research Laboratories of the Department of Supply) in 1949 and was famous for his 1953 paper which explained the process of fatigue in aluminium alloys. This allowed the life-span of an aircraft component to be predicted and the component withdrawn from service before a catastrophic failure occurred. He transferred to the CSIRO Division of Tribophysics in 1957. Head was elected a Fellow of the Australian Academy of Science in 1971 and a Fellow of the Royal Society of London in 1988. He died in 2010.

Dr Alan Walsh (aged 52) was the Assistant Chief of the CSIRO Division of Chemical Physics and one of Australia's most famous scientists. In 1952 he invented atomic absorption spectroscopy.[4] Hilger and Watts, a UK company, sold its first atomic absorption instrument in 1958 and the Australian company Techtron Appliances Pty Ltd produced the first all-Australian atomic absorption instrument in 1964 (this incorporated a straight line diffraction grating monochromator produced on a ruling engine by CSIRO). Australia has a thriving scientific instruments industry stemming from Walsh's activities. Among his many awards and distinctions Alan was elected a Fellow of the Australian Academy of Science in 1958, a Fellow of the Royal Society of London in 1969, a Foreign Member of the Royal Swedish Academy of Science in 1969 and a Fellow of the Australian Academy of Technological Sciences and Engineering in 1982. He was made a Knight Bachelor in 1977. He died in 1998.

Dr J. Paul Wild (aged 45) was the Director of the CSIRO Solar Observatory.[5] He had secured funding from the Ford Foundation in the US to build a large radiotelescope at Culgoora, designed to look at the sun. This radioheliograph enabled astronomers to study the sun's very hot upper atmosphere. Wild went on to become Chief of the CSIRO Division of Radiophysics then Chairman of CSIRO from 1978 to1985. He was one of the inventors of the aeroplane landing system Interscan, and a very enthusiastic proponent of the very fast train between Sydney and Melbourne. He was elected a Fellow of the Australian Academy of Science in 1964, a Fellow of the Royal Society of London in 1970 and a Fellow of the Australian Academy of Technological Science and Engineering in 1977, and was made a Commander of the Order of the British Empire in 1978 and a Companion of the Order of Australia in 1985. He died in 2008.

Dr John C. Ward (aged 44) was Professor of Theoretical Physics at Macquarie University.[6] He came to Australia from the UK with a formidable reputation in theoretical physics. He had made fundamental contributions to quantum electrodynamics and, when working at Aldermaston, conceived a model for the hydrogen bomb. He was elected a Fellow of the Royal Society of London in1965 and won its 1983 Hughes Medal for his highly influential and original contributions to quantum field theory, particularly the Ward identity and the Salam-Ward theory of weak interactions. He died in 2000.

Professor Ken G. McCracken (aged 35) was Professor of Physics at the University of Adelaide and the University of Texas.[7] He was Australia's most famous space scientist, having made a seminal contribution to our understanding of the interplanetary magnetic field. He went on to become Chief of the CSIRO Division of Mineral Physics and Director of the CSIRO Office of Space Science and Applications. He was elected a Fellow of the Australian Academy of Technological Science and Engineering in 1979 and a Fellow of the Australian Academy of Science in 1987. He was appointed an Officer of the Order of Australia in 1989.

Dr Sefton D. Hamann (aged 47) was Chief of the CSIRO Division of Applied Chemistry.[8] He was internationally known for his contributions on the physico-chemical effects of pressure but had broad scientific interests. He is one of the few Australians to be invited by the Swedish Academy of Sciences to present a paper at a Nobel Symposium. He was elected a Fellow of the Australian Academy of Science in 1966 and died in 2009.

For the Thredbo meeting, the Bank invited two more scientists with particular expertise.

Dr Neil B. Lewis (aged 68) had just retired from his position as Head of the Research Department, Kodak (A'Asia) Ltd, a position that he had held since 1930.[9] Lewis graduated from the University of Melbourne in 1923 and worked with A.C.D. Rivett on heterogeneous equilibria until 1924, when he went to Oxford on an 1851 Exhibition Scholarship. He worked with N.V. Sidgwick on the properties of salts of beryllium and obtained his PhD in 1926. He spent two years with T. Svedberg in Uppsala (commencing in the year that Svedberg won the Nobel Prize) before working as a physicist on the Imperial Geophysical Experimental Survey. In 1930 he was appointed by Kodak to establish the Kodak Research Laboratory in Abbotsford, Victoria. He held that position until he retired in 1967, although by then Kodak had moved to a new site at Coburg, another Melbourne suburb. He died in 1984.

Dr David H. Solomon (aged 37) was a Principal Research Scientist at the CSIRO Division of Applied Mineralogy.[10] While not the youngest guest, he was certainly the most 'junior'. Solomon had worked for Dulux Australia (or its predecessors) from his leaving school until joining CSIRO in 1963. His path to a research career was unusual in that he had completed his PhD part-time while working for Dulux. His book *The Chemistry of Organic Film Formers* had just been published and he was developing a strong polymer group. He had been involved in all aspects of product development at Dulux and was keen to see his research at CSIRO go to the market. Dulux had sent him overseas to the parent company in England in 1959 and he became aware that there was no need for any cultural cringe by Australian scientists. His time in industry exposed him to the downsides of Australia's tariff policy. Under this policy, which was aimed at import replacement, technology was imported under highly restricted agreements. The agreements allowed the Australian companies to have access to technical developments from overseas but usually any Australian developments were given to the overseas licensor. Solomon could see that the Bank operated on the same sort of model. It imported all its technology, expected suppliers to provide the most advanced technology and was prepared to share any improvements it developed with anyone who would listen. The Bank saw its task as only supplying the Australian market for banknotes. Solomon knew that a project of the scope articulated by Coombs would not succeed if it was going to address only the Australian market. Solomon was very active in the Royal Australian Chemical Institute and was well known to Price. He was a Foundation Fellow of the Australian Academy of Technological Science and Engineering in 1975, elected a Fellow of the Australian Academy of Science in 1975 and elected Fellow of the Royal Society of London in 2004. His work on the banknote project was recognised by the award of the Australian Bicentennial Science Achievement Award in 1988 and the CSIRO Chairman's Medal (jointly with the Bank's Don Addison) in 1987. He was appointed a Member of the Order of Australia in 1990 and awarded the Prime Minister's Prize for Science (jointly with Dr E. Rizzardo) in 2011.

Dr E.G. (Taffy) Bowen (aged 57), who was Chief of the CSIRO Division of Radiophysics, was an obvious candidate to be invited to the April 1968 meeting and was involved with Prunster in the earliest discussions of possible scientific work on forgery proof notes.[11] He did not attend the April 1968 meeting because of prior commitments in the UK concerning the Anglo-Australian Telescope but clearly kept thinking about the problem and, as will be discussed later, sent a diffraction grating to his contacts in the Bank in September 1971. He has been described as 'one of the most dynamic and influential of the wartime generation of British physicists.'[12] He played an important part in the early development of radar in Britain and was involved in the US development of microwave radar. He was instrumental in building the Parkes radio-telescope. Bowen was elected a Fellow of the Australian Academy of Science in 1957 and of the Royal Society of London in 1975. He was appointed Commander of the Order of the British Empire in 1962 and died in 1991.

The Bank representatives

The Bank representatives at the two meetings were an equally impressive group of career central bankers. Two were later Governors of the Reserve Bank.

Dr Coombs (aged 64) was the first Governor of the Reserve Bank, holding that office from January 1960 to July 1968.[13] The Thredbo meeting was one of his last activities as Governor. Coombs was an economist by training with a BA and MA from the University of Western Australia and a PhD from the London School of Economics.

He had a distinguished career as an economist with the Commonwealth Bank, the Treasury, the Department of Post-war Reconstruction and the Reserve Bank. He became a Fellow of the Australian Academy of Science by special election in 1969 and was a Foundation Fellow of both the Australian Academy of the Humanities in 1969 and the Academy of the Social Sciences in Australia in 1971. He died in 1997.

Mr (later Sir) Harold (Harry) M. Knight (aged 46) was Deputy Governor Designate.[14] He became the third Governor, from July 1975 to August 1982. Knight was an economist with a Master of Commerce degree from the University of Melbourne. He joined the Commonwealth Bank in 1936 and worked with the Commonwealth/Reserve Bank until 1982 apart from serving in the AIF (1940–43) and the RANVR (1943–45) and on a secondment to the International Monetary Fund (1955–59). He was awarded a Distinguished Service Cross in 1945 and appointed a Knight Commander of the Order of the British Empire in 1979.

R.A. (Bob) Johnston (aged 43) was the Manager, Investment Department. He was an economist by training with a Bachelor of Commerce degree from the University of Melbourne. He became the fourth Governor, from August 1982 to July 1989. Johnston had been with the Commonwealth then the Reserve banks since 1940 except during 1943–46 when he was in the RAAF. He was seconded to the International Bank for Reconstruction and Development in 1976 and returned to the Bank in 1978 as Secretary until his appointment as Governor in 1982. He was appointed a Companion of the Order of Australia in 1986.

W.H. (Bill) Wilcock (aged ~62) was a distinguished banker and General Manager of the Note Issue Department. He had been seconded to the Bank Negara Malaysia where he was the first Governor, from January 1959 to July 1962. On his return to Australia he was appointed General Manager of the Note Issue Department until he retired in 1969. He was appointed a Commander of the Order of the British Empire in 1970.

J.G. Menzies (aged ~60) was also a distinguished banker and Manager for Victoria. He had been Chief Accountant of the Bank before his secondment to the Bank Negara Malaysia as Deputy Governor. He was appointed Manager for Victoria on his return to Australia in 1966 and remained in that position until he retired in 1967.

L.P. Kearney was Superintendent of the Note Issue Section of the Note Issue Department. This was his highest position in the Bank.

Ron W. Prunster (aged 57) was the Bank's Science Liaison Officer. He had joined the Bank in 1961 as Science Liaison Officer in the Research Department at its Sydney office after a career as a scientist in the CSIR/CSIRO Division of Plant Industry. He retired from the Bank in 1973.

M.F.W. (Monty) Brown (aged 53) was Works Manager at the Note Issue Department. He was a printer by training who had joined the Bank as Works Manager in 1962. His title changed to Manager Printing in 1969, Manager, Research and Development in 1972 and Chief Manager, Research and Development in 1976. He retired from the Bank in 1978. He was arguably the only person at both meetings who knew anything about the production of banknotes.

Bankers' Clubs

Meetings such as these were quite an unusual event for the Reserve Bank of Australia and probably for note printing authorities anywhere in the world. The Bank was a member of various 'Bankers' Clubs', one of the most important of which was the Four-Nation Anti-Counterfeiting Group, the four nations being Canada, Australia, the UK and the US.[15] Representatives of the note printing authorities of these countries met on a regular basis to discuss note security issues and new technologies to tackle them. These were free-ranging discussions which provided the ideas for much of the security in the original paper decimal notes. The technology was usually owned by the companies supplying the machines, paper, inks and devices rather than by the note printing authorities themselves. Given this background, it was probably not surprising that McCracken came away from the two meetings with the impression that he was there to contribute ideas but that he would not hear from the Bank again. None of the participants signed any confidentiality agreements. The Bank was free to do whatever it pleased with the ideas generated at the two meetings. The Bankers' Clubs had served the Bank well and it is not surprising that Bank staff wanted to contribute ideas that would benefit members of its club rather than build a new manufacturing industry in Australia.

The first meeting

In his opening remarks at the first meeting, in April 1968, the Governor indicated that advances in colour photography and the ready availability of commercial office printing equipment had conferred advantages on the forger. He said 'Accepted security features like the watermark, metal thread and intaglio printing could not be faithfully reproduced but could now be adequately imitated to pass.'[16] He explained that the object of the meetings was to see if the assembled distinguished company could devise techniques to produce notes which would be more difficult to counterfeit. He thought it desirable not to restrict the areas of study and to bring other minds to bear on the problem. He planned that the group would meet again in mid June.

The implication of Coombs' remarks was that he intended a brain-storming interaction with the scientists, after which the Bank's own technical people would implement the ideas.

The minutes recorded that many topics were raised, including:[17]

1 whether consideration had to be restricted to the use of paper-like materials for currency notes, and the decision that it need not be. The recent development of plastic-based 'paper' was mentioned;

2 dissection of the cost of currency note production into capital, labour and material components;
3 the prospect of mechanising the counting of withdrawn notes (it was suggested that if the hole borings through withdrawn notes could be arranged at an angle through the bundle it would provide a longer and 'stepped' arrangement which might be mechanically counted);
4 the possible use of diffraction gratings or moiré interference patterns to indicate inaccurate registrations in printing. This posed several questions in obtaining absolute measurements of such characteristics as:
   - the relationship between width and depth of graves in an engraving plate for the finest lines that can be resolved in printing and the deepest grave for ink deposit by intaglio;
   - the precision in printing register between printings on each side of the sheet. What is the relative precision in this between the Simultan® presses and commercial office equipment? What would be the relative rejection rates in obtaining 'precise' register with one type of equipment and the other?;
   - the finest lines that can be resolved by the intaglio and by Simultan® presses;
   - will the paper distortion caused by intaglio printing distort the registration of patterns printed in register earlier on opposite sides of the sheet by Simultan®? What is the likely variation in distortion between one end of a sheet and another?;
5 the prospect of electronic scan of dot and line etchings and their transfer to engraving plates by laser beam;
6 some physical and chemical characteristics of currency note paper and that used in the recent forgeries (each visitor was given several samples of randomly selected sheets of each type of paper so that they might undertake their own determinations);
7 the prospect that a behavioural scientist might be briefed and invited to join the next meeting, and that someone with photography expertise should also be included.

It is clear from the notes of the meeting that much of the discussion involved incremental improvements on the existing processes. Some, e.g. point 3 above, seem in retrospect to have little or nothing to do with improving banknote security. However, it was consistent with the Bank's business model and is a good illustration of the notion that an entrenched business model can inhibit innovation.

The only radical suggestion was the possible use of plastic paper that Solomon had discussed with Price. Price suggested that Solomon be invited to Thredbo. Solomon thought, while reading the minutes of the first meeting, that since the 1966 forgery had been readily accepted by the general public then if only incremental improvements were made to conventional techniques they probably would not bring the result that the Bank needed.

Recollections from Thredbo

The Bank arranged for a second meeting to be held at Thredbo on the weekend of 15–16 June 1968. It circulated additional notes for Thredbo in early June with some data relevant to points 2 and 4 above as well as brief notes on other matters.[18]

In response to point 2, the Bank provided a dissection of the costs in currency note production. Material, labour and indirect costs comprised 26, 36 and 38% respectively. Paper costs were 21.6% of the total. What the group did with this information is not revealed.

Brown, it was reported, had made many measurements related to the thickness of printed lines and the depth of the graves of the intaglio dies. He had also printed two moiré patterns to indicate the variations between printing in correct register and out of register. More significantly, some simple experiments had been done to obtain photographic simulation of diffraction grating effects. This experiment was not foreshadowed in the notes of the April meeting but may have come from informal discussions with Walsh, who had worn a diffraction grating tiepin to that meeting.[19]

Why was Solomon invited to the Thredbo meeting? He was very much the junior scientist of the group, having been in CSIRO since 1963 and holding a classification equivalent to an Associate Professor at a university.

Price had indicated to the Bank in early discussions the need to include a polymer scientist in the group. Polymer science was not a large component of Australian academic research in the 1960s. Indeed, when Solomon was interviewed in 1963 by Price, then Chief of the CSIRO Division of Organic Chemistry, for a position in that division he was told that CSIRO had no interest in research to understand polymerisation reactions. He was not offered that position but Price must have been impressed with his potential because his application was forwarded to the Division of Applied Mineralogy, which wanted a scientist with industrial experience to work in a group studying mineral-organic complexes. Fortunately for this story, Solomon was offered and accepted that position.

Price later told Solomon that, when thinking about the possible ongoing needs of a banknote project, he perceived that some industrial experience would be essential. In 1968 there were ~500 CSIRO staff in the Industrial Chemistry Laboratories at Fishermens Bend in Melbourne but, despite the lab's name, few of the staff had any industrial experience. Only Solomon had both industrial experience and knowledge of polymer chemistry.

In 1968 Solomon was Chairman of the Polymer Division of the Royal Australian Chemical Institute (RACI). He had invited Professor Seiko Okamura from Japan to be an overseas speaker at the Polymer Division's annual symposium. Okamura consulted for a Japanese company and had invented a synthetic paper made from polyvinyl alcohol fibres. The business card that he had presented to Solomon was printed on this synthetic material and was on his desk when Price visited his office in 1968. Conscious of the need to impress his boss, Solomon suggested that the material may be suitable for a banknote. Price immediately encouraged Solomon to develop this idea as a matter of urgency, and be prepared to discuss it at the Thredbo meeting. Solomon wrote to Okamura requesting samples of synthetic paper; these arrived in early June. Solomon gave some samples to Brown a few days before the Thredbo meeting.

No minutes of the Thredbo meeting were circulated, at least to the external participants. Only two of the guests were still alive in 2013. McCracken remembers a discussion of the use of diffraction gratings as a security feature.[20] He was of the opinion that the Thredbo meeting was his last contact with the Bank. His recollection was that if any further work was needed the Bank would go to CSIRO. Solomon does not have a clear recollection of a discussion about security devices. Both have clear recollections of two things. They both remember that Lewis, the photography expert, reacted to most suggestions with the mantra 'If you can see it you can photograph it' and therefore, by implication, make a printing plate. Both recall that there was no discussion of any next steps. There was no sense of urgency in the Bank and no sense that anyone would do something about the problem. Johnston was present at both meetings. He remembers that at the Thredbo meeting everyone saw Walsh's diffraction grating and that Coombs thought 'they couldn't be put on paper'.[21]

Solomon recalls landing at Thredbo airport in a small chartered plane with the other delegates and finding a gift bottle of Scotch in his room at the hotel. He did not drink spirits and found this welcoming gesture by the Bank at variance with a weekend focused on a serious problem. At the formal discussion sessions, Solomon was anxious to see the results of printing on the plastic paper he had obtained from Japan, but Brown did not provide them until well into the weekend. In the discussions, Solomon remembers an atmosphere of negativity from the Bank's Note Printing Branch staff and from the implication by the former Kodak manager, Lewis, that if a note can be photographed then colour separation technology makes it possible to make printing plates and hence forge the notes. This comment must have registered subconsciously in Solomon's mind. He also recalls that towards the end of the meeting, Brown produced several $1 and $2 notes that he had printed on the synthetic paper from Japan. The notes were very good and could have easily been mistaken for genuine notes, therefore Brown was reluctant to allow Solomon to take them away from Thredbo. Solomon was very encouraged by the quality of the plastic notes but surprised that Brown had not communicated with him before the meeting.

Solomon did, however, learn an important lesson from this incident. The PVAl $1 and $2 notes were unique and the Bank could have arranged for a special grade of the plastic paper for use in banknotes. The plastic notes were also expected to be more durable. However, the uniqueness was not evident and so failed the 'recognised by the person in the street' test. Similar reasoning applied to most of the other ideas from Thredbo. For example, the Bank could have improved its print quality with very fine lines but these were not obvious to the public. Indeed, the 1967 forgery illustrated that the public would accept print inferior to that of the genuine notes.

Solomon did not leave the Thredbo meeting having simply enjoyed a pleasant weekend away. Rather, he thought that he should go away and do something! So did Hamann. He and Solomon continued to explore various ideas for more secure banknotes. If the other participants did likewise their ideas were not communicated to the Bank.

The background of the two organisations: CSIR/CSIRO and the Bank

Before continuing the story of how Solomon and Hamann developed their ideas, it is worth reflecting on the two organisations involved in the project. The two decades during which plastic note development took place were decades in which both institutions were experiencing great change. The development of the plastic banknote was of the highest priority for the scientists and engineers involved but it may not have been for the senior managers of either organisation.

History of CSIR/CSIRO

CSIRO was formed in 1949 from the Council for Scientific and Industrial Research, which had been created in 1926 following the recognition after World War I that Australia needed to develop its own research and development capacity. The history of both the CSIR and the CSIRO has been well documented.[22,23,24]

The period from 1949 to the election of the Whitlam government in 1972 was when Australia developed its civil research and development capacity from a fairly low base. It was a period of technological optimism brought about in part by Vannevar Bush's 1945 report to President Truman *Science: The Endless Frontier*. He wrote that basic research was 'the pacemaker of technological progress' and 'New products and new processes do not appear full-grown. They are founded on new principles and new conceptions, which in turn are painstakingly developed by research in the purest realms of science!'

CSIRO had a large investment in research into agriculture, including wool, and had strong support from rural communities and their political representatives. It was a time of growing resources. Sir Frederick White, CSIRO Chairman from 1959 to 1970, remarked that those were times when research 'money was easy to obtain and the increase in our annual appropriation from the Commonwealth government was quite large so growth, therefore, followed suit.'[25]

CSIR/CSIRO was structured around autonomous divisions established to address the research needs of a particular industry – rather like its modern National Research Flagships. CSIR/CSIRO developed all the disciplinary capabilities within those divisions that it thought appropriate for the needs of that industry. This meant some duplication of capabilities but this was tolerated in the interests of the efficiency and because of the ready availability of funding. Notions of technology transfer or commercialisation were foreign to those times. This was partly because of the view that technological progress would follow automatically from scientific discoveries and partly because the small community involved in the industries in those times generally knew what was going on.

The election of the Whitlam government in 1972 was the beginning of change in CSIRO. The new government's support base was firmly in the metropolitan areas and the union movement, and this inevitably led to a greater emphasis on the manufacturing and mining industries. The 1973 oil crisis started in October 1973 when Iran, Iraq, Abu Dhabi, Kuwait, Saudi Arabia and Qatar unilaterally raised the price of Saudi light marker crude by 17% and announced production cuts – those countries wanted to 'punish' the US decision to resupply the Israeli military during the Yom Kippur war. The oil crisis caused a major disruption to the world economy and, of course, to the Australian economy. The government proposed transferring the Minerals Research laboratories of CSIRO to the Department of Minerals and Energy. This move was strongly resisted by CSIRO and eventually defeated.[26] The incident did raise the issue of the need for a comprehensive research organisation and whether taxpayers were getting value from their investment. Another policy decision of the Whitlam government which had a profound effect on CSIRO was the decision in June 1973 to cut tariff protection of industry immediately by 25% as a means of restraining inflation. This led to the demise of some manufacturing firms and to a rethink of the place of local research and innovation. Solomon's experience at Dulux had made him very well acquainted with the effect that high tariff barriers had on local innovation. When operating under a regime of high tariff protection it made good business sense for a local company or the local branch of an overseas company to license technology rather than to develop it in-house. The company could manufacture the product only for the Australian market and compete with imported products under tariff protection. Under these arrangements any local innovation was usually owned by the licensor. There was therefore little incentive for local innovation. Solomon understood that the Bank was used to importing all its technology and using its monopoly position to produce notes for the Australian market. He knew that developing a new technology required considerable investment which would need access to more than the Australian market to recover the investment.

The Fraser government was elected in 1975 and, in its first Budget in 1976, announced that it was setting up an independent inquiry into CSIRO, to be chaired by Professor A.J. Birch. The inquiry's report to the government in 1977 recommended a shift away from fundamental research towards strategic mission-oriented research.[27] It also recommended measures to involve end-users in the processes for the allocation of resources to research. The *Science and Industry Research Act* was amended to replace the flat divisional structure with a two-level Institute and Division structure which grouped together divisions operating in similar sectors of the economy. Solomon's Division of Applied Organic Chemistry was included in the Institute of Industrial Technology and Solomon reported to the Institute Director rather than directly to the Chairman. The new Executive, which included the Directors of the Institutes, established an external review committee of CSIRO's technology transfer processes. The committee reported in June 1983.

The government changed in March 1983 and the new Minister for Science and Technology, Barry Jones, took a very active interest in CSIRO, particularly in its research for the 'sunshine industries' involving information and communications technology, and biotechnology. The Executive considered the technology transfer review, noting the Minister's interests. It decided not to follow the committee's recommendation to form an Innovation Support Service within CSIRO, deciding instead to form a company, Sirotech. This company would assist in meeting CSIRO's technology development and commercial assessment needs. The company existed from 1984 to 1993 and played a role in the banknote story. The government must not have been satisfied with CSIRO's progress in meeting its policy objectives, however, as in May 1985 it announced that it had requested the Australian Science and Technology Council (ASTEC) to report on 'Future Directions for CSIRO'.[28] ASTEC recommended 'that CSIRO's main role be the conduct of applications-oriented research combined with a commitment to ensuring the effective transfer of its research results to end users.' It also recommended that CSIRO be managed by an independent Board that had the power to appoint the Chief Executive. The first Board Chairman was the former Premier of New South Wales, Neville Wran QC. In 1988, the government formally required CSIRO to earn 30% of its appropriation budget from external sources. This requirement influenced the later stages of the Bank project.

History of the Bank

The Reserve Bank of Australia is an older institution than CSIR/CSIRO. Its origins go back to 1910.[29]

At the time of Federation, paper currency circulating in Australia consisted of notes payable in gold coin and issued by trading banks and Queensland Treasury notes. The *Australian Notes Act 1910* prohibited the circulating of states' notes as money and the *Bank Notes Act 1910* imposed a 10% tax on banknotes issued or reissued by any bank.

The Commonwealth Bank was established by the *Commonwealth Bank Act 1911*. The legislation allowed for commercial and savings bank functions but no central banking or note printing functions. The Commonwealth Bank opened for business in 1912. Responsibility for note issue was transferred to it in 1920 under the control of an independent Notes Board. In 1924, a Commonwealth Bank Board was established and the control of note issue passed to the Bank Board, where it has remained ever since. When the control of note issue passed to the Commonwealth Bank, the notes had to bear the promise that the Treasurer would redeem the notes for gold on demand at the Head Office of the Commonwealth Bank. This provision was abolished in 1932, after which the notes had to state only that they were legal tender throughout the Commonwealth.

The Australian Treasury established its note printing works in the Old Kings warehouse at the western end of Flinders St in Melbourne. In 1912 it appointed Thomas S. Harrison, an Englishman with extensive knowledge of security printing, as the note printer. The first notes were ready for numbering on 1 May 1913. The rising demand for notes led to the need for larger premises, which were established in the Melbourne suburb of Fitzroy in 1924. This site was expanded by the acquisition of an adjacent property previously used as a car dealership. The area was known as the Bayford site and, as we will discuss later, was where much of the Bank's work on this project was carried out. The premises were used until 1981 when the Note Printing Branch moved to its current location in the outer Melbourne suburb of Craigieburn. The Fitzroy premises are now a campus of the Australian Catholic University.

The global depression sparked by the 1929 stock market crash hastened the development of the central banking functions of the Bank. These functions were formalised in 1945 with the passing of the *Commonwealth Bank Act* and the *Banking Act* in that year. The *Reserve Bank Act 1959* changed the name of the 1924 body to the Reserve Bank of Australia and formalised its powers in relation to the administration of monetary and banking policy and exchange control. The commercial and savings bank activities were transferred to a new entity, the Commonwealth Banking Corporation. The new structure commenced on 14 January 1960.[30]

As B.W. Fraser, Governor of the Reserve Bank from 1989–96, said in a foreword, 'These were decades of massive change for Australia, in terms not only of economic development but also of economic ideas. By the end of the period, Keynesianism had given way to monetarism, and we were on the road towards financial deregulation and floating exchange rates'.[31] But in the 602-page book in which those sentences appeared, the author devoted only seven pages to note printing issues.[30]

Sources of tension

It is worth reflecting on three broad issues relating to the development of new products. The first is the models that companies and research organisations use in thinking about how to connect technical potential with the realisation of economic value. The second issue is how companies and research organisations expect to fund the activity. The third is how to test new products before they enter the market place. It is our view that the lack of clarity on each of these was the principal source of tension within the Bank project and a major contributor to its slow progress. Twenty years is a long time from conception to market.

The need for a suitable business model

Chesbrough and Rosenbloom, in their major study of the Xerox Corporation's spin-off companies, proposed that the heuristic logic that creates the connection between technical potential and economic value is the organisation's 'business model'.[32] According to Chesbrough and Rosenbloom, the functions of a business model are to:

- articulate the value proposition, i.e. the value created for users by the offering based on the technology;
- identify a market segment, i.e. the users to whom the technology is useful and for what purpose, and specify the revenue generation mechanisms for the firm;
- define the structure of the value chain within the firm required to create and distribute the offering, and determine the complements needed to support the firm's position in this chain;
- estimate the cost structure and profit potential of producing the offering, given the value proposition and the value chain chosen;
- describe the position of the firm within the value network linking suppliers and customers, including identification of potential complementors and competitors;
- formulate the competitive strategy by which the innovating firm will gain and hold advantage over rivals.

Chesbrough and Rosenbloom claimed that a business model can unlock latent value from a technology, but its logic constrains any search for new, alternative models for other technologies. Business model certainty can constrain discontinuous innovation within a company, leading it away from technical uncertainty. Companies that are aware of these constraints often engage with publicly financed research institutes (PFRI) or other companies to explore new approaches for innovation.

Publicly funded research institutes thrive on technical uncertainty. Their employees are usually rewarded for publishing papers in the international literature, not necessarily for endeavouring to capture the economic value of their work. In recent years governments around the world have been forcing their research institutes to concentrate more on commercialising their research outputs. Gilding, Thompson, Spurling, Simpson and Elsum canvassed some of these issues in their study of the commercialisation of three CSIRO technologies.[33] They concluded that PFRIs are most successful in commercialisation when they tackle projects with high technical uncertainty and where their commercial partner has a well developed business model. In 1968 neither the Bank nor CSIRO had business models particularly suited to the task that they were about to embark on.

Erwin Frand summarised the dilemma faced by CSIRO and the Bank in his comment, 'I have often said that in new business development evolutionary change can come from within, but revolutionary change always comes from without.'[34]

The Bank's 1968 business model

In 1968 the Bank had a well developed business model for its note printing operation. By calling the first meeting, Coombs implicitly acknowledged that this model was constraining innovation. In terms of the Chesbrough and Rosenbloom definition, the Bank's value proposition was that it produced high-quality, well designed banknotes for distribution in Australia and some near neighbours. It had a monopoly in this market segment and had no incentive to explore other markets. It understood its position in the value chain of the note printing business and concentrated entirely on two aspects: the artistic design of the notes and the quality of their production. Given the Bank's monopoly position it was not overly concerned with the cost structure and profit potential of the operation. Its business model relied completely on other firms in the value network to make the technical innovations needed to remain ahead of the forgers. The Bank saw its competitors as the forgers rather than the other legitimate producers of banknotes. Its competitive strategy was to be part of the various Bankers' Clubs and freely exchange information and ideas on the improvement of banknote security. To implement this business model the Bank needed to engage top-quality artists to design the notes and top-quality printers to manage production of the notes. Brown was a printer by training and at the time of the April 1968 meeting was Works Manager of the Note Printing Branch. He was the Bank's senior technical officer at all the initial meetings with CSIRO. Solomon recollects that in all their discussions Brown assumed that the established business model would prevail; that is, the Bank would continue to be responsible for the design and printing of the notes and any technical advance from the project would be shared with other banks and firms in the value network. In the established business model there was no particular economic advantage for the Bank to develop any new technology. On the contrary, it probably enhanced its position in the Bankers' Clubs if it freely discussed any developments at the meetings. Solomon recalls this issue being discussed both formally and informally on three occasions early in the project life. Only one of those discussions is reported in the minutes of any meeting.

A technical committee meeting in March 1973 concluded that it was feasible to produce a plastic note with optically variable security devices. At a convivial lunch after the meeting, Solomon recalls Brown stating that the Bank would share these ideas freely with friends in other banks and that it would be a great contribution to human welfare. Solomon's entirely sober response was to the effect that the Bank did not entirely own the technology and that CSIRO would want a fair return on its investment. Indeed, at that stage of the project CSIRO's investment far exceeded that of the Bank. Solomon was then asked by Brown 'Whether, if CSIRO invented a cure for cancer, would the Organisation want a return on that?' When Solomon said that it certainly would, Brown expressed strong disapproval of Solomon's values and behaviour. The issue of confidentiality was discussed again after the CSIRO/Reserve Bank committee meeting in June 1974 when the committee was preparing a major submission to the Governor. It was raised again at the committee's July meeting, when Solomon requested Paul Grant, an officer from CSIRO Head Office who was secretary of the committee, to review the formal relationship between CSIRO and the Bank concerning exploitation of the results of the joint project.[35] The minutes recorded:

> Mr Brown again pointed out his preference for the basic information about the new notes to be made freely available to the other central banks around the world in accordance with the pattern of the free information exchange which had been cultivated by the 'Central Bankers' Club' in the past. Grant commented that, if such exchange of information amounted to a complete transmission of knowhow together with a free licence to proceed to manufacture of the new notes, a basic policy difference appeared to exist between CSIRO and the Reserve Bank which would need to be resolved at Ministerial level. It was hoped that a compromise would be possible wherein the broad features of the new note would be disclosed and discussed within the Club in sufficient detail to avoid any suggestion of bad faith on the part of the Reserve Bank, but that if another Bank wished to produce the same type of note, detailed knowhow and assistance should be offered by the RBA under a written agreement at a negotiated price.

The CSIRO 1968 business model

In 1968 CSIRO was under no pressure from the Commonwealth government to earn money from commercial activities; its value proposition to the government was that it would conduct high-quality scientific research which would be published and used for economic benefit by firms if they wanted to. The CSIRO market segment was the companies or entities that either chose to work with CSIRO or to exploit its work after publication. All other elements of the Chesbrough and Rosenbloom model were not the concern of CSIRO. As we will see later, this model was made quite explicit in the first agreement that CSIRO had with the Bank. In that agreement CSIRO said the

Bank could do whatever it liked with the results of the research if it agreed that CSIRO retained the right to publish the results. So in the beginning this seemed to be an ideal project. It had high technical uncertainty, making it of great interest to the scientists, and, in the view of the Bank, high business model certainty.

But as the technical uncertainty decreased the business model uncertainty increased. It took a long time for both the Bank and CSIRO to come to terms with this. The business model uncertainty increased for several reasons. Although the first meeting was in 1968 and the first agreement between CSIRO and the Bank was signed in that year, the project did not commence in earnest until 1972. By then the CSIRO value proposition to the government was being challenged. CSIRO was coming to the view that it needed to be more actively engaged in the commercialisation of its research, including more actively engaging firms in the selection of its research programs.

As CSIRO decreased the technical uncertainty, the Bank's business model started to break down. There was no evidence that its traditional technology suppliers were interested in taking up the results of the research. Neither its technical officers nor the more traditionally trained Bank officers managing the project had any experience in dealing with companies outside the rather small group of companies involved in the manufacture of the paper substrate, the production of the specialist banknote printing machines and the suppliers of the special inks.

Solomon's business model

Solomon always held the view that CSIRO should actively engage with firms to select research projects and research directions. He was never comfortable with the idea that CSIRO's task was over when it had published its research. He had a strong conviction that CSIRO needed to conduct research that would support existing firms within the Australian economy and develop new firms and even new industries as a result of its research. Evidence that this was possible came from the scientific instrument industry that was developing as a result of Walsh's invention of atomic absorption technology and from Solomon's experience at BALM Paints where he had been involved in patenting new paint systems and in preparing the business case for their movement to development and production.

Solomon's ideas were first set out in a public document in the 1982 Division of Applied Organic Chemistry Research Report:[36]

> We have taken several steps aimed at exploring ways in which our inventions can be commercialised by Australian manufacturing industry and ways of obtaining closer collaboration with industry. These include continuing discussions with the Australian Chemical Industry Council (Research Sub-Committee) and technical discussion meetings on specific topics organised in conjunction with the Royal Australian

> Chemical Institute and involving people from CSIRO, industry and academia. We also have a program of inviting companies to send technical representatives to visit the Division to see and discuss the Division's programs and the companies' interests.

The value proposition implicit in this statement is that CSIRO would do research in close collaboration with Australian companies with the expectation that one or more of those companies would commercialise the research with subsequent benefit to the Australian economy. For Solomon's division, he identified the market segment as the chemical and plastics industry. The other aspects of the Chesbrough and Rosenbloom model would be the concern of the collaborating company. His vision for the Bank project was that an Australian entity or entities would not only design and print the notes but would manufacture all the components needed. But, as outlined above, the Bank's understanding of its place in the value chain meant that it was unlikely to have an interest in manufacturing the various components needed for the new notes or even be in contact with other firms in Australia which might have an interest.

Attempts to resolve this business model uncertainty were the cause of much of the tension between CSIRO and the Bank.

The banknote and security document value chain

Before discussing how both the CSIRO's and the Bank's business models evolved, it is worth outlining what we now understand as the whole value chain of the banknote and security document business. Security documents include cheques, credit cards, passports and other identification systems.

Production of all these documents commences with the manufacture of the substrate. Until 1988 paper was the only substrate used for banknotes (apart from the use of Tyvek®, a fibrous plastic used in the Isle of Man). Paper is a very common commodity that can be made from a variety of cellulose sources. The paper used in banknotes is usually made from cotton and is made by specialist manufacturers. For example, the paper for US banknotes has been made by Crane & Co. in Dalton, Massachusetts since 1879 and paper for UK banknotes has been made by Portals since 1727.

The next step is to incorporate security devices into the substrate. Some document security devices are built into the substrate and some are incorporated at the printing stage.

An important step in banknote and security document production is, of course, the artistic design of the document, its colours and symbols. This step is usually the province of the central bank or the owner of the document, but can be done by an independent contractor.

With the substrate and security devices selected and the design agreed upon, the next step is to print the banknote or document. Initially, this involves preparation of the printing plates, a step that may involve an entity independent of the printer. For example, the printing plates for Australia's first decimal banknotes were made by Organisation Giori in Milan.

Of all of the processes involved with the production of banknotes and security documents, the actual printing is the most likely to be done by a government agency. For example, US notes are printed by the Bureau of Engraving and Printing. Notes for the Bank of England were for many years printed in the Bank's own printing works but in 2003 De La Rue signed a seven-year contract to print and supply Bank of England currency, thus taking over the bank's manufacturing operation. The contract was renewed in 2009.

The notes need to be distributed to retail banks, collected after they are no longer suitable for circulation, authenticated and destroyed. Any of these activities can be performed either by a government agency or by a private contractor.

The design and manufacture of the printing machines needed to print banknotes and security documents is a specialised business in itself. Some companies include this in the overall package that they offer to a central bank.

The CSIRO–Bank 1979 business model

The passage of time forced both the Bank and CSIRO to think about these matters, and they did so together. The result was a document dated 10 January 1979, entitled 'Proposals for charter and lines of operation for an entity to carry forward the CNRD project'.[37] The project had been called the Currency Notes Research and Development (CNRD) project since 1974.

The proposal was to establish an entity within the Bank or under its control but with CSIRO having an explicit share of effective ownership. The entity would develop the scientific and technical work of the CNRD project, develop the pilot scale production, organise the means of production in collaboration with the Bank's Note Issue Department, keep up a research program and negotiate commercial deals. This proposal was submitted to the CNRD Committee but was never discussed. Instead, the Governor decided to establish a Forward Planning Group to provide advice in relation to the project.

The document was silent on how the entity would be funded and whether it would be able to employ the wide range of professionals necessary to carry out the defined task. It was really a combination of the existing CSIRO and bank business models with all their weaknesses still in place.

The Fink report business model

As we will discuss further in Chapter 10, the Forward Planning Group established in 1979 and chaired by Professor Tom Fink recommended that the Bank proceed with the CNRD project and aim to have a note in circulation in three to four years.[38] It proposed a three-stage process for achieving this. In the definition phase, the Bank would appoint an interim Project Manager and start the process of appointing a permanent Project Manager. During this phase CSIRO would consolidate its work and assist the Bank in defining the specifications of the new note. At some point the project would enter the decision phase, at which the Project Manager would take charge. In this phase CSIRO would assist the Bank in technology transfer. CSIRO would not be involved in the implementation phase. The report recommended that the Bank and CSIRO consider creating a joint venture to deal with export opportunities. The report did not specify the exact timing of the three phases.

He who pays the piper calls the tune

Governments invest in R&D because it is a significant contributor to innovation in the functions it performs and because there are spillovers, benefits that cannot be captured by the innovator. The risk of spillovers tends to decrease as a project goes from basic research to strategic research then to experimental development, so governments tend to concentrate their spending on basic and strategic research. Government R&D agencies and universities understand the risk inherent in research but also understand that there are rewards from successful innovations. Both CSIRO and the Bank are government agencies. CSIRO is funded by the government to do research because of the spillover argument. The Bank uses its money to do research because it believes that innovation will improve its functions. Both CSIRO and the Bank expect to benefit from successful projects, CSIRO from royalties, the sale of intellectual property or the setting up of local industry and the Bank from improvements in the security and efficiency of its provision of services.

Over the life of a project like the one described in this book it would be expected that the Bank and CSIRO might share the funding of the research phase of the project but that the Bank would fully fund the development and production phases. A rule of thumb is that there is a 1:10:100 ratio for expenditure in the research, development and production phases respectively of a successful project. Most of the risk is in the research phase; expenditure in this phase of a successful project is usually well rewarded.

As we will see, CSIRO was a major contributor to funding this project right up to the production phase and had every right to consider that it should have a strong say in the exploitation of the work. It is not surprising that when the Bank indicated that it considered that it had the sole right to determine the exploitation of the technology, that attitude was resented by CSIRO.

Testing procedures

When developing a new product it is very important to know the criteria for success. A high percentage of the world's expenditure on R&D is funded by pharmaceutical and motor vehicle industries and in these two areas markets and testing procedures are well defined. For pharmaceuticals there are clear procedures for testing laid out by national regulatory bodies, for motor vehicles there are both industry and company standards. For the Bank project there were no such guidelines and procedures; all of these had to be developed by the project team.

Paper notes had been in use for hundreds of years so it was unlikely that anyone knew what would be required to introduce a radical innovation in this area. In *Details of Requirements of Commonwealth of Australia Banknotes Commissioned by the Reserve Bank of Australia* for the 1966 decimal notes, there was no discussion at all of the physical properties of the paper.[39] The document assumed that paper would be used and that its properties were acceptable. There were no standard tests which simulated field performance of the note. There were quality control tests for some of the desirable properties of banknotes, such as,durability, tear strength or folding. However, the Bank had such faith in the supplier that it rarely checked that the paper being delivered actually met the specification. The Bank did not even have the equipment to do many of the tests. Senior officers of the Bank understood the reputational and economic consequences of introducing a faulty note and that contributed to their reluctance to commit to introducing the new technology.

Endnotes

1 NAA: B5609, 3/1.
2 D.J. Collins, G.W. Simpson, D.H. Solomon and T.H. Spurling (2004) *Historical Records of Australian Science* **15**, 95–120.
3 P. Humble (2010) *Historical Records of Australian Science* **21**, 221–223.
4 P. Hannaford (2000) *Historical Records of Australian Science* **13**, 179–206.
5 R.H. Frater and R.D. Ekers (2012) *Biographical Memoirs of Fellows of the Royal Society* **58**, 327–346.
6 <http://www.eoas.info/biogs/P000862b.htm>.
7 <http://csiropedia.csiro.au/display/CSIROpedia/McCracken>.
8 T.H. Spurling and D.H. Solomon (2009) *Historical Records of Australian Science* **20**, 255–271.
9 R.W. Home (1990) *Physics in Australia to 1945*. Dept of History and Philosophy of Science, University of Melbourne/National Centre for Research and Development in Australian Studies, Monash University, Melbourne. Also, personal communication from I.H. Coopes.
10 <http://csiropedia.csiro.au/display/CSIROpedia/Solomon> and personal notes.
11 R. Hanbury Brown, H.C. Minnett and F.W.G. White (1992) *Historical Records of Australian Science* **9**, 151–166.
12 R. Hanbury Brown, H.C. Minnett and F.W.G. White (1992) *Historical Records of Australian Science* **9**, 151–166.
13 F. Fenner and S.F. Harris (2000) *Historical Records of Australian Science* **13**, 67–81.
14 The careers of the Bank officers have been constructed from the Reserve Bank of Australia Annual Reports 1959–1980.
15 NAA: B5609, 1/10, 11/3.

16 NAA: B5609, 3/1.
17 NAA: B5609, 3/1.
18 NAA: B5609, 3/1.
19 Personal correspondence from S.D. Hamann to T.H. Spurling, 21 January 1992.
20 Personal communication to T.H. Spurling.
21 Personal communication to T.H. Spurling.
22 G. Currie and J. Graham (1966) *The Origins of CSIRO: Science and the Commonwealth Government, 1901–1926.* CSIRO Publishing, Melbourne.
23 C.B. Schedvin (1987) *Shaping Science and Industry: A History of Australia's Council for Scientific and Industrial Research, 1926–49.* CSIRO Publishing, Melbourne.
24 B. Collis (2002) *Fields of Discovery: Australia's CSIRO.* Allen & Unwin, Sydney.
25 F.W.G. White (1976) *Nature* **261**, 633–636.
26 D.J. Collins, G.W. Simpson, D.H. Solomon and T.H. Spurling (2004) *Historical Records of Australian Science* **15**, 95–120.
27 A. Birch (1977) *Report of the Independent Inquiry into CSIRO.* Parliamentary paper 283/1977, Canberra.
28 ASTEC (1985) *Future Directions for CSIRO: A Report to the Prime Minister by the Australian Science and Technology Council.* AGPS, Canberra.
29 <http://www.rba.gov.au/AboutTheRBA/History/historyoftherba.html>.
30 C.B. Schedvin (1992) *In Reserve: Central Banking in Australia, 1945–1975.* Allen & Unwin, Sydney, p. 294.
31 C.B. Schedvin (1992) *In Reserve: Central Banking in Australia, 1945–1975.* Allen & Unwin, Sydney, Foreword, p. v.
32 H. Chesbrough and R.S. Rosenbloom (2002) *Industrial and Corporate Change* **11**, 529–555.
33 L. Thompson, M. Gilding, T.H. Spurling, G. Simpson and I.R. Elsum (2001) *Innovation: Management, Policy and Practice* **13**, 327–340.
34 E.A. Frand (1978), *Industrial Research/Development*, December, p. 19.
35 NAA:B5609, 1/10.
36 CSIRO Division of Chemicals and Polymers, Annual Report 1982. CSIRO, Melbourne.
37 NAA: B5609, 1/38.
38 P.T. Fink (1979) *Report of Forward Planning Group*, August. A copy of this report is not in the National Archives of Australia collection but is in the possession of the authors.
39 NAA: B5609, 6/17.

Chapter 5
What to do next?

The Forest Products project

Both Sefton Hamann and David Solomon returned from the Thredbo meeting enthusiastic about improving the security of banknotes.

Hamann was interested in the quality of the paper used in banknotes and how this affected the resolution of lines printed by the intaglio process. He was specifically interested in how the properties of the natural fibres in paper affected the quality of the printing, and continued discussions with the Note Issue Department of the Bank and with his colleagues at the CSIRO Division of Forest Products including the Chief of that Division, Roy Muncey.[1] By August 1968 they had developed some ideas and decided to make an official approach to the Bank. Their contacts at the Note Issue Department advised that the best thing to do was for the Chairman of CSIRO to write to the Secretary of the Bank, A.C. McPherson. So on 23 August 1968 Jerry Price wrote to McPherson confirming arrangements 'made by telephone for a meeting in Melbourne between representatives of the Bank and certain CSIRO officers.' The officers were Hamann, Arthur Gaskin (Chief of the Division of Applied Mineralogy and therefore Solomon's chief), Muncey and Price. Further discussions must have taken place because on 10 December 1968 John Shelton, Secretary of the CSIRO Physical Sciences Branch, wrote to the Bank referring to discussions between CSIRO and the Bank concerning the Bank's proposed sponsorship of a research program to be undertaken by CSIRO in the field of currency note production. The nature of this research was not specified in the letter sent to the Bank confirming the arrangement but it was noted that the work would be undertaken in the Division of Forest Products under the general direction of the Chief, Muncey. The Bank paid CSIRO $11 000 (about $120 000 in 2013 dollars) for a one-year research project. There was no mention in the letter of any work on synthetic paper but the presence of Gaskin at the meeting indicates that CSIRO was aware that Solomon had continued his investigation of the possible use of synthetic polymers in banknotes. This project had nothing to do with the minerals industry but nevertheless had Gaskin's support as a project in the national interest.

The CSIRO–Bank agreement

The 10 December letter was the only 'agreement' between CSIRO and the Bank. Its contents give a good insight into the attitude to commercialisation that was dominant in CSIRO in 1968. Shelton noted that:

> As far as practicable, CSIRO retains its right to publish any scientific results of the sponsored research. However, before making any such publication or a disclosure of any substance to a third party, CSIRO will submit in writing to RBA a copy of the proposed publication or outline of the information to be disclosed. If RBA request CSIRO not to proceed with the publication or disclosure of whole or part of the information on the grounds that the security of its currency note operation may be prejudiced then CSIRO will delay publication or disclosure for such period as is specified in writing by RBA.

In 1968, CSIRO's main concern was to preserve its right to publish. It had no concerns about commercial exploitation of the results. Solomon remembers being surprised that two agencies of the Commonwealth needed a formal agreement to work together. He thought that both would be working for the common good of the Australian taxpayer. Of course, in their own view, both were! Coming to a common view of what constituted the 'common good' was the subject of much discussion between the two agencies.

T.J. Bartley, the Secretary of the Bank, responded to the CSIRO letter accepting all the conditions for the collaboration between the Bank and CSIRO. Neither organisation had given any thought to the consequence of success. As will be seen later, some officers of the Bank sometimes viewed the arrangement as collaboration and sometimes as a contract to purchase technology. This caused some tension between the two organisations.

Despite the formal agreement, Hamann must have kept up informal discussions because in March 1969 Monty Brown, Works Manager at the Note Issue Department, sent him a nickel copper die suitable for intaglio printing. Brown said that it 'should prove an excellent subject for your ink experiments' – indicating that Hamann was continuing to dabble in printing as a follow-up to the 1968 meetings.

The June 1970 meeting and further work

The parties agreed to meet in September 1969 to review progress; at that meeting the Bank agreed to extend the project for six months but did not commit extra funds. At this stage of the project there seemed no sense of urgency. The forged notes had been discovered at the end of December 1966. The Governor's first meeting with the scientists was held in April 1968 and in September 1969 the Bank was willing to extend by six months a project in which it had no real involvement. CSIRO submitted its report on 12 May 1970 and requested a half-day meeting to discuss the report and any proposals for further work. This was arranged for June 1970.[2]

The report consisted of two parts. The first was a detailed report from the Division of Forest Products and the second a half-page report from the Division of Applied

Chemistry (which had received none of the $11 000). In fact Solomon, whose work was being reported, was still working in the Division of Applied Mineralogy. CSIRO was at that time arranging for his transfer to the Division of Applied Chemistry.

The Division of Forest Products reported that it had investigated five techniques:

1 paper made from synthetic fibres which had recently been developed commercially;
2 papers made with special surface properties by introducing wool or other fibres;
3 papers with distinctive surface properties, e.g. rough patterned surfaces;
4 papers with built-in patterns, e.g. distinctive thick and thin areas;
5 colour contrasts from the use of bleached, unbleached and dyed fibres.

The Division of Forest Products concluded its report with the prophetic comment:

> There appears to be no difficulty in devising ways in which unusual characteristics may be imparted to whole sheets or selected areas of a sheet, although some specifications may require intricate and specialized processes to be developed.
>
> A major requirement is for the Reserve Bank of Australia to state, quite explicitly, their requirements both for the next few years and on a long-term basis. For example, it would be appropriate to have an indication of the extent to which the Reserve Bank is willing to accept innovation in note composition and printing procedure and design, and at a later stage their possible replacement by some other specialized token. Some indication of the way in which the public would react to such innovations should also be considered.
>
> Until these points are clearly defined, any further research or development work will be random and relatively unprofitable.

Work on plastic substrates was not mentioned in the letter of agreement between CSIRO and the Bank and no money was allocated to the Division of Applied Mineralogy. Nevertheless, Solomon continued to investigate synthetic papers made from polyvinyl alcohol fibres supplied by Sansho Mercantile of Japan. Hamann discussed the work with Solomon and invited him to meetings to review the work being done at the Division of Forest Products. Solomon's own work was 'skunk works' in that it had nothing to do with the research programs of the Division of Applied Mineralogy. Attached to the report from the Division of Forest Products was an addendum from the Division of Applied Chemistry reporting Solomon's preliminary work on the unusual printing characteristics of the synthetic papers. Like the Forest Products work, variations in thickness were used to show different colour effects from ink.

It concluded:

> We suggest that a profitable approach to the problem of forgeries would be to develop a unique paper consisting of strips of different fibres of distinct types, for instance synthetic and natural fibres, and to exploit their different printing characteristics. The fibres could be chosen to produce both a unique appearance and an unusual feel in the printed notes.

Gaskin was not able to attend the June meeting and requested that Solomon go in his place. At this meeting the Bank indicated that it did not think that the work on conventional paper should continue, but it encouraged Solomon to do further work on synthetic paper and report back in June 1971. The Bank did not offer any funds to continue the work. Solomon continued investigating the properties of the polyvinyl alcohol fibres that he had obtained from Okamuru.

In 1970, CSIRO decided to transfer Solomon's polymer group from the Division of Applied Mineralogy to the Division of Applied Chemistry.[3] The letter announcing the move to the staff concerned indicated that it was a strategic decision by the Executive to expand the Division's efforts in polymer chemistry. However, it was almost certainly the result of Solomon's increasing involvement in the Bank project. The project was shrouded in secrecy. Soon after Solomon's group transferred to the Division of Applied Chemistry, Hamann prepared a case for the promotion of Solomon to Chief Research Scientist, the highest career level for a scientist in CSIRO. The case was largely based on Solomon's contributions to polymer chemistry but included the following paragraph: 'I have been associated personally with Solomon in some of his work and been enormously impressed by the extent of his knowledge of chemistry, his originality, his critical ability and his practical turn of mind.' Even in a confidential submission to the CSIRO Executive Hamann only alluded to the Bank project!

Solomon and his team prepared 'paper' from polyvinyl alcohol fibres supplied by Sancho of Japan. They printed on the samples using the inks and dyes supplied by the Bank and experimented with different techniques to produce unusual effects in the paper. The report prepared for the Bank contained eight samples of their work. Sample 8 showed aluminised polyester film incorporated in the paper.

In his 9 June letter to the Bank attached to the report, Shelton asked the Bank to comment on the report as soon as possible because Solomon was going overseas in July and would like to visit possible suppliers in Japan and the US. He also noted that CSIRO was 'a little out of pocket' in preparation of these samples.[4]

The Bank delays its response

The Bank sent a quick reply on 16 June, encouraging Solomon to investigate the overseas suppliers but by November 1971 had not made a considered response to the report. On 5 November, Shelton wrote again to the Bank requesting the return of the samples and noting 'Regretfully, we have come to the conclusion that the interest and initiative that prompted the Bank in the first place to encourage CSIRO to work in the area is no longer maintained.'

On the contrary, the Bank replied on 22 November, it was still interested. We can only speculate why, if it was interested, it took so long to reply. Shelton sent his letter to the Secretary of the Bank at the Head Office in Sydney. At that time the Bank's Research Department (to which Prunster, the Bank officer who organised the first think tank, belonged) was an economic research group not a research group interested in the technical aspects of banknote research. The letter would have made its way to the Note Issue Department in Fitzroy, Melbourne, which at that time did not have a research laboratory and was entirely responsible for the production of the notes. It was around this time that the Bank received a letter from E.G. Bowen, Chief of the CSIRO Division of Radiophysics, who suggested incorporating a diffraction grating into a note – that may have sparked the Bank's reaction. Its reply reported that the Bank was taking steps to increase its R&D capacity at Fitzroy and that it had examined the plastic samples. The 1971/72 Annual Report of the Bank indicated that it had increased its R&D capacity – but only by changing Brown's title to R&D Manager.[5] This is a good indication of the Bank's failure to recognise the magnitude of the task in front of it.

In particular, the Bank expressed interest in Solomon's Sample 8 (see Fig. 3.2), which included an aluminised polyester film:

> Sample No. 8 presents a unique feature with the incorporation of an aluminized polyester film. Such a feature could not be adequately simulated by any conventional printing process known to us. Such an application to a bank-note could be sufficiently unique as to be a complete deterrent to potential counterfeiters. In view of this we should like to see some further work undertaken in this particular application not necessarily undertaken in conjunction with 'paper' fibres but produced in a manner that would allow some appreciation to be made of what production methods would be required to form the base material either in sheets or reels.

The Bank project was on its way.

Hamann's response to the first positive sign from the Bank was typically restrained. He wrote to Shelton on 2 December 1971 saying, 'I think we should now have another discussion with their people to plan further action. I hope they will come to it with clearer ideas than they have in the past, of what they want done.'

The February 1972 meeting and its results

That meeting was held on 21 February 1972 – nearly four years after the initial meeting at Fitzroy. No minutes of that meeting are in the CSIRO records but there is an account of the meeting written by Hamann in December 1991.[6] He recalled:

> That meeting was held on February 2, 1972 and was attended by M F W Brown, R A S Bywater, S D Hamann, R W Prunster, J P Shelton, D H Solomon, and a few others.
>
> At some fairly dull stage of the meeting, M F W Brown suddenly produced – with no fanfare but with a very characteristic flourish! – a most remarkable experimental banknote that he had recently 'pasted together'. It is shown in Figure 1.
>
> Brown's note was a complete break from the kinds of things we had been thinking of. It had the following important and original features, which were all later incorporated in the 1988 Commemorative $10 Note:
>
> 1. It was made of transparent (birefringent) plastic film;
> 2. To provide a background for printing, some areas of the film were rendered nearly opaque with a surface coating of pigment;
> 3. The clear areas of the note contained a spectacular diffraction grating, embossed on thin film, metallized, and sandwiched between two main outer films;
> 4. The grating was a patchwork composite of sections of non-linear rulings (they turned out to be sectors of spiral rulings of several different pitches);
> 5. The grating was visible from both sides of the note;
> 6. The printing on the opaque areas was of a fine quality.
>
> Brown explained that the diffracting film (or 'rainbow' metallized film, as it was then known) had been sent to R W Prunster from London by Dr E G (Taffy) Bowen, with an injunction to 'forge this if you can'. Bowen had picked it up at the Army and Navy Store, in September 1971, as a decorative wrapping material, at about $1 a square foot. He suggested in a letter to Brown that a similar embossing technique might be combined with holography to give 'a passable multi-colour 3D picture of Elizabeth R'.

Plate 11 shows an image of Brown's note. It is not dissimilar in appearance to Solomon's Sample 8 in Fig. 3.2.

In a letter to Hamann dated 28 March 1972 Bowen expanded his comment about the Queen: 'which could only be reproduced if the forger also persuaded the Queen to sit in front of a laser beam! However this would involve a few extra tricks which are not entirely in the bag yet.'[7] He also noted that 'Paul Wild is interested in this letter and may have some ideas.' Dr Paul Wild had succeeded Bowen as Chief of the Division of Radiophysics and later became involved in the project as Chair of CSIRO. There is, however, no evidence that he contributed ideas on security devices to the project.

Solomon's recollection of the February 1972 meeting is different from Hamann's. He remembers Monty Brown suddenly producing the note with a very characteristic flourish and saying 'Look, you don't even need printing!' As can be seen from in Plate 11, there was printing on the note, which was made from Mylar®. Hamann described it as 'fine printing' but Solomon noted that it was not intaglio printing and therefore, by Brown's standard's, not 'fine printing'. The note was described by Monty Brown at this meeting as an 'idiot sheet'. By this he meant that the note included the optically variable device as the only security feature and did not need the detailed patterns and intaglio printing of conventional notes. Solomon also recalls Brown mentioning the 1945 Bank of England £5 note as an example of an 'idiot sheet' that had been in circulation for 12 years.[8] That note had monochrome printing on one side only and a metal thread; it was hardly an example of a secure 'idiot sheet'. The quest for an optically variable device dominated the project for two decades. Users of the current Australian notes will be well aware that a highly secure plastic note can be produced without an elaborate optically variable device.

It is worth going back to the Bank's comments on Sample 8 in Solomon's addition to the CSIRO report.[2] These were written after the Bank had received Bowen's commercial diffraction grating. Brown's subsequent production of the note makes it likely that one of the 'further unique features' that the Bank thought might be developed was a diffraction grating.

The records do not reveal whether CSIRO included the aluminised polyester film in Sample 8 with the idea of developing further unique security features. We assume that this was the case, otherwise there was no point in the aluminised patch. Hamann and Solomon had already consulted colleagues at the Division of Chemical Physics about their straight line gratings, at least before Hamann's letter of 16 March 1972 to Bowen in which he said: 'David Solomon and I are fairly sure that we can produce this kind of effect – in fact we have already done so in a crude way using diffraction gratings from Chemical Physics and pressing them into thermoplastic films.' A footnote explained that 'Our gratings are a bit too good. They have 70 000 lines to the inch, where your example has ~15 000.'

The exchanges indicate that in 1971 the two organisations were not being entirely open with one another. The Bank had clearly not revealed to the CSIRO scientists at Fishermens Bend that their former colleague from the Division of Radiophysics had sent an interesting sheet of diffraction gratings; the group at Fishermens Bend did not divulge why they were interested in aluminised films. It also reflected the Bank's tendency to worry about production methods before it was clear what was going to be produced – an attitude that had a great influence on the project.

As mentioned earlier, Bowen bought the diffraction gratings from the Army and Navy Stores in London. With the renewed interest from the Bank, Hamann tried to find the manufacturer of the product. He wrote to the Australian Scientific Liaison Officer in London, Dr G.N. Lance, to see if he could help. Lance's obvious first step was to contact the Army and Navy Stores, which denied ever having sold the product! Hamann then contacted the Scientific Liaison Officers in Washington and Tokyo and eventually tracked down the manufacturer – Toppan Printing in Tokyo. The product was imported to Australia by Half Moon Products, a small company in Northcote, a suburb of Melbourne.[9]

Establishing the project

It took another month before Shelton wrote to the Bank concerning the outcomes of the February meeting.[10] On 24 March 1972 he wrote to Bywater:

> My apologies for the delay due to pressures in this office in following-up the helpful discussions recently held with you and your colleagues.
>
> We would like to suggest for your consideration, a grant from the Bank to CSIRO, for use in the Division of Applied Chemistry to enable appointment to be made of an Experimental Officer for 2 years. An appropriate appointment would be in the range of Experimental Officer Grade I or II, and, depending on the qualifications and experience of the person concerned, would be in the salary range of $4,714 p.a. – $8,421 p.a. An additional sum of, say, $2000 per annum would assist towards non-salary expenses, such as consumable stores.

The Bank did not reply; Shelton rang Bywater on 21 April and quickly got the following response:

> I confirm our telephone conversation of this morning, namely that the Bank has approved the proposal to reimburse CSIRO (up to a maximum of about $21,000 sought) to cover the appointment of an experimental officer for research on the Bank's behalf on the basis outlined in your letter of 24 March 1972.
>
> We should like to know in due course details of the appropriate timing and procedure for reimbursement payments. I understand that you prefer quarterly reimbursement, but would like to know the commencement date when this is known.
>
> As discussed with you, I feel that there will be considerable merit in an arrangement for regular quarterly meetings between Drs. Hamann and Solomon and Mr Brown and myself to discuss progress of the research and redirect it as necessary. This of course, would be apart from any normal day to day contacts on specific aspects.

> We are looking forward greatly to this revival of our collaboration and I hope that your officers as well as ours will find the project interesting and stimulating.

The position of experimental officer was advertised and, to comply with the secrecy of the project, the duties were 'to undertake the synthesis and characterisation of polymers and to investigate methods of modifying the surface properties of polymers.' The new appointee was to work in Solomon's section.

Note that Bywater wanted regular quarterly meetings to 'redirect' the research as necessary. It is not clear what he meant by this. The overall direction of the project was well understood, i.e. to produce a polymer banknote with an optically variable security device. The two Bank officers on the committee had no technical expertise and the Bank made no effort to recruit any scientists to the project. Its ability to redirect the research was always quite limited.

Endnotes

1 NAA: B5609, 5/3.
2 NAA: B5609, 5/3.
3 D.H. Solomon, CSIRO Personal History file, accessed by the authors.
4 NAA: B5609, 5/3.
5 RBA Annual Report 1971/72.
6 Personal correspondence from S.D. Hamann to T.H. Spurling, 21 January 1992.
7 Letter given to T.H. Spurling by S.D. Hamann.
8 See <http://www.bankofengland.co.uk/banknotes/Pages/denom_guide/nonflash/5-white-2.aspx>.
9 NAA: B5609, 6/17.
10 NAA: B5609, 5/3.

Chapter 6
1972 to 1974

Another letter of agreement

The only formal confirmation of the new arrangements was a letter dated 21 April 1972 stating that the Bank had 'approved the proposal to reimburse CSIRO (up to a maximum of about $21,000 sought) to cover the appointment for two years of an experimental officer for research on the Bank's behalf on the basis outlined in your letter of 24 March 1972.'[1] That letter referred to recent 'helpful discussions' and proposed the said appointment. In reply to the Bank's letter, CSIRO agreed with the proposal to hold quarterly meetings to review progress and noted that the initial work would be 'directed to the use of diffraction rulings in plastic laminations.' None of the correspondence between the Bank and CSIRO discussed how the research would be exploited so it must be assumed that both were working under the December 1968 condition that 'as far as practicable, CSIRO retains its right to publish any scientific results of the sponsored research' but won't prejudice banknote security. As noted in Chapter 3, David Solomon was working towards not only securing the Australian currency but also establishing a new industry in Australia. He, perhaps naively, assumed that his superiors in CSIRO and his collaborators in the Bank were also working towards these twin goals so was not at all concerned that the project started without a new agreement being negotiated.

The Bank's requirements

The Reserve Bank never did take the advice of the Division of Forest Products to 'state, quite explicitly, their requirements both for the next few years and on a long-term basis.'[2] However, their requirements were clear enough to Solomon and Hamann. They understood in general terms that the Bank wanted a banknote made from plastic with an optically variable security device that would be extremely difficult to forge, and that is what they set about to achieve.

As noted in Chapter 3, banknote security features are generally classified as primary, secondary or tertiary devices. The Australian notes issued in 1966 relied entirely on primary security devices. They contained a watermark on the cotton fibre paper, a metallic strip and intaglio printing. As was clearly demonstrated by the 1966 forgeries, all these devices could be simulated quite well. The 'feel' of the note is largely due to the intaglio printing and this was not successfully simulated by the forgers. The forgers had added a wax coating late in production to try to simulate the feel of the genuine note but that was the very aspect that caused suspicion in the Ashburton milkbar owner who raised the alarm. The mock-up note presented by Monty Brown, Works Manager at the Note Issue Department, was the simplest possible. It relied entirely on the diffraction grating for its security. It did not have intaglio printing, hence the printing could be easily reproduced by a commercial printer. Brown called this note an 'idiot sheet' because in his view it solved the problem in a very simple way. He was adamant that one 'can't print on plastic'. By that he meant that it was not possible to get quality printing, such as intaglio print, on plastic. This was not necessary on his idiot sheet which clearly had high enough quality printing for the user to identify it as a banknote. Brown was a very influential voice in all the technical discussions between CSIRO and the Bank and his quest for a suitable diffraction grating was a preoccupation of the project.

Paper or plastic?

Brown had used plastic in his mock-up note, all the CSIRO work after the initial Forest Products project was based on the use of a plastic substrate and the March 1972 letter had clearly specified 'plastic laminations', but it was not clear that the Note Issue Department in Fitzroy had kept the Bank's Head Office in Sydney fully briefed on all the implications. A letter from the Governor, J.G. Phillips, to Hamann on 26 February 1973 is instructive:[3]

> I gather from comments coming to us following the regular meetings between CSIRO and the Bank that both you and our Fitzroy people believe that some form of plastic substrate would lend itself to the uniqueness we seek for our currency.
>
> In principle, we are not opposed to the use of plastic of some description. I must add however, that even when you have made a real break-through in your researches, there will almost certainly be the need for a very full evaluation by us of the material before we could be satisfied about its suitability for all processes through which currency must pass in the hands of the Reserve Bank, the other banks and the public.

While this letter was very encouraging, it does illustrate that the Bank saw CSIRO as the 'researchers' and the Bank as the 'evaluators' rather than CSIRO and the Bank collaborating on a joint project. It also shows that there may not have been great communication between the Note Issue Department in Melbourne and the Sydney Head Office.

Establishing proof of concept

It proved to be difficult to arrange the 'quarterly' meetings. The first wasn't scheduled until August 1972, so Solomon and Hamann had six months to develop and test their ideas.

Diffraction gratings

As noted in Chapter 5, Hamann used his network of international contacts to try to find the source of the diffraction gratings that E.G. Bowen, Chief of the CSIRO Division of Radiophysics, had sent to the Bank. This turned out to have been unnecessary because Brown had found that Half Moon Products in Northcote (a suburb of Melbourne) imported the Toppan material. Hamann and Solomon visited the company and obtained a few sample gratings that Mr Littauer, the Managing Director, had had for several years. The CSIRO team quickly established that these were spiral gratings pressed into plastic (either polyethylene terephthalate (Mylar®) or cellulose acetate), coated with aluminium and with a backing paper applied to the aluminised side. Littauer obtained further samples, all made from aluminium-coated Mylar®. Some were gold in colour from using coloured Mylar®. The team quickly devised methods of producing gratings from an existing Mylar® grating by direct pressing or by replication onto a metal back for pressing. The technical details of this work are described in Chapter 3.

The team made different patterns of gratings by cutting straight line gratings into pieces and reassembling them into different patterns. They also produced novel optical effects by coating the back of the grating with black ink and by producing crossed gratings. They produced embossed plastic notes and notes that included both temperature- and pressure-sensitive liquid crystals, and demonstrated that plastic sheets could be laminated with a mesh or strip sandwiched between to produce visual or 'feel' effects.

On 31 July 1972 John Shelton, Secretary of the CSIRO Physical Sciences Branch, wrote to Hamann with the following information:

> The Annual Report of Canadian Patents and Development Limited contains a reference to 'a new security system for currency, credit cards or documents is based on an optical interference coating on a plastic film. The coating gives colour shift patterns that are unique and are almost impossible to decipher and duplicate.'[4]

Shelton noted that Canadian Patents and Development Ltd was set up as a company by the Canadian National Research Council (NRC) to handle inventions from NRC and other government-sponsored research organisations. CSIRO did not have such a company in 1972. It established the technology transfer company Sirotech Ltd in 1984, but in 1972 was still searching for its role in commercialising technology.

The substrate

Solomon recalled:

> In order to achieve a substrate with great versatility and durability we also studied reinforced laminates using a variety of plastics and synthetic

CSIRO at Fishermens Bend

When CSIR was formed in 1926, its work was mainly concerned with primary industry. An exception was the Division of Forest Products, which was one of the original divisions and was concerned with paper manufacture and other timber processing. One of the initiatives of the 1930s was to investigate establishing a 'secondary industry laboratory'. In 1938 it was decided to establish a Division of Aeronautics and in 1940 a Division of Industrial Chemistry, both at Fishermens Bend, a Melbourne industrial suburb. The Division of Aeronautics left CSIR to become part of the Department of Supply and Development when CSIRO was formed in 1949.

The first Chief of the Division of Industrial Chemistry was Dr Ian Wark, who held the position from 1940 until 1958. Between 1958 and 1962 it was divided into several divisions including the Divisions of Physical Chemistry, Organic Chemistry and Applied Mineralogy with Chiefs Dr Keith Sutherland, Dr Jerry Price and Arthur Gaskin respectively. Dr Sefton Hamann became Chief of the Division of Physical Chemistry in 1960.

In 1966 Price was promoted to a Member of the Executive and one of his first actions was to combine the Divisions of Physical and Organic Chemistry to form the Division of Applied Chemistry, appointing Hamann as Chief. In June 1970 it was decided to transfer Solomon's polymer research group from the Division of Applied Mineralogy to the Division of Applied Chemistry.

In 1973 Hamann announced that he was going to resign as Chief and 'go back to the bench'. The position was advertised but in February 1974 CSIRO announced that it had decided to split the division to form the Division of Applied Organic Chemistry with Solomon as Chief and the Division of Chemical Technology with Dr D.E. Weiss as Chief. When Hamann was first appointed Chief in 1960 it was understood that he would hold that position until he retired or resigned. By 1974 Chiefs were generally appointed on seven-year terms with the provision that at the end of the term they could be reappointed, or revert to a position as a Chief Research Scientist with a reduction in salary. Hamann was asked by Price to become Chairman of the Applied Chemistry Laboratories Committee with no drop in salary and no authority over the two new Chiefs but with the task of encouraging collaboration and contact between the two new divisions. Solomon reported to the Chair of CSIRO rather than to Hamann. This management structure was puzzling to people within CSIRO and possibly even more so to Bank officials. Hamann remained in that position until 1978 when, following the Birch report, the government restructured CSIRO into Institutes. Dr Hill Worner was the first Director of the Institute of Industrial Technology to which both divisions were assigned.[5]

woven meshes. (We actually purchased a range of materials from a women's fashion shop for brides which caused great amusement to the team. The scientists who made the purchase were teased mercilessly. It also gave me great amusement to present the bill to our administrators; the purchase of bridal materials!!!)

Chapter 3 contains an account of the technical details of this work.

The first 'quarterly' meeting

The first 'quarterly' meeting was held at Fishermens Bend on 18 August 1972.[6] By now Solomon was a Chief Research Scientist in Hamann's Division of Applied Chemistry. The first item on the agenda was the election of a chairman (it was an all-male committee). The Bank officers were astonished that the senior CSIRO representative, Hamann, was not the CSIRO choice as chairman – Solomon was. This reflected two aspects that affected the project over the next 20 years. The first was the different approaches of the two organisations to their hierarchies. The Bank would have automatically had its most senior person as the chairman; CSIRO would usually have done the same but with an initial discussion of who would be most suitable. The second aspect was to do with the personality of Hamann. He was not a typical senior manager. He had a life-long habit of coming to work on the first available public transport, usually arriving at work around 6am, well before anybody else arrived. He always left work around 2pm even if this meant leaving during a meeting! He never sought management positions. He was invited to be Chief of both his Divisions and left the post in 1974 when it became more 'managerial'. He was always reluctant to formulate a CSIRO position on technical issues connected to the project. Hamann had an extensive network of collaborators around the world and by the end of his career had published papers co-written with over 100 different scientists. But his method of collaboration was essentially on a one-to-one basis rather than as part of a team. Solomon, on the other hand, had come to CSIRO from an industrial background and understood the importance of working in teams.

The meeting agreed with Solomon's suggestion that Jean Swift, one of the CSIRO scientists working on the project, be co-opted to the Committee as Secretary.

R.A.S. Bywater, General Manager of the Note Issue Department, reported on his visits to the Bank of England and Bank of Canada. He informed the committee that the Bank of England was contemplating 'attaching diffraction gratings to normal paper banknotes in the form of a metallized plastic strip with the grating inwards to the paper of the bank note' and that the Bank of Canada was investigating the use of a 'pattern of holes, produced by a laser beam, which when held up to the light produced a diffraction pattern'. Solomon suggested that, based on the results that he was going to report later, the Bank of England approach was of doubtful value.

The CSIRO team then reported on the considerable progress of the previous six months. Curiously, there was no mention that Bank funds had been used to appoint Dr Colin McLean to the project.

CSIRO was able to report that 'Whilst no single feature we have outlined is unique, a combination of these features can be extremely difficult to reproduce and would require expertise and expensive equipment in a variety of different fields.'

In other words, CSIRO had demonstrated a proof of concept. If the collaborator had been a large technically competent firm, at this point the management and direction of the project would have been taken over by that firm under a renegotiated contract. However, as indicated in the previous chapter, the Bank was not such an entity. It had no experience in research and development on the scale required to develop a completely new technology. All its technical experience was in buying and operating state of the art printing systems and the materials required to produce banknotes. While never explicitly stated, the early expectation of the Bank was that the CSIRO would produce a 'turn-key' system for the Bank to purchase.

Discussion of the CSIRO report concluded by agreeing that all the present ideas should be further developed and that the possibility of a unique grating design should be explored. The Bank must have remembered Bowen's letter describing an optically variable device based on a laser hologram of the Queen because Bywater expressed a desire to see an engraved portrait pressed over a grating. A sophisticated version of this was incorporated in the 1988 commemorative note.

Solomon and Hamann agreed to contact the CSIRO Division of Chemical Physics regarding the use of lasers for grating manufacture, particularly the development of a portrait. The issue of using a portrait to produce a recognisable diffraction grating became a recurring theme. On one hand it restricted the use of other images and abstract designs in the diffraction grating, but on the other hand it provided the impetus for the development of the technology that became known as 'catpix' (an abbreviation of catastrophe pixel).

Bywater noted that when designing the new notes the following points should be borne in mind:

1 ease of manipulation;
2 ease of counting;
3 ease of stacking.

These points were of particular significance because of the CSIRO proposal to change to a plastic laminate. This was a strange choice of language. As mentioned earlier, the idea of a plastic laminate was first suggested at the April 1968 meeting; it was encouraged by the Bank in the extension of the first contract between CSIRO and the Bank and was the essential feature of Brown's 1972 mock-up note. The proposal to change to plastic was not a CSIRO proposal but the very basis of the agreement between the Bank and CSIRO. Maybe the Governor had expressed some concerns to Bywater.

It continued to be difficult to arrange quarterly meetings. The second meeting was held eight months later on 5 March 1973; CSIRO again reported significant progress particularly in the thinking about security devices.[7]

Producing diffraction gratings

CSIRO reported that they had tried three different approaches to producing a diffraction pattern that was clearly recognisable but not available from commercial sources. The simplest method was to manually piece gratings together to form a pattern. Pieces of metal were cut to suit the chosen design. Using available gratings, replications onto the cut pieces were made such that the gratings could be used to their best advantage. The pieces were then matched together to form the unique design and a master produced from this.

The second method was highly innovative. If a coarse grating pattern with 75–150 lines/cm could be drawn on a large scale and photographically reduced to give 2000–4000 lines/cm, then any pattern could be produced. With this in mind, Hamann and Solomon visited the Division of Chemical Physics because of its experience in producing straight line gratings for use in spectroscopy. Staff were doubtful that it could be done. This, of course, spurred Hamann and Solomon to try to do it.

Their efforts highlight the difficulty of carrying out a 'secret' project which required extensive consultation with firms and institutions outside CSIRO and the Bank. Solomon first consulted the literature. The *Encyclopaedia of Chemical Technology*[8] referred to the National Cash Registers' (NCR) PCMI (Photochromic Microimages) system which was capable of reducing all the pages of the Bible to fit on 25 cm^2, about a 50 000-fold reduction. The local branch of NCR didn't know much about the technology except that it required a highly specialised laboratory, and volunteered to contact its US associates if CSIRO desired. The CSIRO team decided that it would be better to make further inquiries within Australia before engaging with the US parent company without being able to explain why a chemistry research group was interested in the technology. Kodak Australasia was contacted regarding the limits of the resolution of photographic techniques. It indicated that 4000 lines/cm was within the limits of photographic technology. Kodak knew of a local firm, Technic Photo Services, that had achieved 1500 lines/cm but was constrained by lighting problems and the limited size of commercially available drawings.

The problem was to produce artwork of suitable size and quality. As discussed in Chapter 3, the CSIRO team was aware that the Munitions Factory in Maribyrnong had a Gerber Plotter with a maximum plotting area of 3 ×2.5 m. It was computer-controlled and easily capable of drawing 80 lines/cm. It would be possible to draw a portrait on this plotter, albeit at considerable expense. The plotter at the Munitions Factory was the only one in Australia and using it to produce a security device would prevent a forger from obtaining similar artwork.

The most technically advanced photographic set-up in Australia at that time was at the Weapons Research Establishment at Salisbury in South Australia, which could make a 25:1 reduction with a resolution limit of 20 000 lines/cm. CSIRO entered into a formal agreement with the WRE which had already produced, from parallel straight lines of 60 lines/cm, negatives with 1750 lines/cm. The CSIRO team was able to produce masters from the negatives and press the grating into plastic film.

The third way of producing the master was by directing a beam of electrons onto plate coated with a thin polymer film. If the beam could be accurately controlled, it should be possible to produce gratings with any pattern. This was the beginning of the use of an 'electron beam writer' or using the electron beam of an electron microscope as a 'printer'. CSIRO had been involved with the development and use of electron microscopy since 1945 when Dr A.L.G. Rees had imported an RCA electron microscope as the first instrument in his newly formed Chemical Physics Section of the Division of Industrial Chemistry. By 1972 the groups investigating the more fundamental aspects of electron microscopy had moved to other sites but the Division of Applied Mineralogy still had a JEOL scanning electron microscope for use in its mineral work. This instrument was operated and maintained by a Technical Officer, Alan Wilson. He operated it rather like an organist playing a pipe organ and was willing to experiment and extract the best possible performance from the instrument. Wilson was very keen to experiment in electron beam writing even though neither he nor his division was officially involved with the project. Solomon had worked closely with Wilson when both were in the Division of Applied Mineralogy so collaboration was easy; Wilson's contributions were frequently acknowledged in Solomon's papers.[9]

Other security devices

CSIRO reported work on five other security devices.

Liquid crystals are partly ordered materials in a state somewhere between their liquid and solid phases. CSIRO carried out and reported its extensive testing on the use of cholesterol ester liquid crystals as banknote security devices. In one example displayed at the March 1973 meeting numbers become visible when the colour of the liquid crystal was changed by the heat of the body. Liquid crystals were quite stable in the laboratory but seemed to fade in a few days when incorporated into the ink used on the note.

Embossing could be used to give a distinctive feel or texture to the note. This would not only be a security device, since embossing machines are not readily available, but would also make the note recognisable by feel and therefore by blind people.[10] Later this was abandoned in favour of a polyurethane varnish which contained silica. This was used to control feel and protect the banknote.

Hamann had given considerable thought to theory of the generation of moiré patterns and their use as security devices but had not developed ways of incorporating them into the note. Solomon and his group took over this aspect. This could be done in several ways including:

- one line pattern would be incorporated in the note which could be matched against a standard pattern, e.g. at a cash register, to produce a distinctive moiré pattern;
- the line patterns could be incorporated in the ends of the notes so that when the note was folded in a certain manner a distinctive moiré pattern was produced;
- the line patterns could be aligned within the note to give a moiré pattern which varied with the angle of viewing.

While these methods worked on a macroscopic scale in a non-production environment, they were not for mass production.

For moiré patterns to be difficult to forge, the lines need to be closer together than the normal resolution obtained by printing. It was proposed to achieve this by either:

- embossing the design into the plastic;
- applying a photographic emulsion to the note and exposing it to a suitable negative.

CSIRO eventually lodged a patent covering this invention.[11]

The photographic emulsion could be useful in incorporating other fine line work (if not a moiré pattern) into a note, thus forcing the forger to use an additional technique.

The fifth device was to change the nematic liquid crystals mentioned above from transparent to translucent by the application of a voltage. This would be done by incorporating a metallic coil into the note and generating the current by passing the note across a magnet possibly attached to a cash register. This was a secondary security device and was not carried any further.

All the security devices discussed above could either only be used in a plastic note or would be optimally used in a plastic note. In March 1973 the CSIRO team was not committed to either a single sheet or to a laminate. They favoured a laminate as it would be more difficult for a forger to produce and some of the security devices described could be within it. A laminate also made it possible to match the paper note for thickness and various mechanical properties.

Patenting the invention

Although not discussed at the March meeting, the CSIRO team had been thinking about lodging a provisional patent covering the general concept embodied in the new note. Apart from protecting the intellectual property, Solomon had the view that gaining an international patent would allay the scepticism he had observed in the Bank that a group of Australian scientists working at Fishermens Bend could be as good as the scientists and technologists working for the banks and companies associated with the Bankers' Clubs. Hamann and Solomon met with Grant, from the CSIRO Head Office Commercial Group, on 2 May 1973 to discuss the possibility of drafting a provisional patent. Solomon and Grant quickly drafted the patent. Solomon's recollection is that it was during this drafting that Grant came up with idea of calling the proposed security devices 'optically variable devices'. Shelton sent the draft patent to Hamann on 11 May. In his covering letter, Shelton made two interesting points.[12] He said 'a provisional patent has been drafted as a basis for further discussion between ourselves and, *perhaps* [emphasis added], with the Reserve Bank.' He concluded 'In any event, as we believe a Bank Officer is to be designated as an inventor, we will need to come to some understanding with the Bank about the development and commercialisation of the invention before the application is filed. Preparatory to such a meeting we will need to decide among ourselves about the degree of independent licensing which we would like to exercise.' Solomon had written to Bywater on 3 May 1973 informing him that CSIRO was preparing a provisional patent and broaching the question of the need to renegotiate the agreement between the Bank and CSIRO which expired in July that year.[13]

Agreements

It is not clear why CSIRO thought that the agreement expired in July 1973. The first agreement was for one year, commencing 1 November 1968. This was extended by six months in September 1969 until 30 May 1970. At the meeting held in June 1970 it was agreed that CSIRO would further explore the possibility of using synthetic paper for banknote production. In June 1971, a report on this work was forwarded to the Bank with the comment that 'we are a little out of pocket in preparation of these samples and perhaps we should discuss at some time the possibility of a small grant from the Bank if further work along these lines seems to be desirable.' The June 1971 report was finally discussed with the Bank in February 1972 and in April 1972 the Bank formally 'approved the 'proposal to reimburse CSIRO (up to a maximum of about $21,000 sought) to cover the appointment for two years of an experimental officer for research on the Bank's behalf.' It requested to be informed of the commencement date but CSIRO may not have done so. The advertisement was placed in the press in April 1972 and, as noted earlier, McLean commenced work in May 1972. So the 'agreement' actually expired in May 1974.

No formal reply to the 3 May letter was received by CSIRO so on 1 June Shelton tried again. He attached the draft provisional patent for comment and set out a framework for a formal agreement.

The inventors were Hamann, Solomon and Brown.[14] The practice at Fishermens Bend was to list authors on papers and patents in alphabetical order and, in the case of patents, to list organisations involved in alphabetical order. The patent was concerned with the production of banknotes, credit cards, tickets and similar security tokens of value. The introduction noted that the widespread availability of equipment for photographic reproduction had made forging easier and cheaper and that advances in paper technology had made high-grade papers more readily available so that the paper used in banknotes had lost some of its distinctiveness. It also noted that any technique to overcome these advances needed to be easily recognised as genuine by an unskilled person.

The invention consisted of a security token (which could be a banknote, cheque or credit card) comprising a laminate of at least two layers of plastic sheeting intimately bound together, at least one optically variable device enclosed between the layers and at least one transparent window above or below the device so that it could be viewed. The idea that a transparent window was by itself a security device was not presented in this patent.

The patent, since it also covered security tokens that did not need to be flexible, indicated that a wide variety of plastic material could be used – either thermosetting or thermoplastic. Various epoxy resins could be employed where flexibility was not required 'whereas thermo-plastic sheeting produced from plastics materials such as polyacrylates, polyvinyl chlorides, cellulose acrylates, polyolefines (this includes polyethylene and polypropylene), polyethylene teraphthalates, cellulose acetates and polyesters have been found to be suitable for the production of flexible paper-like notes etc. It is also envisaged, of course, that the sheet material can be embossed, dyed, printed, texturised or otherwise treated before or after lamination.'

The patent also noted that 'it is obviously necessary for some portion of the laminated sheets to be transparent'.

The patent listed an impressive array of optically variable devices – diffraction gratings; liquid crystals; moiré patterns and similar patterns produced by cross-gratings with or without superimposed, refractive, lenticular and transparent grids, such as Fresnel lenses; spaced partially reflective (and partially transparent) coatings yielding variable interference patterns or the like; birefringent or polarising layers; zone-plates and the like. The patent included details of three embodiments of the invention:

- a distinctive seal including a diffraction grating for application to a document;
- a form suitable for use in share scrip, security bonds and other valuable documents. This form included a diffraction grating as well as 'liquid crystal ink';
- a laminated banknote incorporating a liquid crystal, a diffraction grating and a moiré pattern.

The broad scope of the patent, covering all security tokens, all plastic materials and a large array of security devices indicated that CSIRO had ambitions for the technology beyond its use in banknotes. Whether the Bank shared these ambitions at that time is unclear, but unlikely given its general approach.

The extent of CSIRO's ambitions was revealed in the letter that Shelton sent to the Bank on 1 June 1973 when he forwarded the draft patent.[15] Shelton noted that CSIRO was sufficiently encouraged by the progress that had been made and by the Bank's positive reaction, to think that pilot-scale production would be worthwhile. He revealed that the CSIRO team was already assembling the necessary equipment and made the obvious point that any new agreement should cover the pilot-scale development.

He expressed in quite strong language that CSIRO would be reluctant to sign an agreement before both parties were quite clear about the criteria to be used in judging the acceptance of the new notes. He said, 'While we appreciate that it is not possible to state all such criteria in the form of objective tests, it would be helpful to review once again the important factors so that we have our goal as clearly defined as possible.' These words were strangely similar to the plea of the Division of Forest Products in 1970.

The letter also discussed the details of the pilot-scale project including that CSIRO did not expect it to cost more than about $50 000–60 000. Shelton noted that CSIRO:

> would also like the agreement to provide that, after the specified number of sample notes have been submitted for evaluation, the Bank will report the results of the evaluation to CSIRO in full and will advise CSIRO whether it intends to take steps to bring the new notes into production. If the notes are clearly not satisfactory we would need to seriously consider whether further work was justified; if, on the other hand, the notes were deemed to be satisfactory but the Bank does not intend to take steps to bring them into production, we would like to retain the right to exploit the development independently by licensing or collaboration with others.

Direct contact with the Governor

Some informal discussions took place between Shelton and McPherson and a luncheon was arranged between the senior management of the Bank and representatives from CSIRO. The guest list is instructive. The CSIRO guests were Hamann, Shelton and Solomon. The Bank hosts were Governor Phillips and Deputy Governor Knight. The Bank guests were Bartley, Bywater, McPherson, Parr and Prunster. Note that neither Price from CSIRO nor Brown from the Bank was invited. The luncheon was held at the Sydney office of the Bank on 27 July 1973.

The luncheon must have gone well. On 31 July McPherson wrote to Shelton:[16]

> As you could gather the Governor and Deputy Governor were greatly impressed by the work and the enthusiasm for it.
>
> We are sufficiently encouraged to wish to press on urgently with the next stage and will be pleased to receive from you a detailed proposal covering objectives and costs estimates.
>
> As we said we will co-operate fully to the extent of our resources both within our Fitzroy works and in the Bank generally and will shortly designate a representative to liase with your people on all aspects of the project.

> With respect to patenting we agree an application for letters patent in our joint names should be proceeded with forthwith and in this regard perhaps it would be helpful if your people were to go through the provisional specification in detail with our Messrs Bywater and Brown.

Note that there was no mention of a new agreement.

CSIRO quickly developed a proposal for the Bank to contribute $60 000 over two years.[17] This was given to Bywater on 10 August 1973 along with the draft patent application. The Bank fulfilled its promise to appoint a Project Officer; Peter Morriss was introduced to Hamann and Solomon at the meeting. Morriss visited Fishermens Bend on 21 August to meet the CSIRO staff and review technical points. He was a distinguished note and stamp designer but had no technical qualifications.

The Bank approved the provisional patent application and it was duly lodged on 26 September 1973. The full patent was lodged one year later and the patent granted on 18 November 1977.

It was around this time that Solomon realised that if he was going to succeed both in solving all the technical problems and in commercialising the technology in Australia, he would need more support and understanding from the CSIRO Head Office. He proposed that Paul Grant, an Assistant Secretary in Shelton's area, replace Swift as Secretary of the committee. Grant was a patent attorney and had been involved with the preparation of the joint patent. He attended the 27 April meeting as an observer.[18]

The first meeting with Grant as Secretary was held on 11 October 1973.[19] The Bank was silent on the question of a new agreement. It did raise the issue of its presentation to the Pacific Rim Conference which was to take place from 29 October to 7 November. This conference had representatives from the note printing authorities in Australia, the US, Canada, Mexico, Indonesia and Japan. CSIRO argued that there should be minimal disclosure of the work at the meeting, particularly because much of the technology would be know-how. Eventually it was agreed that any disclosure should not go beyond the contents of provisional patent specification. To control this as much as possible Solomon provided the Bank with a set of 35 mm slides.

At the next meeting, which took place on 5 November, the Bank reported that the work on the new note had created quite an impression and that delegates thought that further effort by the Australian team was well worthwhile.[20] It was clear from the discussion that the Bank had disclosed more than it had agreed to at the previous meeting. The main negative comments about the new note were:

- oversophistication, i.e. too complex;
- longer note life will lead to a lower rate of forgery detection;
- use of liquid crystals dubious because of questionable shelf life and doubtful value as a security element;
- plastic notes are likely to be too limp and difficult to count.

Apart from this, they liked it!

Commercialisation issues

As discussed in Chapter 4, the implications of the different business models in the minds of its members were an underlying issue at the Committee meetings. The minutes of the meeting held on 4 June 1974 record that Brown 'again pointed out his preference for the basic information about the new notes to be made freely available to all other central banks through the world in accordance with the pattern of free information exchange which had been cultivated by the central banker's club in the past', and record Grant's response that such a basic policy difference between CSIRO and the Bank it had to be resolved at ministerial level.[21] Grant referred the matter to the CSIRO Executive Officer in Canberra, Dr J.A. Allen.

Allen was the Executive Officer of CSIRO from 1971 to 1976. He was educated in chemistry at the University of Queensland and Bristol University and served in the RAAF from 1943–45. He was a Senior Lecturer in Chemistry at the University of Tasmania (1952–55), Section Leader at the ICI (Australia) Central Research Laboratories (1955–59), and Associate Professor then Professor and Deputy Vice Chancellor at the University of Newcastle (1959–1971) before taking up the position at CSIRO. He left CSIRO to become Chairman of the Board of Advanced Education of Queensland.

Allen put forward the following proposition in a letter to McPherson on 10 October 1973:[22]

> Firstly, you should be reassured that CSIRO would not wish in any way to seek royalties from the Bank for its own use of the invention. Similarly, it would seem futile for CSIRO to attempt to negotiate licences in the banknote area with foreign banks. Thus, we feel that you should be primarily responsible for the exploitation of the patent rights in the bank note area, but we suggest that we should be advised before any licensing arrangements are concluded and that any royalties recovered from such arrangements should be nominally split 50:50. In the area of security tokens other than bank notes, we would also be happy for you to seek industrial interest, but here, we would like to have the right to proceed independently. Once again, we will advise you before any agreements are concluded and would agree to split any royalties obtained on a 50:50 basis. The same basic philosophy would be applied to new inventions arising from the collaboration and, at the present time, we are considering filing applications on two or three inventions made by Hamann for the production of novel Moire gratings.

Allen then introduced the notion of consulting with the Australian Industry Development Corporation over the exploitation of the patent rights overall and sought the Bank's views on this matter. The AIDC had been established by the Gorton government in 1970 to facilitate the development of Australian industries, including providing financial services to those engaged in the industries and by participating in enterprises or projects.

In 1973 CSIRO was in the early stages of developing its approach to commercialisation of technologies. Chiefs of divisions reported directly to the Chairman and were responsible for all aspects of the work of their divisions. The Chairman and the two full-time members of the Executive had a Secretariat at the Head Office in Canberra to assist in their management of the organisation. The Secretariat had an Industrial and Physical Sciences Branch that dealt with issues arising from the mining and manufacturing divisions. Shelton was the Secretary of that branch and had three Assistant Secretaries including Grant. Secretaries of branches had no decision-making authority and no budget. The decision-makers were the Chief of the division and the Chairman of CSIRO. It was probably confusing to the Bank to have letters from the Chief, Secretary and Chairman. The 1977 independent inquiry into CSIRO, the Birch Inquiry, recommended great changes in the structure of CSIRO and in the way that it approached the commercialisation of its research.[23] In 1979 a Commercial Group was formed as part of a new Bureau of Scientific Services. Grant was appointed Officer-in-Charge of the Commercial Group. At the same time the divisions were grouped into Institutes with the Chief now reporting to an Institute Director. Dr Hill Worner, who had been one of the full-time members of the Executive, was the first Director of the Institute of Industrial Technology. Neither the Institute Director nor the Officer-in-Charge of the Commercial Group was able to make decisions about resource allocation; that remained with the Chairman and the Chief. These arrangements were changed in November 1984 when CSIRO established Sirotech Ltd. This was a company, wholly owned by CSIRO, whose purpose was to provide commercial support for CSIRO divisions by promoting the results of their research to Australian industry. Sirotech ceased to exist in July 1993. Its functions were taken over by CSIRO and external contractors.[24]

McPherson replied to the 10 October 1973 letter on 13 November, carefully avoiding any commitment on the issues raised by Allen.[25] He said:

> As you know, our paramount interest is to obtain maximum protection against forgery of Australian currency notes and, if the project is a success, the preservation of that interest would be vital to us.
>
> Therefore, whilst in broad sympathy with your comments, the Bank considers further discussion should await the outcome of the pilot development and other research.

The CSIRO–Reserve Bank Committee continued to meet on a regular basis. The first meeting in 1974, which was held on 22 March, was a very important one.[26] The meeting agreed that sufficient progress had been made that it was worthwhile to proceed with prototype note production on a continuous pilot machine. Brown emphasised that, quite apart from the security features, it was becoming apparent that a major advantage of the new note was going to be the great reduction in production costs and the great increase in production capacity. The meeting agreed to aim for pilot-scale production by June 1974 (only three months away) with a view to convincing the Governor to proceed to small-scale commercial production. They agreed to have a further meeting on 22 April to plan the details of the pilot-scale production.

Solomon again expressed concern that the Bank had not assigned Morriss full-time on the project.

At the 22 April meeting it was decided to:[27]

- press ahead with pilot-scale production at Fishermens Bend;
- aim to hold a high-level joint meeting in July 1974 at the Bank in Sydney;
- present information orally at the meeting with the aid of charts, diagrams and samples, together with a colour movie film (with sound) showing prototype note production.

The minutes reflect a degree of excitement and optimism among participants. There seemed to be a genuine feeling that they were onto something and that new notes may well be in production sooner rather than later.

Preparing for the Governor's meeting and the role of Don Parr

That possibility was dampened at the next meeting of the committee, on 24 June 1974, by the intervention of Don Parr, one of the Governor's advisers from Sydney.[28] Solomon was confident that all the research problems had been solved and that it was time to decide whether or not to proceed with the development of mass production techniques.

The minutes of the meeting record Solomon as arguing that proceeding to mass production would presuppose an in-principle commitment by the Bank to work towards the production of the new notes and would require a substantial financial commitment by the Bank and CSIRO. The purpose of the high-level meeting in July was, therefore, to put this issue forward for decision by the Bank. In retrospect it is clear that CSIRO did not appreciate that when the Bank used the words 'mass production' it was not agreeing to issue the notes. The question of whether to issue notes was a completely separate decision.

Parr put a damper on the general enthusiasm. He pointed out that if a major decision was really going to be put to the Bank on 18 July, the supporting documentation would need to be very thorough and go well beyond a technical progress report. The nature and scope of the development phase, together with the additional resources required, would need to be spelt out in considerable detail. Furthermore, Parr suggested that since the matter of security would normally rest within the Bank with the Note

Issue Department, it was important for the submission to cover this question explicitly. He suggested the need for detailed information on the likely plant costs, and gave his view that it would be better to postpone the meeting than go with inadequate documentation. He also stated his view that it was probably unreasonable, at this stage, to expect the Bank to make a clear yes-or-no commitment to commercial production of the new notes in a given year; the Bank was serious about the project and the question would be how much should be committed and in what way towards development over the next, say, two years.

Grant was given the task of producing a first draft of the joint report for circulation before the next meeting, which Parr would attend.

The 5 July meeting was still not happy with the draft.[29] In particular, Parr thought that the document was inadequate to support a major decision by the Bank. He favoured an integrated and comprehensive report of the history of the project, the progress made, the results achieved and the resources required for development and then for production. The task of drafting the report was assigned to Morriss, Hamann, McLean and Solomon, a joint CSIRO–Bank team.

Reporting considerable progress

The report prepared for the meeting, which was eventually held on 16 September, was very convincing. It outlined the considerable progress in the various areas of the project.[30]

It suggested that the basic structure of the note was to be a five-component system containing a centre of woven Terylene® or nylon mesh to improve the strength of the laminate. On either side of this mesh would be a highly pigmented, low-density polyethylene film. This would constitute the centre laminate, giving the note the required opacity. Holes to receive optically variable devices were to be punched into the laminate and after suitable treatment the surface would be printed. The final two layers were the outside laminate of high-density polyethylene that seal the optically variable device in the note. The report stated that this basic structure should be regarded as first-generation only. The team at CSIRO were already thinking about alternative substrates. Each layer could be changed as further work was done. It nevertheless offered advantages over conventional banknote papers in terms of durability and cost. The laminate as described in this report was unique and therefore offered some minor security in itself.

The report discussed the wide range of optically variable devices that had been considered for inclusion in the CSIRO notes. These were practical devices which:

- would be difficult and costly to duplicate;
- could not be photographed, i.e. they exhibited optical variability;
- would force the forger to master a second high-technology field in addition to mastering plastics technology.

The report designated the following as already practicable:

Diffraction gratings
A thin-film metallised diffraction grating in the form of a unique diffraction pattern, or a montage of individual gratings, offers high security and (because of the past development effort) immediate practicality. The pattern or montage can be readily recognised by 'the man in the street' but cannot be duplicated without access to equipment worth hundreds of thousands of dollars.

Shiny metal band
This is a simple device which can be applied with little cost or difficulty and is analogous to the metal thread now used in paper notes. The security offered is substantially less than the diffraction grating since the metal device could be fairly readily produced by the potential forger.

Liquid crystals
This device simply consists of the application of micro-encapsulated liquid crystals over a dark back-ground device – such as the Coat of Arms. The effect offered is a change of colour under, for example, body heat. Though security may be regarded as doubtful because encapsulated liquid crystals of this nature may be on the market at any time, it is highly unlikely that commercially available liquid crystals would withstand the temperatures and pressures associated with heat lamination.

Moiré figures
Security devices based on Moiré figures are still undergoing intensive development and a practical fabrication technique still remains to be devised.

The report was accompanied by a film demonstrating that the new notes could be produced by state-of-the-art technology, including segments filmed in actual factories to emphasise the feasibility of the process. It noted that the incorporation of the security devices into the note was a matter of 'straight forward development, rather than research.' It also noted that the scale of note production envisaged meant that it would be economic for the Bank to produce the substrate within the Bank, thereby improving the security of the notes. The production plan assumed that the notes would be web-printed, thus offering considerable savings in production costs. It was not planned to use intaglio printing on the notes so, unlike conventional notes, print quality would not need to be a security feature. This would also offer considerable savings in production costs. So the Bank supported Monty Brown's original idea that the new notes did not need intaglio printing as a security device. Brown always had the view that it was not possible to do intaglio printing on plastic. This was not true, but Brown's view prevailed within the Bank until his retirement.

The report included a four-step development program.

1 Development of a production prototype note and associated mass production techniques should proceed concurrently with research and development effort on the most promising security devices – in particular the moiré patterns.
2 Because plastics technology was new to the Bank, it was proposed that the development team be located at Solomon's Division of Applied Organic Chemistry, but be staffed by officers recruited by the Bank so as to ensure continuity and efficient knowhow transfer in the event of a decision to proceed with production on Bank premises.
3 Experience with web-printing of plastic sheet should be built-up concurrently within the Note Printing Branch.
4 The pre-production development stage should be completed within 18–24 months, with a decision point at the 18-month stage concerning the purchase of certain items of full-scale equipment.

The Chief Executives' meeting

Attending the meeting at the Bank's Head Office in Sydney on 16 September 1974 were, from the Bank: Sir John Phillips (Governor), H.M. Knight (Deputy Governor), A. McPherson (Senior Adviser), D. Parr (Chief Manager and Adviser), R.A.S. Bywater (General Manager, Note Issue Department), P. Morriss (Superintendent, Engraving Section, Note Issue Department) and Mr Bevan (Manager, Currency and Banking, Note Issue Department).[31] It was one of the few meetings which Brown did not attend. The following staff from CSIRO were present: J.R. Price (Chairman), D. Ford (Member of the Executive), J.A. Allen (Executive Officer), S.D. Hamann, D.H. Solomon, P.A. Grant, C. McLean and R. Seccombe (CSIRO Film Unit).

The Governor welcomed everyone to the meeting and called upon Price to reply on CSIRO's behalf. Solomon then ran the meeting and asked Bywater to outline the Bank's view on the need for a new note. Solomon then made the detailed technical presentation.

CSIRO had devoted considerable effort to preparing Price's speech and the main presentation to be given by Solomon. This included commissioning the CSIRO Film Unit to prepare a movie illustrating the history of the project and the progress that had been made. The then Victorian ABC news presenter, Jeffrey Raymond, read the commentary. This film can be viewed at <http://www.publish.csiro.au/Plastic_banknote>. In addition to the film, CSIRO had prepared an impressive array of 26 exhibits and demonstrations of all aspects of the project.

Price's speech included the following paragraph:

> Finally, it might be of some help to explain that, while the CSIRO Executive is very conscious of the need to maintain first-class long-term research within CSIRO, it is also CSIRO policy that potentially useful results of its research should be carried to a stage where their commercial feasibility can be reliably assessed. You can see therefore that Dave faces something of a dilemma in this project: he has a team of first-rate organic chemists whom, I am sure, are anxious to see a return to research chemistry; but on the other hand, he is very conscious of the obligation to pursue this development project so long as there is a realistic chance of the results being applied commercially. The purpose of this meeting is, of course, to allow the Bank (and, I suggest, CSIRO) to assess the project in this light.

The Memorandum of Meeting issued by the Bank on 17 September was quite succinct:[32]

> After presentation of the report and screening of a supporting film there was general discussion on the potential of the project. The Governor indicated the Bank's agreement, in principle, to proceed to the development stage on a substantial pilot scale with appropriate check points incorporated in the necessary planning.
>
> It was agreed that there was need for an expanded committee to administer the project. This committee should, as a first step draw up a detailed action plan. The Governor nominated Mr A C McPherson as Chairman of the committee with other nominations from both parties to be confirmed within a week. An inaugural meeting would be called as early as practicable thereafter.

More informative were Grant's notes on the meeting.[33] He reported that, when summarising the situation, Solomon said that the research stage had been substantially completed and that successful development should be possible using established technology. He pointed out that since the development stage would be considerably more expensive than the research stage, it should not be undertaken unless production was seriously contemplated.

The Governor expressed appreciation for the effective presentation of the issues, and noted that a competent adviser would be needed to decide upon the style and content of the new note, thus pre-empting his decision to continue the project! The Governor was also concerned that the Bank and CSIRO may face with a recruitment problem if it decided to go ahead, but was reassured that that was the least of anybody's worries. Solomon thought that the principal difficulty was the matter of security. He had overcome this in the past by appointing new recruits to existing CSIRO projects and transferring permanent CSIRO personnel to the project. He would be able to continue this but might need to use some misleading advertisements. Ford stressed that, if there was a decision to go ahead, it would be essential for the Bank to set out its objectives very clearly and to consciously manage the project to achieve those objectives. Allen noted 'that the Bank was in a difficult position with respect to a company marketing a new product in that he could not see any valid way of test marketing notes.' He stressed that some of the peripheral benefits of the new notes – e.g. improved handling, sorting and destruction – could be evaluated in realistic trials conducted in-house.

Parr, possibly sensing the enthusiasm of the meeting, cautioned that a decision in principle to proceed with the project by the Bank did not carry a firm commitment to production by a given date; that is, there would have to be several intermediate decision points where progress was seriously reviewed. Allen confirmed that CSIRO understood this and again stressed the need for a joint steering committee formed by the Bank and CSIRO to undertake control and review of the project and, if necessary, recommend the abandonment of the work. Whether Allen understood that 'production' did not imply 'issue' is not clear from the minutes.

In retrospect this was the meeting at which business model issues should have been discussed. Ford was correct in saying that the Bank needed to set out its objectives very clearly. What was equally true, but not said, was that CSIRO needed to do likewise.

Endnotes

1 NAA: B5609, 5/2.
2 NAA: B5609, 5/2.
3 NAA: B5609, 6/18.
4 NAA: B5609, 6/18.
5 Compiled from CSIRO Annual Reports, personal recollection of D.H. Solomon and biographical memoirs of S.D. Hamann, T.H. Spurling and D.H. Solomon (2009) *Historical Records of Australian Science* **20**, 255–271 and Weiss, T.H. Spurling (2011) *Historical Records of Australian Science* **22**, 152–170.
6 NAA: B5609, 1/6.
7 NAA: B5609, 1/6.
8 *Kirk-Othmer Encyclopedia of Chemical Technology*, 4th edn, John Wiley & Sons, New York, 1996, contained no such reference. The earlier edition was not available.
9 See for example D.H. Solomon, B.C. Loft and J.D. Swift (1967) *Journal of Applied Polymer Science* **11**, 1593–1602.
10 NAA: B5609, 1/6.
11 D.H. Solomon and D.G. Hawthorne, *Fine line photographic transfers*. WO1983/000750.
12 NAA: B5609, 5/3.
13 NAA: B5609, 5/6.
14 S.D. Hamann, D.H. Solomon and M.F.W. Brown, Australian Patent 488 562, publication date 1 April 1976.

15 NAA: B5609, 5/6.
16 NAA: B5609, 5/1.
17 NAA: B5609, 1/7.
18 NAA: B5609, 1/6.
19 NAA: B5609, 1/7.
20 NAA: B5609, 1/8.
21 Paul Grant, a patent attorney from the CSIRO Commercial Group in Canberra, later became Secretary of the Technical Committee.
22 NAA: B5609, 1/7.
23 *Report of the Independent Inquiry into the Commonwealth Scientific and Industrial Research Organisation*, August 1977, Australian Government Publishing Service, Canberra.
24 Compiled from CSIRO Annual Reports 1973–1994.
25 NAA: B5609 1/8.
26 NAA: B5609 1/9.
27 NAA: B5609 1/10.
28 NAA: B5609 1/10.
29 NAA: B5609 1/10.
30 NAA: B5609 3/2.
31 NAA: B5609 3/2.
32 NAA: B5609 5/2.
33 NAA: B5609 5/3.

Chapter 7
The Mornington think tank

Invitees (and exclusions!)

Solomon got to work quickly. The meeting between the Governor and the Chairman was held on 16 September and by 2 October he had organised a two-day off-site 'think tank' at a location in Mornington, Victoria.[1] There were three unusual aspects to this. At that time CSIRO typically did not do its research in teams, meetings were seldom held off-site and workshop staff were not usually considered as part of the group. A fourth observation is that although the September meeting had agreed that the Bank would take over the overall management of the project, no Bank person was invited to the think tank.

Those attending were D.H. Solomon (now Chief of the Division of Applied Organic Chemistry), S.D. Hamann (although he only attended part of the second day), Colin McLean and Mario Girolamo (newly recruited scientists), Ken Clark (research assistant), Jack Ross (Divisional Engineer), Bob Brett (Division Draftsman), Laurie Julius and Ted Sorani (fitters and turners from the workshop) and Graham Quint (the workshop's computer programmer).

Solomon was well aware of the contribution that the workshop was making to the project, hence the workshop contingent at the meeting. Ross was the Engineer in Charge of the CSIRO workshop at Fishermens Bend and had been recruited by Solomon as soon as he realised that CSIRO would need to take the concept from the research phase to development. Ross brought a keen intellect and a practical bent to the project and was crucial to its success. His contribution to the project was recognised by his promotion to Principal Research Scientist in 1980. It was most unusual for a CSIRO workshop engineer to achieve this promotion.

Solomon intended the two days to be team-building, informative and a way of planning future research. Note that Hamann only attended part of the second day. He was never comfortable being part of think tanks and team-building exercises. Indeed, he did not participate in team meetings and often submitted independent reports to the CNRD Committee. The management relationship between Solomon and Hamann was uniquely CSIRO: as noted in Chapter 6, Hamann used to be Solomon's boss but was now his colleague on the Applied Chemistry Laboratory Committee, a committee that had no authority. Solomon had no budget to support Hamann's research and no management authority over Hamann but willingly provided the resources that Hamann needed for ongoing research projects from the Division's appropriation budget.

Purpose of the meeting

Solomon opened the meeting by outlining the central dilemma of the project. He noted that in the next two years about $1 000 000 would be available to produce between one and five million banknotes for in-house testing by the Bank. While CSIRO knew that the Bank wanted a plastic banknote with at least one optically variable security device, it did not know what the Bank considered to be the desirable properties of the banknote nor its timetable for its release. CSIRO would have to decide on the direction of the research. In hindsight, it may well have saved a lot of time and anguish if some of the key Bank people had participated in the think tank. Who from the Bank should have been invited? The Bank's production business model meant that it had no employees with the expertise in research and development needed to make a contribution to the technical discussions. A senior manager may have been able to shed light on the Bank's thinking on when and how to introduce the new technology.

CSIRO knew that there were different views within the Bank on the design of a banknote containing the new technology. At one end of the spectrum there was the Monty Brown 'idiot sheet'; a plastic banknote with a diffraction grating and only enough printing to designate its value. At the other end was the idea that the plastic substrate would simply replace paper in the production of a traditional-looking banknote. Some evidence for the dominance of this view was that the Bank had retained the doyen of Australian banknote design, Gordon Andrews, to assist the project. That the first outsider hired by the Bank for the project was an artist and not a polymer scientist was clear evidence that the Bank assumed that the step from the laboratories at Fishermens Bend to its factory at Fitzroy was the least of its worries. Its past experience was that an outside supplier would deliver the material and equipment to the note printing plant. There is no evidence of any discussion of how the new banknotes would be introduced. Would the Bank start with a low-denomination banknote of traditional design on a plastic substrate, would it introduce a high-denomination banknote with all possible security devices or would it introduce a one-off commemorative banknote to test public reaction?

Solomon's research plan

Research could answer only the first of the four broad issues identified above. Researchers could produce a variety of substrates with a variety of physical properties and security devices and put them together in any combination required. The research team was not in control of the visual design of the banknotes or the technology transfer mechanisms and had no influence whatsoever in the release of the banknotes. However, the note release strategy had an important influence on the direction of the research. Solomon devised a research plan to cover all possibilities. He proposed that CSIRO produce four banknotes of increasing complexity and called them Mark 1, 2, 3 and 4.

The Mark 1 banknote would be a simple punched and embossed plastic banknote without an optically variable device but with a clear area. A clear area is not an optically variable device, but it is a strong security device in that it is very difficult to replicate in paper. It would be based on the Terylene® mesh/pigmented LDPE laminate. It was thought that this would be used for the $1 and $2 banknotes and introduced to gauge public acceptance of a plastic banknote. The Terylene®-based substrate would be extremely durable and therefore very suitable for $1 and $2 banknotes. Forgers were unlikely to be interested in forging these low-denomination banknotes, thus minimising the need to include more expensive security devices.

The Mark 2 banknote would use the same substrate as the Mark 1 banknote but with security devices that did not require holes to be punched in the inner laminate. For example:

- Mark 2a banknote would have a diffraction grating, introduced by transfer foil technology;
- Mark 2b banknote a gold facing window;
- Mark 2c banknote, thermochromic/photochromic inks;
- Mark 2d banknote, a counting device.

The Mark 3 banknote would have the same plastic laminate as previously but with the inner laminate punched to receive additional optically variable devices, moirés, diffraction gratings and other novel devices.

Finally, the Mark 4 banknote would be based on a new generation of plastic laminate without a woven inner reinforcing layer.

Involving Bank staff

Solomon's plan was developed in the absence of clear direction from the Bank, but was it realistic to think that the Bank would want to have two different plastic substrates in its note printing department? Solomon's strategy was to quickly involve Bank staff in the project by proceeding with the Mark 1 banknote as soon as possible. This would give them some experience in handling and printing on plastic even if the Mark 1 banknotes were never in circulation, since all the equipment and processes would be similar for any other plastic film. The plan was to have Union Carbide supply 10 000 m by 1 m of the inner laminate to the Bank for it to print its designs, either by a commercial printer with suitable equipment or by the Bank if it purchased suitable equipment. At the same time, CSIRO planned to fabricate a 1 m laminator/extruder/embosser to enable the printed inner laminate received back from the Bank to be completed as a banknote by the addition of the embossed outer films. The 1 m wide roll of banknotes would then be guillotined to size and tested by the Bank.

The proposed schedule required close cooperation with the Bank.

By December 1974 the laminate specification would be agreed to by the Bank printers and CSIRO. The Bank would have the option of printing the inner laminate itself or having it done by a commercial printer. Since the main technical prowess of the Bank was printing, it was likely that it would want to print the inner laminate. During this period CSIRO would be ordering laminator/extruder/embosser equipment and checking the best techniques for cutting the material.

Assuming all this worked, by March 1975 CSIRO would order 10 000 m by 1 m of the specified laminate.

It was an ambitious plan that would see the in-house testing of the Mark 1 banknotes completed by December 1975.

The longer-term research program

At the same time as proposing a production process, Solomon was also proposing to continue the longer-term research program for the Mark 2, 3 and 4 banknotes. This would look at five different aspects of the banknotes.

The first was the inner laminate. A range of laminates, including polyvinyl chloride and various grades of polyethylene, would need to be tested before a selection for the Mark 4 banknote was made. It was appreciated that the use of a pigmented LDPE and a PET woven fibre inner layer restricted the placing of clear windows for optically variable devices. The need to punch a hole in the inner layer would complicate the mass production of the banknotes. The meeting noted that a technique for printing the background opacity must be developed as soon as possible. The notes of the meeting imply that this was the responsibility of the Bank. The use of a pigmented plastic was driven by Brown's doubts about printing on plastic. The CSIRO team knew that it was possible to print on plastic but was unable to persuade Brown that this was so.

The second area was the development of optically variable devices. The Mark 1 banknote did not include an optically variable device but did have a clear area. Its security was the clear area coupled with the inherent difficulty of producing the substrate, and the plan was to use it for the $1 and $2 banknotes. At the time of the Mornington meeting, there was no optically variable device yet developed to the stage of being suitable for inclusion in a production line. The optically variable devices being considered in 1974 were:

- gold and/or caesium windows.
  - Two ways of producing this device were to be researched. It could be inserted mechanically into the punched laminate or inserted as a hot stamping foil during the printing process.. It would have been both technically and commercially viable to use an ultrathin gold film. A gold film was included in a $7 banknote (Plate 12). Why caesium was included is

not clear. Caesium is a highly reactive metal with a low melting point and probably not suited for inclusion in a banknote. It is however an indication that in this project CSIRO was willing to consider all ideas no matter how impractical they appeared.

- Diffraction gratings.
  - At this point it was known how to include a diffraction grating into the banknote. It was essentially the same hot stamping foil that would be used to include a gold or caesium window. What was not known was how to design a grating that would survive everyday usage and would have an appearance that was acceptable to the Bank. The tasks were:
    - grating design, including artwork;
    - photoreduction;
    - computer reduction;
    - preparation of masters;
    - designing and producing equipment and pilot plants.
  - The idea of using the scanning electron microscope to produce the diffraction grating was already extant at the meeting.
- Moiré patterns.
  - There were plans for three moiré patterns:
    - Mark 1 was to be produced photographically;
    - Mark 2 was to be produced by mechanical means;
    - Mark 3 was to be a hot stamp version of Mark 2.
  - The central problem was to increase the number of lines to 4000 per cm.
- Liquid crystals and other devices:
  - most could easily be applied in the printing operation. The problem was to select the optimum product.

The third area was the development of inks that would adhere to the plastic films selected for the banknote. The inks needed high opacity to eliminate the need to pigment the substrate but still had to allow excellent heat sealability of the laminating films. This was an area of research that would normally be done in close collaboration between the Bank and the ink suppliers, but because of the lack of suitably trained people at the Bank it would probably need to be done by CSIRO.

The fourth area was the outer protective coats. There was a need to develop an outer layer to protect the security devices, to enhance durability and provide an acceptable feel. The feel of a conventional banknote is partly due to the intaglio printing, but at this point in the development of the polymer banknote there was no plan to use intaglio printing. The feel would have to be generated by the outer coat.

The fifth area was the development of counting devices which could be used to count bundles of banknotes returned to the Bank and to check for counterfeits. Several possible counting devices, including radioactive counters and conductivity methods, were discussed but with no satisfactory solution. This area received little attention in the next few years.

Finally, a great deal of thought and discussion was devoted to engineering and pilot plant operation. Some of the equipment could be purchased; the 1 × 1 m wide laminator/extruder/embosser, the vacuum metalliser and the guillotine were all standard industry equipment and could be purchased off the shelf. Other equipment, such as a high-speed punch, high-speed security device press and the coating machine would need to be designed and constructed in the Division. The whole production line was designed by the CSIRO team with major inputs from Ross and the workshop staff.

During these discussions Julius from the workshop, who was in charge of the high-speed punch and other high-speed device equipment, suggested bluntly that developing a high-speed punch that would scale up to a commercial application would be very difficult and therefore some thought should be given to developing a system that did not require a punched hole in one of the sheets of laminate. Solomon agreed, and the remark probably raised the priority of developing a clear laminate with excellent printing and heat sealing characteristics.

The report had eight attachments outlining the research projects and assigning people to each project.

One was Project 5, Research and Design of Laminates, Lacquers and Textures. This would be led by Girolamo, one of whose duties was 'To specify properties and construction of alternative banknote materials with particular reference to producing a clear laminate with excellent printing and heat sealing characteristics.' This was the first hint of the use of polypropylene.

Polypropylene!

While the use of polypropylene in the substrate was not mentioned in the report of the Mornington meeting, it was one of the plastics considered for use as the clear film in the laminate in 1973 and was probably in the minds of Solomon and Girolamo when they thought about alternative banknote materials. The first detailed mention of polypropylene was in Report CNRD 374 dated 19 November 1974 and titled 'Report on Pilot Production Developments'. Section 4.0 discussed 'Laminates'. It summarised the dilemma identified at Mornington:

> Our original banknotes used highly pigmented LDPE to get the necessary opacity. This method limits the introduction of clear areas. It is highly desirable to be in a position to print the inner laminate because this would enable clear areas to be placed anywhere in the banknote and for their shape to be irregular. Two methods of mass producing the inner laminate are under study:

> 1. lamination of the polyethylene to the Terylene® fabric;
> 2. extrusion coating.
>
> Discussions with Union Carbide are under way on the production of these laminates on a large scale.
>
> Ultimately, we hope to avoid the use of woven Terylene® in a laminate and we have therefore commenced work on other plastic films, particularly highly oriented films such as bi-axially oriented polypropylene. Conventional inks are not formulated to take a subsequent heat-seal or laminate. We have therefore begun work aimed at producing unique, high opacity inks which will be suitable for accepting the outer polythene coating of the banknote. A major unresolved problem is the surface feel and texture of the new banknotes and we have begun work trying to establish a specification for both the surface texture and surface chemistry of our banknotes.

The report was discussed at the second meeting of the CNRD Committee, held on 29 November 1974. The minutes of that meeting mention the surface 'feel' work but not the work on polypropylene.

A coherent team

The Mornington think tank was a major event in the development of the plastic banknote. It established the CSIRO 'team' as a coherent group working for well defined goals. One of us was, at that time, a research scientist in the newly formed Division of Applied Organic Chemistry not yet involved with the project. There was a distinct feeling of excitement at Fishermens Bend as word got out that a group had been off-site planning activities for the 'secret project'. Although it was meant to be secret, most knew that the Division was working with the Bank on a plastic banknote. The existence of the project gave a sense of relevance to the rest of the Division. This was important as the project developed and more Division staff became involved in different aspects of the research. Everyone was willing to drop whatever else they were doing to take part in the project.

As Chief of the Division in the 1970s, Solomon had almost total control over the allocation of its resources. The Division had almost no resources contracted to external companies, so individual scientists could be readily taken from their curiosity-driven project and deployed to the Bank project. In the 1980s, when external earnings targets were imposed, the flexibility of the Chief to reallocate resources was considerably reduced. In research, as in life, timing is everything!

Endnote

1 NAA: B5609 3/9.

Chapter 8
The hard grind

Establishing the Currency Notes Research and Development Committee

If Solomon was quick to arrange the Mornington think tank, the Bank and CSIRO showed an unusual sense of urgency in appointing and calling the first meeting of the steering committee.[1] This was held at the Reserve Bank in Melbourne on Friday 11 October 1974.

Attending the meeting were, from the Bank, A.C. McPherson, M.F.W. Brown, R.A.S. Bywater and D.R. Parr, present as the Governor's nominee as alternate to the Chairman. From CSIRO, there were J.A. Allen, S.D. Hamann and D.H. Solomon. N.T. Bevan, from the Bank, was present as Secretary. Only Brown, by now the Manager, Research and Development at the Note Issue Department, and Hamann and Solomon had been with the project from its beginnings in 1968. None of the new members from the Bank had a technical background.

A.C. McPherson was a career banker and in 1974 was an Adviser to the Governor of the Bank.[2] He had been the Secretary from the establishment of the Bank until 1968 and was an Adviser until he retired in 1976.

R.A.S. Bywater was General Manager of the Note Issue Department. He had been the Planning and Research Manager of the Department from 1962 until his promotion to Assistant General Manager in 1969 and then to General Manager in 1971.

D.R. Parr was Chief Manager of the Accounting, Operations and Services Department. In 1960 he was the Assistant Secretary, was promoted to Superintendent, Capital Market Section in 1961, Senior Economist in 1965, Deputy Manager of the Banking Department in 1966, Manager of the Banking and Finance Department in 1969, Manager of the Securities Market Department in 1971, Chief Manager of the Securities Market Department in 1971, Chief Manager of the Accounting, Operations and Services Department in 1973 and General Manager of the Note Printing Department in 1981. He was an Adviser to the Governor from 1976 to 1982.

Why Hamann?

There is no indication in any letters on file or in the minutes of the CSIRO Executive meetings how the CSIRO members of the committee were chosen. Allen was clearly there as the representative of the Chairman, Price. He was the Executive Officer of CSIRO and, while not a member of the CSIRO Executive, attended all the Executive meetings. He was the Executive Officer from May 1971 to February 1975. He was not replaced on the CNRD Committee until the eighth meeting, which was held on 26–27 February 1976. His replacement was V.D. Burgmann, a full-time member of the Executive. Solomon was, by then, Chief of the Division of Applied Organic Chemistry and had overall responsibility for the CSIRO effort in the project. So these were obvious appointments. Hamann was one of the early drivers of CSIRO's involvement in the project, but by 1974 had no direct managerial or policy responsibility. In fact, he had resigned from his position as Chief of the Division in order to avoid being involved in such matters. In 1974 one of the part-time Members of the CSIRO Executive was D.L. Ford, R&D Manager of Union Carbide (Australia), who was an expert in polymer technology and in the commercialisation of science and technology. He was present at the 1974 presentation to the Governor and Chairman and was very interested in the project. In fact, some of the sequences in the film presented at the 1974 meeting were filmed at the Union Carbide plant in Sydney. He would have been a valuable addition to the CNRD Committee. While the Bank and CSIRO both had three members on the committee, the records show that Parr attended most of the meetings. To balance this CSIRO sent a representative of its Chairman to many of the meetings.

The Currency Notes Research and Development Committee

The committee agreed to call itself the Currency Notes Research and Development Committee and to adopt the following charter:

> The Committee is charged with the overall responsibility for the promotion of the currency notes research project through the development stage to substantial pilot production and subsequent evaluation of that production.

At the time, the CSIRO representatives agreed with the charter. They thought that 'production' implied 'issue'. As we shall see, the ability to produce a note did not mean that the Bank would issue the note.

The first meeting canvassed many aspects of the project. It established a technical group to work 'within the committee proper'. The members of the group were Hamann and Solomon from CSIRO and Bywater and Brown from the Bank. The committee was told that Gordon Andrews, the artist responsible for the design of the original decimal currency, had been contacted by McPherson and arrangements had been made for him to visit Fishermens Bend. The meeting agreed that 'inputs covering the interaction between technical and design requirements were an essential priority component of any action plan.' If Andrews agreed to commit to the project, the Bank would cover all the cost.

CSIRO identified three priority areas to which staff resources would need to be allocated – chemical, technological and physics.

CSIRO would support the physics area from its own resources by recruiting appropriately qualified staff to the Division of Applied Organic Chemistry. CSIRO suggested that, as a first step, the Bank take direct responsibility for the engagement of McLean and his assistant and for the project leader. The Bank representatives did not commit to this and referred the matter to Mr Crozier (Assistant Secretary – Staff, CSIRO) and L.T. Hinde (the Bank's Chief Manager, Personnel) to determine remuneration and contractual details. The Bank's reluctance to employ the personnel needed to carry out its part of the project was a constant source of conflict between the two organisations. CSIRO was convinced that it was on a technology transfer path which, to be successful, would require a considerable increase in the science and engineering capacity of the Bank. The Bank, despite agreeing to the continuation of the project, had clearly not made a decision on the long-term future of the product.

CSIRO outlined the four-stage approach developed at Mornington. The meeting neither agreed nor disagreed with these plans. It instructed the technical group to develop a critical path plan.

The Bank did agree to draw up a document detailing the tests and standards the new note should meet to fit established systems for issue, storage and distribution.

Missed opportunity

Neither the Bank nor CSIRO used the opportunity to outline how they thought that the research program would eventually lead to a product in the hands of the public.

The Bank was still operating on the business model outlined in Chapter 4. It saw itself as a printer and issuer of banknotes, not as a manufacturer of substrates and security devices. Furthermore, it did not seem to have an ongoing problem with forgeries so the urgency displayed in 1968 had abated. On the other hand, the potential for forgeries continued to exist so it would have been an unwise decision to abandon the project. Under these circumstances it made no sense for the Bank to employ the scientists and technical staff needed to take the research project to production. In fact, it would have been irresponsible for the Bank to offer continuing employment to professionals who did not fit into its long-term plans. It was entirely consistent for the Bank to continue to fund the project at CSIRO and to employ project staff at the Bank on short-term contracts. The Bank was spending a relatively small amount to maintain an activity that it might need in the future. It was cheap insurance!

This left CSIRO in something of a dilemma. It had spent a considerable amount of its own resources developing the proof of concept for a product that it saw had the potential to revolutionise the banknote and security document business worldwide. It could see that more work needed to be done on the design and manufacture of diffraction gratings but, as Solomon stated at the meeting with the Governor and the Chairman, the research phase of the project was complete. CSIRO at that time and indeed, still today, did not usually proceed to the pilot plant stage of a project without the clear commitment of a commercial partner. It seldom committed its own resources to this stage of the project. In the Bank project CSIRO was convinced that it had very valuable intellectual property and a committed partner, so it decided to continue down the development path. In 1974 this decision was made by Solomon as Chief of the Division involved, after some informal discussions with the Chairman, Price.

In an ideal world, the first meeting of the CNRD Committee would have spent time discussing these longer-term issues. Instead it spent its time on the shorter-term issues arising from the research activities.

The role of Gordon Andrews

Developing a new product requires strong interaction between scientists, engineers, designers and in some cases artists. When the Bank introduced the 1966 decimal currency it bought all the technology and did a brilliant job in the artistic design of the banknotes. Officers in the Bank probably had that model in mind when introducing the artist Gordon Andrews to the Bank project. But the project was still in the research and development phase and if it needed non-scientific input, it needed it from an industrial designer rather than an artist. An industrial designer may well have looked at the project and decided, as the Bank itself did in 1993, that the clear area provided a security level equal to or better than an optically variable device.

Andrews visited the Fishermens Bend site on 22 October 1974.[3] He was accompanied by Bevan (Secretary of the CNRD Committee). Andrews spoke with Solomon and Hamann and with Jack Ross, who was site engineer at the time and later the chief project engineer. The Bank's note on the visit recorded that 'We were shown the pilot production facilities, the engineering workshop facilities and a wide range of optically variable devices developed by Dr Hamann'. In fact Hamann was only responsible for the moiré patterns and, as discussed in Chapter 3, those had not yet been reduced to a size suitable for inclusion in a banknote. Solomon's team had developed all the other devices. The Bank reported that the discussions were wide-ranging and very frank and that Andrews established excellent rapport with the team.

Andrews raised some important issues that took a long time to resolve. He expressed doubts about the robustness of the diffraction gratings and whether, even if the pattern was unique, the visual effect was dissimilar enough from commercially available gratings. He thought that while moiré patterns might ultimately provide the most security there was a long way to go. Andrews had some previous experience with moiré patterns and Hamann indicated that he would like to visit Andrews' studio when next he was in Sydney.

There was an interesting discussion on quality. The CSIRO people wanted specifics from Andrews but he was thinking of aesthetics – an intuitive and rather subjective judgement for which it was difficult to formulate specifications. He was not convinced that the new substrate could simulate banknote paper feel, and asked to be supplied with a range of plastic surfaces. Andrews queried the requirement for punching a hole to house the diffraction grating. Ross was confident that any manufacturing problems could be solved. In fact, this issue had been discussed at Mornington (see Ch. 5).

CSIRO noted that their four simultaneous strands of development were aimed at eliminating the need for the Terylene® insert.

Solomon and Hamann visited Andrews in his Sydney studio on 15 November. Much of the conversation was about printing on plastic.[4] Andrews had devised a printing assessment pattern designed to evaluate various methods of printing on plastic. Solomon was bemused by both Andrews' and Brown's assumption that printing on plastic was something that needed new technology – the packaging industry was already printing quite high-quality text and images on a variety of plastic surfaces. Why Andrews, the artist, was issuing technical challenges to CSIRO in areas where CSIRO knew that there were no problems is not clear. As promised, Andrews demonstrated his own moiré patterns. The group agreed that there was a need to develop more spectacular patterns.

Also, as promised at the Melbourne meeting, Solomon showed a variety of plastic films for comment on the surface feel. It was noticed that the random modulation produced a noise when handled. The possibility of non-random surfaces, with variable modulations being used to produce a sound spectrum, was discussed. The aim would be to produce a different surface pattern for different denominations, enabling denominations to be identified by a distinctive sound achieved by rubbing a thumbnail across the surface.

Progress on diffraction gratings

The CSIRO team continued to work on diffraction gratings. They persuaded the Munitions Factory (then under the control of the Department of Manufacturing Industry) to modify its Gerber Drafting Machine to suit the requirements of the project for large-scale drawings of the diffraction patterns. Solomon had enough discretion over his budget to pay the Munitions Factory $10 000 towards the $23 000 needed to upgrade the input system to enable magnetic tape to be used. In return the Munitions Factory agreed to allocate 250 hours of plotter time and to allow high-priority access to the plotter for the duration of the project. In all the correspondence with the Munitions Factory the project was described as a 'special confidential project'.[5]

Subsequent meetings

The second meeting of the CNRD Committee met as planned on 29 November.[6] Much progress was reported. McLean and his assistant, Ken Clark, had accepted three-year contracts with the Bank and were to commence the new arrangements on

6 December. The discussions between the personnel departments of the two organisations had not resolved how to transfer continuing CSIRO appointees across to continuing Bank employees. Crozier did not at any time contact Solomon to discuss his ideas on this matter. Solomon's vision was that McLean and Clark would form the basis of the Bank's ongoing R&D group. He was disappointed when they were offered three-year contracts and predicted that they would try to obtain longer-term employment elsewhere. It was agreed that CSIRO would handle the recruitment of the Project Leader. CSIRO and the Bank had agreed that the area allocated at the Bank's Bayford site in Fitzroy was sufficient and all necessary alterations were going ahead. Work on the Critical Path Plan was quite advanced and would be tabled at a later meeting. The Governor had given McPherson full financial delegation for the project and both the Minister of Science and the Treasurer had been briefed.

The main business of the meeting was to discuss the assessment of security features in banknotes. Hamann presented the hierarchical classification of security features. Class 1 features could be identified by the 'person in the street', Class 2 features could be identified at point of sale by a technical device and Class 3 features could be identified only at the central bank. There was general agreement with this classification and with the view that comparisons should first be confined to individual features within the same class, and that classes themselves should be separately evaluated.

The Bank presented what it considered to be desirable features of security devices. It was agreed that the Bank would expand its classification to include a 'desirable/essential' spectrum and to nominate features that were 'technical' and those that were 'people-oriented'.

The third meeting was held on 14 February 1975.[7] The 'guide montage' for a diffraction grating, developed by Andrews as an outcome from the earlier meeting with Hamann and Solomon, had been made available to CSIRO. Hamann tabled some comments based on computer simulations of the visual effects. Since Andrews was not at the meeting, it was agreed that Hamann should talk once again to Andrews.

The meeting noted progress in recruiting the Project Leader and in the alterations of the Bayford site.

Recruiting the Project Leader

The Project Leader had to be recruited without any details of the project being revealed to applicants. CSIRO had agreed to manage the recruiting process and the following advertisement appeared in *The Australian* on 18 January 1975:[8]

> CSIRO has been asked to advise an Australian Government Authority with which CSIRO is co-operating in a development project on the appointment of a Project Leader.

> This project is based on research work and laboratory investigations in CSIRO which have now reached the stage at which it is appropriate to embark on the development phase. This will involve initially the establishment by the co-operating authority of a pilot plant and the proving of the process and the product on a substantial scale.

The advertisement said that the Project Leader would initially be located in the CSIRO Division concerned and later with the Authority itself. It did not specify the term of the appointment but anyone reading the advertisement would be justified in assuming that the position had long-term prospects. Applications closed on 31 January.

The advertisement did not attract many suitable applicants. CSIRO had anticipated this and had had a preliminary discussion with Jan Kolm, a Director of ICI (Australia). Kolm was well known to both Allen and Solomon and, according to the file note, 'had some limited knowledge of the project and a very quick and accurate appreciation both of the nature of the task ahead and of the requirements in a project leader.' Kolm saw little difficulty in identifying someone in ICI (Australia) who would be suitably qualified for the position, but anticipated that it might be difficult to persuade them to take leave of absence from ICI for, e.g., three years, given the known difficulty of re-establishment in the company. However, Glenn Wischer, a 45-year-old senior engineering manager at ICI (Australia), saw it as a very interesting career move and, after an interview, was recommended for the position.[9] Wischer had an arrangement with ICI that he could return to the company within three years. He did return to ICI in 1978, frustrated 'that the Bank was too slow'[10] in making a decision to proceed with production of the banknote. Governor Knight noted this at a Chief Executives' meeting, where he 'stated his immense respect for Dr Solomon and his innovative work and accepted that at times Dr Solomon had at times been frustrated by the Bank machine'.[11]

The fourth meeting of the CNRD Committee was held on 11 April 1975 in Sydney.[12] Andrews and I.D. Whittaker, Chairman-elect of the Assessments Panel, attended for specific items.

Andrews, who was gaining enthusiasm for the project, gave a presentation with the broad theme that the new concept of security devices called for an equally new concept of note design. He thought that the new note should be an interesting but simple design leading the public to concentrate on the primary security device or devices. The minutes do not record the meeting's reaction to this notion. The design of the $10 commemorative note and of the new plastic banknotes show that the Bank did not entirely adopt the idea.

Solomon and Brown had underlying differences on this issue. Solomon's aim was to develop a wide range of substrate and security device technologies to give maximum flexibility to the designers. Brown was committed to his 'idiot sheet' which depended on a diffraction grating as the only security device, with no need for intaglio print.

Whittaker was present for the discussion on the role of the Assessments Panel. The meeting agreed that more work needed to be done to prepare for the first meeting of the Panel. The committee Secretary, Bevan, and Whittaker were to draw up the agenda and draft a questionnaire for the first round of assessments.

Solomon reported that the Terylene® fibre had been delivered and that the 12 inch laboratory laminator was nearing completion. The laminator would produce Strand 75, a development of the original substrate. It was a five-layer laminate suitably embossed and cut. CSIRO had examined methods of applying diffraction gratings to the substrate and had established that commercial foils were not suitable. Work was proceeding on formulating a unique foil.

The Committee visits Fishermens Bend

The CNRD Committee visited the CSIRO laboratories at Fishermens Bend and the Munitions Factory in Footscray on 24 April 1975.[13] It was a comprehensive program. By this time, Ross was the day-to-day manager of the project at Fishermens Bend and hosted the visit. The Committee saw all the main aspects of the research program.

Girolamo and Clark explained the development, properties and evaluation of the plastic laminates, John Evans the research on optically variable devices, and Les Dalton and Stephan Demerac the work on photochromic inks. M. Seuret explained the problems of incorporating optically variable devices into note materials, Julius and Brett showed all the engineering equipment including the laminators and the corona dischargers, Bryan C. Loft demonstrated extrusion coating and Wilson the scanning electron microscope that was being developed to draw the diffraction gratings. The Committee then went to Footscray where Quint demonstrated the Gerber Plotter printing the diffraction grating images ready for photo reduction.

The visitors must have been pleased with what they saw because they requested that a new forward plan be produced by CSIRO with estimates of the dates for which responsibility of certain areas of the project could be handed over to the Bank. This sounded good, but there was nobody of a suitable level or experience in the Bank to accept the handover. The Bank representatives thought that the Governor should visit Fishermens Bend. He did so on 7 July 1975, the same day as the next Chief Executives' meeting. Figure 8.1 shows photographs of the visit.

The Assessments Panel gets to work

The Assessments Panel had been foreshadowed at the fourth meeting.[14] It met for the first time on 17 June 1975. It had five members. Two were Reserve Bank nominees: I.D. Whittaker (Sub-manager (Note Issue), Currency and Banking Operations Department)

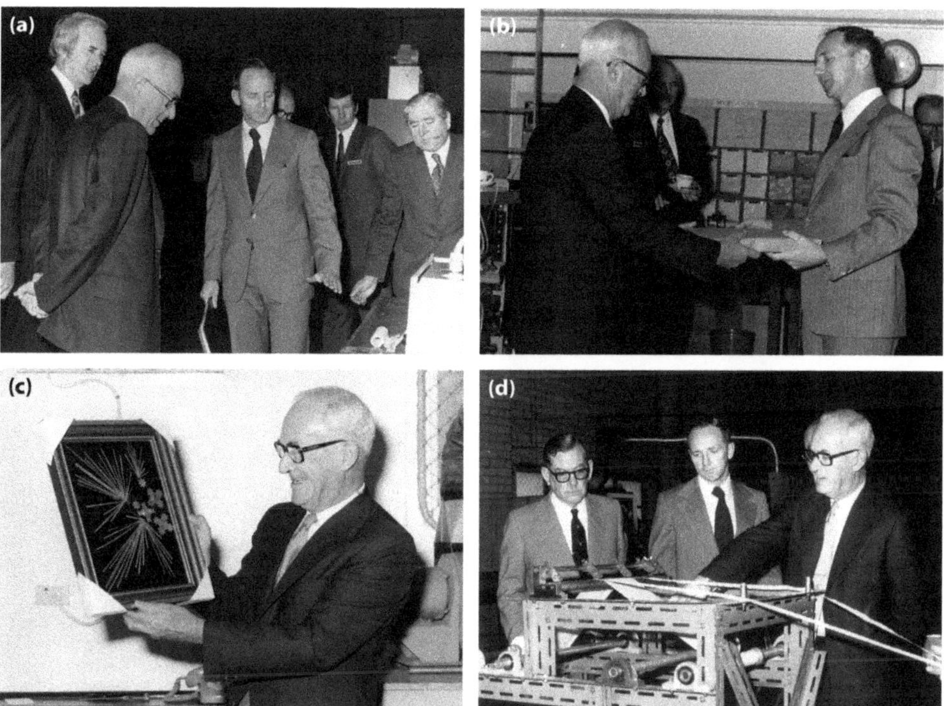

Fig. 8.1: The Governor's visit to Fishermens Bend. (a) Governor viewing production of moiré patterns at Fishermens Bend. Left to right: Knight, Phillips, Solomon, Wischer and Hamann. (b) Solomon presenting the Governor with a diffraction grating montage. (c) Governor viewing montage. (d) The Governor and Price viewing laminate production. Left to right: Price, Solomon and Phillips.

and J.B. Boxshall (Sub-manager (Issuing Division), Note Issue Department). The three CSIRO nominees were F.J. Lehany (Director of the CSIRO National Measurement Laboratory), R.W. Viney (Senior Assistant Secretary, (Finance and Property), CSIRO Administration Branch) and design consultant Gordon Andrews.

The National Measurement Laboratory was formed in 1974 by merging the Divisions of Physics and Applied Physics.[15] Lehany had been Chief of the Division of Applied Physics since 1961. Curiously, no one from the two CSIRO physics divisions had been invited to the Dr Coombs' original meetings in 1968.

Prior to the meeting, each member had been sent 400 sections of paper, 100 pieces of four different sizes (65 × 130 mm, 70 × 140 mm, 70 × 150 mm, 75 × 150 mm). They were asked to answer seven questions (note that this is an odd collection of criteria. It applied equally well to paper).

1 On the score of transactional convenience, how do you rate the various sizes submitted?

2 On the score of personal convenience, how do you rate the sizes submitted?
3 If you were required to hand-count bundles of banknotes, how would you rate the sizes submitted?
4 Do you see any inconvenience to users arising from adoption of the concept of standardisation? If 'yes', please elaborate.
5 If the sizes of all denominations are standard, do you see a requirement for discrete colours as a means of differentiating denominations?
6 Assuming that a strong distinction can be made by design without using different colours, do you think that this would be a satisfactory solution to the problem of differentiating denominations? If no, please elaborate.
7 If new banknotes are to be issued in standard size and colour, on balance, do you see advantages in introducing both size and standard colour from the outset? Please set out major issues influencing your conclusion.

The overall assessment was that the 65 × 130 mm was the worst on the size questions, and that the panel was generally not in favour of standardisation.

The dimensions of the plastic banknotes are: $5, 65 × 130 mm; $10, 65 × 137 mm; $20, 65 × 144 mm; $50, 65 × 151 mm; $100, 65 × 158 mm.

The second assessment test was devised by Spurling, of CSIRO, based on the notion that there was a psycho-physical concept the 'feel of a banknote'; it tested where various samples fitted that concept. The test showed clearly that the plastic banknotes did have the 'feel of a banknote'. The Governor took part in the test during his visit to Fishermens Bend (see Fig. 8.2).

Looking back, it is not clear why the Bank and CSIRO were so interested in the size and colours of the new banknotes at this stage of the project. Those issues could be settled much closer to production and were unrelated to the immediate issues of substrate selection and the development of new security devices. Also, it is not obvious that a panel of senior Bank and CSIRO officials were appropriate people to ask about the effect of size on the handling of banknotes. CSIRO did need an agreed dimension for its first production run, but that did not need to be dimensions of the final note.

It is, however, clear why CSIRO was interested in the 'feel of a banknote'. Ever since the suggestion of making the note out of a plastic material there had been an undercurrent that plastic would not have the 'quality' feel that was required for a banknote. CSIRO had the view that much of the feel of a banknote came from the surface treatment (both physics and chemistry) rather than from the properties of the substrate. The experiment conducted with the Assessment Panel confirmed that view.

The Assessment Panel report was considered at the fifth meeting of the CNRD Committee.[16]

Fig. 8.2: Spurling conducting the 'feel' test with Governor Phillips.

The CSIRO Forward Plan

The fifth meeting also considered 'A Forward Plan of the CNRD Project as at 6th May 1975', which had been requested from CSIRO during the committee's visit to Fishermens Bend on 24 April.

What had been requested was 'a forward plan of the project as seen by CSIRO' together with staff requirements and estimated dates for which responsibility of certain areas of the project could be handed to the Bank. CSIRO was adamant that 'Equally important is the need to set dates by which the Bank should furnish information and results from the areas of their responsibility so that research and development of the note is continued towards mutually acceptable goals.' Note that the development of suitable inks was the Bank's responsibility. There was a suggestion by Brown that the Bank might contract out this work – an admission that it didn't have suitably qualified staff.

The plan stated that the research and development of the note project fell into six broad categories:

1 the format and artistic design of the note;
2 the production of a suitable plastic laminate;

3 the selection of printing process and ink technology;
4 the development of a variety of security devices and their incorporation into the note;
5 the development of a suitable outer covering;
6 the testing and assessment of the note and note components.

The categories are obviously interdependent, and the plan reviewed this as well as delineating the respective responsibilities of the Bank and CSIRO.

Categories 1, 3 and 6 were identified as clearly the responsibility of the Bank. The plan noted that many engineering design details were dependent on the note design, and that CSIRO needed the following data before the end of June:

- the dimensions of the banknotes;
- the desired dimensions of the security devices;
- the location in the note of the security devices.

Looking back, it is not obvious why CSIRO required this information so urgently. The complete development of a prototype note could take place with the information already available to CSIRO. Solomon recalls that demanding the information was a way of keeping the Bank engaged with the project.

The plan still envisaged the use of the Strand 75 laminates, with their design to be finalised by July 1975.

The development of the long list of security devices mentioned in previous reports was considered a medium- or long-term project. CSIRO promised to produce a third Strand 75 incorporating a simpler security device, e.g. a clear area, watermark or printed pattern.

The plan summarised the various substrates that were to be produced by CSIRO and Bank staff.

Strand 75		Date
75/1	The basic five-layer laminate, embossed and cut to $1 size by CSIRO and supplied to the Bank for in-house testing of subjective properties	Mid June 1975
75/2	Printed 75/1 Strand. CSIRO to supply 14 inch laminator to Bank mid June. Bank staff to produce three-layer laminate and carry out extensive printing trials. Bank to supply CSIRO quantities of printed inner laminate for incorporation of optically variable devices and covering trials	September 1975
75/3	Variations by CSIRO on Strand 75/2. Some element of security, e.g. a clear area, watermark, printed patterns	August 1975

Strand 76		
76/1	Incorporation in Strand 75/2 and 75/3 of a diffraction grating, based on commercially available materials	September 1975
76/2	As above but with CSIRO unique design gratings	February 1976
Strand 77		
	Incorporation into Strand 76 of thermo and/or photochromic inks	
Strand 78		
	Incorporation into Strand 77 of a moiré pattern	

The plan ended with a note on the long term, which included Solomon's offer to house a background research group in his division:

> Given that plastic laminates become a commercial reality there will be a need for continuing research into all aspects of the note manufacture ranging from plastics technology through to new optically variable devices.
>
> There are variations in processing conditions which will require constant study and review, particularly as economics change, e.g. the major cost in the notes at the present time is the reinforcing Terylene® mesh and we are using curtain-grade material. It would be desirable to investigate more open weaves and alternative fibres such as nylon (which we have already shown as a satisfactory alternative) and various surface treatments to improve or control adhesion. There are various grades of polyethylene available and these will make marginal differences to the properties.
>
> The other cost factor is that polyethylene film we use is made from pellets by extrusion blowing (as shown in the movie film in September), whereas extrusion coating goes direct from the pellets to the note material and hence would be cheaper.
>
> Also, if our project is successful as we hope, other countries and organisations may well be interested and the Reserve Bank would offer them an expert and continuing consultant service and for this reason I would be prepared to house a background research group, particularly in the polymer area, at the CSIRO Division of Applied Organic Chemistry on the understanding that this group would be financed and supported by the Reserve Bank.
>
> In this way we would avoid the problem of the Bank locating one or two research scientists in an environment in which they may not be able

> to interact with sufficient of their peers. In addition it would give Dr Hamann and me a continuing interest in the project which we would find personally satisfying.

There was no mention of the use of a polypropylene film.

Solomon's offer to house a longer-term background research group was appreciated by the Bank, which promised to make a decision when the project aims were closer to fulfilment. The Bank made no promises with respect to staffing arrangements except to say that it would defer any long-term commitments until the project was further progressed.

Attached to Solomon's plan was a report written by Mario Girolamo, *Progress in Basic Work on Laminates*. There was no mention of polypropylene film in this report.

Polypropylene at last!

But in the *Progress Report to 31 August 1975* there was a brief mention of polypropylene.[17] Under the heading 'Laminate Research and Production' it reported 'Investigation is continuing on alternative laminates as note carriers, e.g. biaxially-oriented polypropylene and random overlaying of spun fibres followed by bonding into sheet form.' Curiously, the accompanying paper outlining the proposed program of work for the pilot production facilities at Bayford did not mention the use of polypropylene. Solomon's plan was to get the Bank involved in the work by using Strand 75. The new clear material was tabled at the sixth meeting but it did not elicit any comment from the Bank.

In the seventh meeting of the CNRD Committee, held on 5 December 1975 in Sydney, the CSIRO Progress Report contained a description of a new clear laminate produced by binding biaxially oriented polypropylene films.[18] The report designated this material as Strand 78, replacing the material described in the May report.

Hamann immediately saw the security potential of this new substrate. He wrote on 31 December 1975 (possibly one of the few people working at Fishermens Bend on that day!):

> By accident – not by design – the transparent plastic laminate known as Strand78 has the properties of an optical quarter-wave plate. These properties occur in thin films of crystalline minerals like mica, but they are very rarely found in plastic films. Given a special, but simple and cheap, optical viewing system, they enable the laminate to be distinguished immediately from non-identical material. They therefore constitute a first-rate tertiary security feature.

This was the first time that Hamann had shown any enthusiasm for a plastic substrate but his idea for a security device was not adopted. Hamann often sent documents to the Bank without prior discussion with Solomon, the designated CSIRO Project Leader. Most of the suggestions sounded good in theory but were not practical. Often the Bank was attracted to the idea but underestimated the problems with practicality. The transmission moiré is a good example – it was an essential requirement of Governor Knight but CSIRO could not incorporate one in a banknote.

A member of the CSIRO Executive joins the Committee

Allen left CSIRO on 2 February 1976 and was replaced on the CNRD Committee by a member of the Executive, Victor Burgmann. Allen was not replaced as Executive Officer. Burgmann had been the Officer-in-Charge of the Physics and Engineering Unit, Wool Textile Research Laboratories from 1949 to 1958, and Chief of the Division of Textile Physics from 1958 until he was appointed an Associate Member of the Executive in 1969. He became a Member of the Executive in 1970 and was Chairman of CSIRO from 1977 until the appointment of Dr Paul Wild in 1978. Burgmann's appointment raised the level of the CSIRO Head Office representative on the CNRD Committee. Allen had discussed his replacement with Hamann before making his recommendation to the Chairman. This raises once again the curious management arrangements in CSIRO at that time. Solomon was the officer in charge of all the CSIRO resources going into the project and the principal CSIRO contact with the Bank. It is not clear why Allen did not consult him as well as or instead of Hamann. But it made no difference to the outcome. Solomon was very pleased that a Member of the Executive was being appointed.

Planning the handover

Burgmann's first meeting was the eighth for the CNRD Committee, and was held on 26–27 February 1976.[19] It was also the first meeting for Geoff Sceats, the new Manager of the Note Printing Branch. It was a very positive meeting. The main items of business were the annual review of the project, discussion of the planned Bank commitment to the project and presentation of a review of progress to the Chief Executives.

CSIRO was very confident that by the 30 September 1976 deadline the viability of the project would have been established and all the strands of research handed over to the Bank for the necessary development and refining. This was in spite of the recognition that in some cases the associated process and engineering development at CSIRO may not have progressed as far as previously envisaged. It was agreed that the project would make better progress with the Bank's early involvement in development work.

The meeting agreed unanimously on the need to establish an ongoing research facility in order to maintain a lead over would-be forgers. The Bank noted that while it appreciated the CSIRO offer to provide the necessary expertise on a continuing basis, the scale of that support would not be known until closer to 30 September 1976.

The Bank reiterated its willing acceptance of the handover program but the meeting agreed that the plan should not be applied too rigidly. It was agreed that the project's success was based on the collaborative efforts of the parties.

At this point Governor Knight and Chairman Price were briefed on progress. The Governor was very positive. He announced that he wanted 5 million 'banknotes' of issue standard to be produced so that in ~24 months a decision on the 'marketing status' could be made.

It was agreed that a design freeze for a Mark 1 note should be set for mid-September 1976 to meet the proposed production schedule.

In retrospect, this was an overly optimistic meeting. The Mark 1 note was still to be made of the polyethylene/Terylene® substrate and a suitable optically variable device had not been developed.

The ninth meeting of the CNRD Committee was held on 23 April 1976 in Melbourne and was an important follow-up to the eighth meeting.[20]

The Bank tabled a memorandum entitled 'Transfer of Research and Development Responsibilities from CSIRO to RBA', which had been written 'in keeping with the February 1976 min which recognised that the concept of "handover" should not be applied too rigidly'. It suggested that the Bank's response to the handover documentation for transfer of each discrete stage of the project should take the form of a simple acknowledgement by the Bank's Project Leader that the Bank agreed to the transfer of further development, testing and evaluation and accepted major responsibility for progressing the stage. At the date of transfer it would be necessary for CSIRO to have demonstrated to the Bank's satisfaction the feasibility of the discrete stage under consideration. This would be demonstrated by the completion of a checklist that would broadly confirm that CSIRO had adequately trained and instructed the Bank staff in the component steps; had provided written instructions, explanations and other relevant documentation associated with the component steps; and had transferred to the Bank's control any purchased or designed, constructed and commissioned, prototype laboratory and pilot plant equipment necessary to the discrete stage.

It would be interesting to see a 'rigid' transfer approach! The transfer memorandum is an illustration of the different cultures of the two organisations. While both the Bank and CSIRO called the project the Currency Notes Research and Development project, it is clear that the Bank saw it as project which would result in CSIRO transferring complete packages of technology which the Bank could start operating. At this stage the Bank had not built up a research and development workforce that could take over a project from a research organisation and had not recruited any permanent staff to work on the project.

CSIRO tabled a memorandum entitled 'Incorporation of Birefringence into Plastic Laminates'. It pointed out that the phenomenon of birefringence can be induced into certain plastic materials provided their molecular chains can retain some degree of orientation and that Strand 78, which consisted of oriented polypropylene, showed this phenomenon. It recommended to the Committee that birefringence be taken into account as a security feature. It now appeared to be accepted that Strand 78 would be polypropylene. The meeting agreed that Solomon and Wischer should, as soon as possible, establish high-level contact with ICI to obtain information on alternative plastic film compositions which could be relevant to the project. It was also agreed that a further meeting of the Assessments Panel should be programmed for late May, and that the items to be assessed should include Strand 78.

The Bank tabled a memorandum entitled 'Diffraction Gratings – Simulations'. Included in the papers were notes of a series of meetings between the Bank, CSIRO and design consultant, Andrews. All the papers discussed an issue that would remain of importance until the launch of the note in 1988 – how to design and incorporate in a note a diffraction grating that had a diffraction pattern that was not only unique but was recognisable by the 'person in the street' and so could not be simulated easily.

The Bank continued to think about this problem and presented a paper, 'Diffraction Grating Design Concept', to the 10th meeting, held on 4 June 1976.[21] That paper summarised the Bank's approach as follows:

1 the diffraction pattern formed by the grating should have simple, easily described and easily recognisable features;
2 the line rulings to give the diffraction pattern should not be circular or straight;
3 line spacings should be modulated where possible;
4 no hard shapes should appear within the grating area;
5 the outer shape of the grating should be simple.

CSIRO again reported on the possibilities of birefringence as a security feature. This possibility arose because of the inherent birefringent properties of the polypropylene film used to make the Strand 78 laminate. Included in the report was a discussion on the security potential of polarising films, using the definitions of primary, secondary and tertiary security devices stated earlier (Chapter 3, p. 26).

CSIRO concluded that neither birefringent (B) nor polarising (P) films held any promise as primary security features, that P films and combinations of P and B films had very great promise as secondary features, that considerable research would be needed to produce and incorporate thin P film on a large scale and that the present birefringent properties of the Strand 78 plastic provided a measure of secondary security, which should be enhanced either by hot embossing or by adding regular strips (not confetti) of polypropylene in the laminating stage.

CSIRO responded at the next meeting to the 'Diffraction Grating Design Concept', paper offering its own expanded list of principles. It had nine principles put into three categories.

- Defence against copying
  1 It is absolutely necessary to avoid straight-line and circular rulings with unmodulated spacings. These are available commercially.
  2 It is highly desirable to use lines of complex mathematical shapes – not simple sine waves, for instance, which an intelligent forger could recognise.
  3 It is highly desirable to modulate the spacings of the lines, again in a fairly complex way (we should move away from simple sine modulation).
  4 It is desirable that the boundary of the grating should not have the same shape as its effective diffracting lines. That is easy to achieve by using a frame of arbitrary shape.
- Defence against simulation
  5 It is essential that the diffraction pattern be quite different from those of straight-line and circular gratings.
  6 It is essential that it be quite different from any that can be produced by cutting and patching straight-line and circular gratings.
  7 It is desirable that it shouldn't look like a toffee paper.
- Recognisability
  8 It is highly desirable that the diffraction pattern should be clear and uncluttered.
  9 It is desirable that it resemble some familiar shape.

In CSIRO's view, 'the above requirements – together with the extreme difficulty of predicting the kind of diffraction pattern that any particular set of lines will give – take the designing of novel basic rulings right out of the sphere of conventional artistic design. It is probably the most specialised job on earth.' The hot stamp technology developed by CSIRO for transferring mosaic patterns would force the forger to develop transfer foils (see Ch. 3).

CSIRO argued against the ban on 'hard shapes' advocated by the Bank. They thought that their use could assist recognisability without compromising security.

The design freeze

By the 12th meeting, in August 1976, progress was such that the Committee agreed to a design freeze.[22] Significantly, the design freeze specified the polypropylene film. All mention of Strand 75 had disappeared.

A note produced using the specifications of the 1976 design freeze would look similar to the 1988 commemorative note. The substrate was polypropylene, it had a diffraction grating as the principal security device and it had a clear area. The 1976 banknote had good-quality printing but not the intaglio printing that was part of the 1988 note. The absence of intaglio printing was not for technical reasons, since CSIRO had demonstrated that intaglio printing on a plastic surface was of equal or better quality to that on paper. It was based on Brown's strongly held view that the optically variable devices provided sufficient security.

Design freeze: proposed note specification

Substrate
Material of construction: ICI 'Propafilm® M'
Thickness: 80 μm
Method of construction: 2 × 25 μm + 1 × 35 μm lamination
Width of web at lamination: 360 mm
Post-lamination: 338 mm
Length of roll: 1000 m
Width and length of note: 75 × 150 mm (two banknotes across web)

Blanking out
Printing process: gravure
Ink: polyamide ink, or otherwise, to be compatible with later printing and coating processes
Printings: two printings on one side of the web
Opacity: transmittance <40% ('Macbeth' Densitometer)
Clear area: Vertical strip. Clear width approx. 30 mm.

Printing
Printing process: dry offset (text). Letterpress (numbering)
Ink: must be compatible with blanking out ink and later coating process
Printings – text: two colours on each side of the web
Numbering: two serial numbers per note on one side of note. To be printed in sheet form

Security devices
Diffraction grating No. 7 'butterfly' pattern. Maximum dimension 25 mm
Inc. by hot stamp or wet adhesive transfer from preformed tape

Moiré zone plate, mosaic type
Maximum dimension 25 mm
Incorporation method:
line pattern – to be advised by CSIRO
mirror – hot stamped foil
Clear area: Vertical strip. Clear area approx. 30 mm
Photochromic ink: based on spiropyran compound
Maximum dimension 25 mm
Printed by gravure
Infrared tracer: compound and method of incorporation to be advised by CSIRO
N.B. Strand 78 material is birefringent, a potential security feature.

Coating
Material: polyurethane type
Method of application: liquid coating
Thickness: 2–5 µm approx. Total thickness of coated note 85–90 µm.

Emboss
Surface gloss: specular bloss (Method 515B of BS2782)
Coefficient of friction: 0.20–0.40 note/note
Surface appearance: pattern or effect to be determined

The design freeze note had both primary and secondary security devices. Secondary security devices were not included in the 1988 note nor in any subsequent plastic banknotes.

The 1976 memorandum

CSIRO and the Bank exchanged a memorandum entitled 'CSIRO/Reserve Bank of Australia Agreement Post September 1976.'[23]

The primary objective in the period to 30 September 1977 was to produce a maximum of 10 000 specimen banknotes of the type specified in the design freeze. The agreement noted that some minor departures from that specification may be necessary, according to developments as work proceeded.

The memorandum also noted that the Bank's secondary objective over that period was to establish as far as possible production feasibility and requirements by using a web process for all stages of pilot production except text printing and numbering. In the process it should be possible to develop ideas and tentative plans for either a tiny commercial plant with prototype printing equipment or a full-scale production plant. Figure 8.3 is a diagrammatic representation of the manufacturing process.

The budget for the period was part of the agreement. On the expenditure side, CSIRO agreed to spend $580 000 and the Bank $265 000. The Bank agreed to

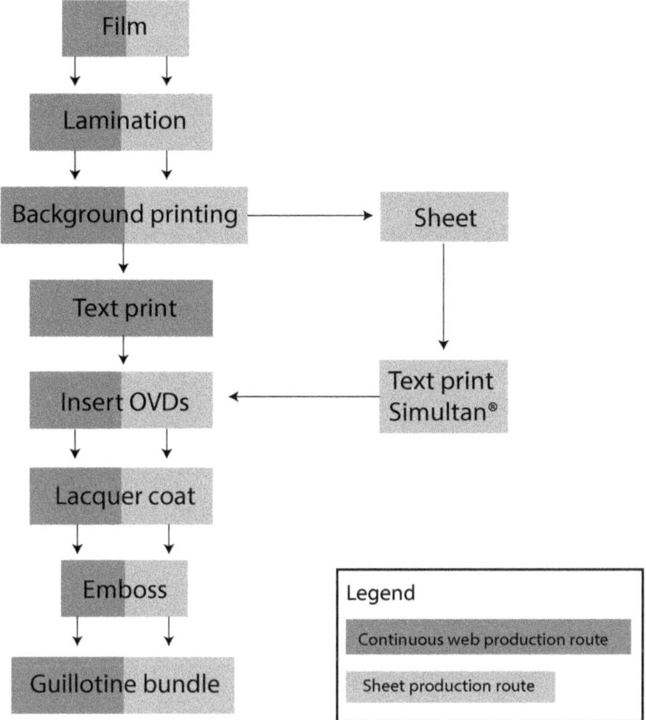

Fig. 8.3: Diagram of the manufacturing process.

contribute $230 000 to CSIRO, making the CSIRO net contribution $350 000 with a Bank net contribution of $495 000. In the discussions leading to this agreement, CSIRO agreed to increase its expenditure by $100 000 from an initial offer of $250 000 'in order to get to a decision point, hopefully by mid-1977 but no later than 30 September 1977.' CSIRO was obviously very keen to proceed with the project. It was prepared to spend $350 000 of its own appropriation funds on a development project for which it had no commercial rights specified in any agreement. A letter confirming the budget agreement was sent to CSIRO by the Bank on 24 December 1976 – 'a useful Christmas present', Solomon wrote in a letter to Pearson on 19 January 1977.

The Bank has second thoughts

However, by the 14th meeting of the Committee the Bank was having second thoughts.[24] The Chairman (now Parr) mentioned three aspects that concerned the Bank during its discussions on the budget.

- It was obvious that the project team was pushing hard to achieve a tight deadline – it would be important to avoid disruption of the general development effort by intruding impossibly tight deadlines for 'go/no-go' decisions. It would admittedly be difficult if the way ahead was not reasonably clear by September 1977 but the Bank did not see a 'go/no-go' precipice at that time.

- Impossibly high technical standards for the design freeze, e.g. in the number of lines per inch for the diffraction grating, should be avoided. This was not to say that the project team should not aim high but it should not lead to undue strain in achieving the Mark 1 note.
- There was still some worry about unduly compressing the time allowed in the critical path for the development of the moiré.

Solomon reassured the Bank that the team intended to do what the design freeze required but explained the importance of concurrent ongoing research. For example, the design freeze required the incorporation of the WRE grating (8000 lines/inch) but it hoped to demonstrate that the Toppan grating (13 000 lines/inch) could be inserted using the same technology. He predicted that work on the JEOL-type grating would show that even higher standards were possible. Burgmann thought that the Bank could do more on the handling of plastic since the production of a plastic note was the object of the exercise, not the inclusion of any particular security device. Parr stressed that a plastic substrate by itself was not sufficient, it must also be demonstrated that the incorporation of a security device was practicable. Parr's comment at this meeting harked back to the 'idiot sheet' proposed by Brown in 1972 and was part of the ongoing argument between the Bank and CSIRO. Solomon always thought that a plastic substrate with a clear area would provide sufficient security. It turned out that he was correct: the only optically variable device in the current Australian banknotes is the clear area. In retrospect, both the Bank and some senior people in CSIRO slowed the introduction of plastic banknotes by their obsession with the high technology of diffraction gratings and moiré patterns.

Hamann spent considerable research efforts on trying to incorporate moiré patterns into a note, entirely due to his own enthusiasm for this technology. Solomon was never convinced that it would ever be possible to print lines with the spacing and alignment required for a moiré pattern to be a suitable banknote security device (see Ch. 3).

Senator Webster's visit: commercial matters

The Minister for Science, Senator J.J. Webster, visited the project on 1 March 1977, both at Fishermens Bend and the Bayford site (see Fig. 8.4). He expressed interest in the project and emphasised that, in view of the magnitude of the Division of Applied Organic Chemistry's commitment to the project, a more formal arrangement regarding the ownership of rights, royalties and other commercial matters was desirable.

In a paper at the 15th meeting, CSIRO recalled that in the early stages of the collaboration, letters had been exchanged between Allen and McPherson relating to those matters.[25] The letters did not resolve the issues and there had been no formal discussions since. However, CSIRO understood from discussions with Bank officials that:

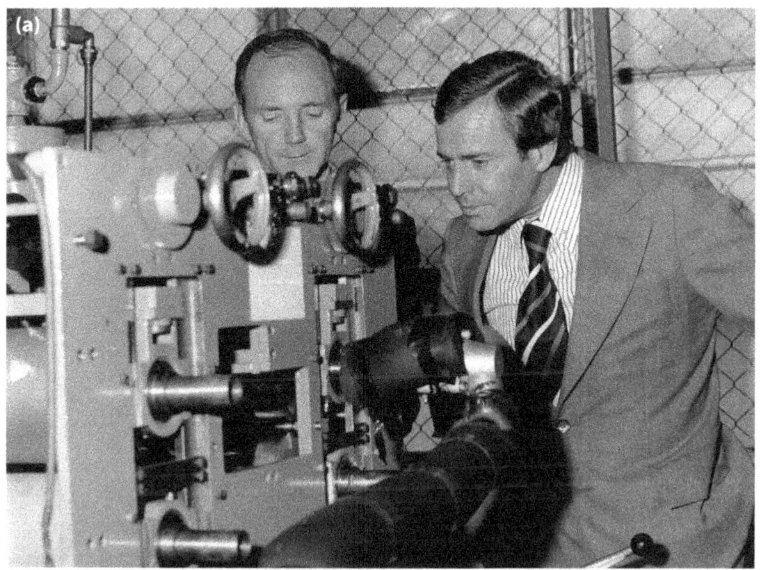

Fig. 8.4: Senator Webster visiting Fishermens Bend. (a) Solomon showing Senator Webster a component of the CSIRO process. (b) Solomon chatting with the Senator. Left to right: Hamann, Solomon, CSIRO Chairman Burgmann, the Minister and Ross (largely obscured).

1 CSIRO had the sole rights to all spin-offs and was free to pursue the development and marketing of spin-offs;
2 any overseas licensing of the bank note technology was to be at normal commercial rates.

This verbal understanding did not clearly specify the rights of each party, so CSIRO suggested that a more detailed agreement needed to be prepared. CSIRO suggested that the agreement should encompass three principles.

> 1. All spin-off technology and developments are the sole right of CSIRO and CSIRO are free to pursue and develop these aspects of the Project as they see fit, however CSIRO gives a firm undertaking to the Reserve Bank that no developments will be entered into which could adversely affect the security of the new banknotes.
> 2. In areas relating to security devices, excluding banknotes, CSIRO and the Reserve Bank would jointly develop the concepts and would share equally in the sale of technology or in royalties from licensing the knowhow. However, if either party should decline to enter into the development of these security areas, the other would be entitled to pursue the subject alone and as a consequence would have sole commercial ownership of the developments. Again from CSIRO's point of view we would undertake not to develop any security devices which would adversely influence proposed banknotes. A reasonable time limit would need to be put on this limitation.
> 3. In the areas of banknote development the Reserve Bank would use the technology and knowhow royalty free in Australia but any overseas agreements or licences entered into would be on a fifty-fifty basis with CSIRO and the Reserve Bank sharing royalties or income from the sale of knowhow. It is likely that in addition to the sale of knowhow, components of the new banknotes could be sold overseas (for example, the plastic substrate and the diffraction grating foils) and in the event of this development CSIRO would expect, in addition to the above, some recognition in the way of profits from the sale of the component. In the event that the Reserve Bank chooses not to pursue the commercialisation of the new bank note technology within five years, then CSIRO would be free if it so desired, to commercialise the technology in any way it sees fit.

Working together at last!

The 17th meeting was held on 10 June 1977. It was the first time that the technical progress reports from the Bank and from CSIRO were combined, although a joint report had been submitted to the Chief Executives' meeting in 1974. The design freeze had brought the two groups together. The exact status of the design freeze was always an issue. Should the project proceed with the exact materials mentioned in the design freeze when a slight change would vastly improve the outcome? A case in point raised at this meeting was a change from Propafilm® M to Propafilm® C. The planned printing on the Simultan® press had been completed using Propafilm® M but CSIRO had obtained better adhesion in its security device transfer line using Propafilm® C. A change would require further testing on the Simultan® press. Sceats was not happy with the prospect of having to interrupt his printing schedules again to test Propafilm® C, but he agreed that it would be possible to schedule the required tests. For the Note Issue Department, the production of banknotes was the first priority. A properly designed research project would have scheduled time on the printer for the research runs and have avoided causing frustration within the research team.

Another issue concerned the testing of various aspects of the banknotes. Solomon said that he interpreted the design freeze as intended to show:

- production feasibility – which virtually existed even though not in a fully integrated line;
- ability of the banknote to stand up to handling – which would best involve separate, incomplete sets of exhibits.

The report of the Technical Committee submitted to the meeting on 5 August showed the intensity of the project activity.

Solomon, Loft and Ross[26] met Lindsay Fortune of Wrightcell and A. Harling of Australian Cellophane, firms that marketed the 'Shorko' range of polypropylene films on behalf of their parent company, British Cellophane. The Shorko films were thought to be a better option because of their improved clarity and crease-resistant properties. The three men reported on the printing trials and the various difficulties, including sheets sticking to the blanket, carryover of black ink into other colours, and poor adhesion to blanked-out areas of the substrate. They did get some good-quality sheets for later optically variable device transfer, coating and embossing operations.

Solomon's three options

In preparation for the August 1977 meeting Solomon prepared a paper, 'On Options and Costs'.[27] He said that after the RBA/CSIRO agreement ran out on 30 September 1977, the Bank had three options. These were to:

1. acquire and commission an integrated mini-production line for the production of the new banknotes;
2. further evaluate the submission and claims presented to the Chief Executives on 12 October;
3. abandon the project.

Solomon sent his draft to Pearson, who sent back some suggested modifications. He clearly wanted a variation of option 2 and suggested wording he thought the Governor of the Bank would accept.

Solomon's draft sparked a lively discussion at the August meeting. A consensus was reached that the report to the Chief Executives should be based on:

- acknowledgment that the project was not quite ready to move to semi-production stage;
- specification of the further work to be done, with expected (short) time dimension and related budget;
- confidence about appropriateness of early move to semi-production along the general lines of that outlined.

It was about this time that Hamann noticed that a Russian postage stamp, the 1976 Ilya Muromets, had very fine printing. He contacted J.G. Downes, Counsellor (Scientific) at the Australian Embassy in Moscow, to find out more about the technology. The Russian authorities refused to give any information 'because of its connection to bank note printing'.

Should an EBX machine be purchased?

Discussion about the possible purchase of the EBX machine was held during this period.

R.A. Lee wrote a note to all concerned explaining the similarities and differences between holograms and diffraction gratings. He pointed out that both were diffractograms. The line pattern produced by the interference of two coherent light beams on a photographic plate is called a hologram whereas if the pattern is produced by a ruling engine or by EBX then the line pattern device is called a diffraction grating. If there is any difference between holograms and diffraction gratings, it is just that holograms tend to have more complex line patterns than diffraction gratings.

An appropriately programmed EBX machine can produce line patterns of unlimited complexity but some patterns can be produced more quickly and accurately by holography. The Fourier transform diffractogram is an example of a security device that is more easily produced holographically than by EBX. On the other hand, 'butterfly' type diffractograms would be extremely difficult to produce holographically.

After the August meeting, the Bank realised that there was a need to ensure that all interactions between CSIRO, the Bank and commercial suppliers were covered by appropriate secrecy agreements. Pearson sent a draft secrecy agreement to Solomon for comments.

The team prepared well for the October review meeting with the Chief Executives.

The report tabled at the meeting noted that:

I. Several hundred banknotes complete with all design freeze elements including outer coating and embossing, and

II. 10,000 banknotes fully printed on Strands 78M and SCC with photochromic device, outer coating and embossing, but without other optically variable devices had been prepared.

In addition the following are partly produced and will be completed at an early date.

III. 20,000 banknotes on Strands 78C and SCX including all elements other than text printing.

On the basis of the report, the Governor approved the continuation of the project until 31 March 1978 and the allocation of $95 000 to CSIRO.

1978 and still a research project

1978 was an interesting year for the project. A perennial issue was the size and type of diffraction grating to include in the note and therefore whether or not to buy an EBX machine.

The Bank contributed a thoughtful piece to the debate in July 1978. Its firm opinion was that it should not have to choose between a series of experimental designs based on different mathematical formulae 'but rather set the machine the task of formulating the chosen styles of grating from the outset.' This misunderstood the fact that the 'machine' could only produce the pattern from a mathematical formula that a person had input! It further stated 'that in the CNRD exercise we have talked in broad terms of uniqueness and ready recognisability as being prime requirements. Associated with these are the questions of durability and production feasibility.'

Neither CSIRO nor the Bank was in a position to make a final decision by September 1978. So CSIRO, with some help from the Bank, proposed a timetable for the period 1 October 1978 to 30 June 1979.

The program was in two parts. The first part was one where alternative optically variable devices, substrates, inks and topcoats would be prepared and demonstrated in a small number of note pieces. The purpose was to prepare samples that looked like banknotes but had been prepared using laboratory processes. The second part was the semi-production phase of a large number of banknotes incorporating the features preferred and accepted by the Bank.

CSIRO felt strongly that a semi-production stage should not be entered into unless or until the Bank accepted and approved, at least in principle, all the components proposed for incorporation in the note pieces. This note would be the basic production note suitable for circulation with minor modifications to some design features.

In response to the growing frustration of the CSIRO with what they perceived as slow decision-making on the part of the Bank, they added a final paragraph with a clear timetable for a final decision by 30 June 1979. In his covering letter to Solomon, Pearson said 'I, of course, retain my doubt that the timing Ross had suggested will prove practicable – especially that involving January next – but we can let the Committee kick the matter around.'

They did so at a meeting between the Chief Executives and the CNRD Committee on 26 February 1979.[28] This was the first such meeting for Paul Wild as Chairman of CSIRO although, as the Governor remarked, he had been at the initial conference at Thredbo (and at the first meeting in Melbourne). It was also the first meeting attended by Hill Worner, a Member of the CSIRO Executive.

Solomon was able to report that:

- he considered that the base carrier system had been resolved, problems having been overcome in respect of pin-holing as a result of exposure to sunlight and unsatisfactory appearance when crumpled;
- testing of the new photochromic compound had not been completed but it had passed the 10 day mark in exposure;
- there remained a need to integrate the various layers of the note to ensure compatibility – the adhesion of the grating and moiré devices had been affected by the outer coating.

Solomon made the point that if he was able to explain the problem to industry the adhesion problem would be more easily overcome. He thought that the main remaining problem related to the effects of crumpling on the diffraction grating and moiré device.

There was a very interesting discussion about diffraction gratings. Morriss suggested that more work was required to ensure that the gratings retained their recognisability when worn. Solomon made the point that there needed to be some agreement as to what crumbling test the note needed to pass. Worner, possibly trying to be helpful, said that he never regarded the grating as the absolute device; rather he thought it could be useful to include it as one of several strands and to accept that other security devices would need to be relied on in some conditions.

The Governor then made an important intervention. He said that, without being finally committed to it, the diffraction grating should be explored further. He considered the introduction of artistic skills to be long overdue since the concept could not be properly tested until the skills of the visual psychologist, graphics artist and scientist/mathematician had been brought together. He stated that even though there were wide limits of tolerance within which the public would accept whatever money tokens were issued to them, there were precedents to caution the note issue authority to ensure that its tokens were within those limits.

The Governor did not say what those precedents were nor how the limits could be determined. His statement was an indication of the caution that, probably rightly, characterised the Bank's approach.

An external review

The Governor then gave his view on the future course of the project. He said that the CNRD project was now regarded as standing within the mainstream of the Bank's research relating to currency notes. He also made the point that because of the importance of the note issue to the community the Bank did not suffer any discomfort about expenditure aspects of the project. Nevertheless, while encouraged by progress, the Bank did not consider that the project was nearing completion. The Bank thought that some aspects required more work before going to pilot plant production. These included:

- production aspects of the moiré;
- introduction of skills from the fields of graphic arts and visual psychology to increase confidence about production of diffraction gratings acceptable to the public.

The Chief Executives agreed to commission a Forward Planning Group with a charter to:

- secure any technical advice and staff necessary to assess the progress and potential of the CNRD product;
- consider possible courses for the future carriage of the project and advise on the most suitable.

Endnotes

1 NAA: B5609 1/12.
2 Biographical notes prepared from Reserve Bank Annual Reports.
3 NAA: B5609 1/13.
4 NAA: B5609 1/13.
5 NAA: B5609 5/4.
6 NAA: B5609 1/13.
7 NAA: B5609 1/14.
8 NAA: B5609 5/12.
9 NAA: B5609 5/12.
10 Personal communication to Solomon.
11 NAA: B5609 1/1.
12 NAA: B5609 1/12.
13 NAA: B5609 1/15.
14 NAA: B5609 1/15.
15 C.B. Schedvin and K. Trace (1978) *Historical Directory of Council for Scientific and Industrial Research and Commonwealth Scientific and Industrial Research Organisation, 1926–1976*. CSIRO, Canberra, p. 61.
16 NAA: B5609 1/15.
17 NAA: B5609 1/16.
18 NAA: B5609 1/17.
19 NAA: B5609 1/19.

20 NAA: B5609 1/19.
21 NAA: B5609 1/20.
22 NAA: B5609 1/22.
23 NAA: B5609 1/25.
24 NAA: B5609 1/25.
25 NAA: B5609 1/26.
26 NAA: B5609 6/26.
27 NAA: B5609 1/29.
28 NAA: B5609 1/38.

Chapter 9
The Tangalooma conference

Dr Solomon's response

At the meetings between the Governor of the Reserve Bank and the Chairman of the Executive of CSIRO held during 1978 Solomon was becoming increasingly uneasy about the Bank's commitment to seeing the project through to issuing the banknotes. He was confident that the Bank would keep funding the research project. Indeed, Governor Knight had once asked him whether it was possible to slow down the research![1] Solomon thought that this indicated that the Bank was using the project as an insurance policy in case of another forgery outbreak. He decided to have another off-site conference where all staff actively involved in the project could critically appraise all aspects of the project. In this way he hoped to be able to mount a convincing argument for the Bank to proceed on a path to issue the new notes.

He chose to have this conference at Tangalooma, on the west coast of Moreton Island ~40 km north-east of Brisbane. It was established as a naval station in September 1943 and used for detecting submarines. It was the site of one of the largest whaling stations in the southern hemisphere from 1950 to 1962, and became the Tangalooma Island Resort in 1963. It was used by CSIRO for in-house training courses in the 1970s and 1980s and was an ideal place for the CNRD team to meet to assess all aspects of the project. The conference was held from 24–27 July 1978.

Who attended the conference?

All CSIRO scientists actively involved in the project attended the conference and, as at the Mornington think tank, all the workshop staff actively involved in the project were also present.

In contrast to the Mornington meeting, which had no Bank representative, the Bank was represented at Tangalooma by Wischer, the former ICI chemical engineer employed to manage the project. Hamann was down to attend for the whole conference but, like the Mornington conference, attended only the sessions concerning the design of diffraction gratings and moiré patterns. However, he left before the final session where important decisions concerning these were made. Worner, the Member of the CSIRO Executive on the CNRD Committee, attended for the final two days.

A thorough internal review

The Proceedings of the Tangalooma Conference noted that 'particular attention was to be given to the role and value of each component of the CNRD banknote, its alternatives and the techniques of fabrication and incorporation into a note.'[2]

The list of topics discussed gives a good idea of the scope of the meeting. Each topic was presented by one of scientists actively involved in the research.

- The carrier system: D.H. Solomon.
- Note life: J.B. Ross and T.H. Spurling.
- Birefringence and polarising film: M. Girolamo.
- Foil design and construction: D.G. Hawthorne.
- Printing and outer coat: J. Hodgkin and M. Linton.
- Design of the grating and moiré pattern: S.D. Hamann.
- Photochromics and spectroscopic labels: J.W. Loder.
- Patent policy and spin-offs: J.B. Ross.
- Aspects of security: G.P. Wischer.
- Alternative optically variable devices: S.D. Hamann.
- Holography and EBX: R.A. Lee, A. Wilson and G. Quint.
- Post design freeze: D.H. Solomon.

In his general introduction to the meeting, Solomon made the point that 'the next six months will be critical as the durability and uniqueness of the grating is to be proven, together with some aspects of production feasibility.' As was the case throughout the project, the concentration of effort on the diffraction grating distracted the attention of both CSIRO and the Bank from the main innovation, the use of plastic as the substrate. Solomon knew that to suggest otherwise led some Bank staff to conclude that CSIRO had a lack of confidence in the OVDs.

What price security?

There was a long discussion on the relative lives of the paper and plastic banknotes. This was a critical issue because the increased cost of producing a plastic banknote (including an OVD) needed to be offset by a longer life. The Bank had never quantified the value of increased security. So, for example, if the life-time of the new banknotes was the same as that of the paper banknotes but they cost more to produce, would the increase in security offset this? CSIRO was never able to get an answer to this question so Solomon circumvented the issue by producing banknotes with vastly increased durability. The Bank had supplied data on the average lives of its suite of banknotes. The average life of the \$1, \$2 and \$5 banknotes was about seven to eight months, whereas the average life of the \$20 and \$50 banknotes were 24 months and 58 months respectively. In his presentation Ross noted that while he was confident the CNRD banknotes could readily achieve double the life expectancy of the low-denomination banknotes, he was not certain that the CNRD banknotes could last the 10 years required to double the life expectancy of the $50 banknote. The serial numbers of Australian banknotes have two letters followed by eight numbers. The first two numbers indicate the year the banknote was printed. We invite readers to check the year the banknotes in their wallets were printed. The results will show that Ross was far too conservative!

But in 1978 the life-span was unknown and since it was impossible to conduct a field trial of the new banknotes they had to be compared with the paper banknotes in a series of tests. Solomon and his team developed this series since the banknote printing industry did not have any such test regime. These tests made up a valuable portion of the intellectual property of the project. They were devised after the CSIRO team had informally quizzed bank tellers and found that paper banknotes were withdrawn largely because they were torn or quite dirty. There were eight main classes of tests:

1. production control – dimensions and weight;
2. physical tests – abrasion, resistance, device and print adhesion, flexural and tensile properties and tear resistance;
3. user tests – handling and counting characteristics;
4. exposure to food and common household chemicals;
5. resistance to writing materials such as organic solvent-based inks;
6. light exposure resistance – 10-day outdoor exposure and exposure to diffuse light;
7. resistance to fungi, bacteria and vermin;
8. miscellaneous tests – personal hazards, flammability and toxicity.

The results showed that the CNRD banknote was superior to paper banknotes in respect of abrasion resistance, adhesion, tensile strength, elastic properties, tear initiation and clean-up. It was inferior only in that it shrank at a temperature of 120°C, it had slightly inferior tear propagation resistance and the OVDs deteriorated in direct sunlight (Fig. 3.13c). The slightly inferior tear propagation resistance is not an issue in practice because of the vastly superior resistance to tear initiation. In fact, the Bank now recommends that the public use the difficulty of initiating a tear as one means of checking for forgery.

The tests listed above did not really simulate the performance of the banknote in actual use so it was necessary to develop a simulated wear test. The CSIRO team, particularly Ross, developed one well controlled test and Hamann devised one that was not well controlled.

The controlled test was the Turbula test. Twenty banknotes had a 9 g rubber weight attached to each corner. They were placed in an oblong container (kerosene tin) with 2 kg of an abrasive (polypropylene beads) and 200 g of a soiling mixture (see Fig. 3.15). The container was rotated at 60 rpm and the banknotes examined at intervals of 1000 revolutions. The banknotes were considered to have failed when any tear exceeded 2.5 cm. Failed banknotes were replaced by a dummy weighted banknote to maintain the same conditions in the container. In this test the CNRD banknotes were found to last four times longer than the paper banknotes. The mean for the paper banknotes was 6.3 hours with a standard deviation of 2.2 whereas for the CNRD banknotes it was typically 24.1 hours with a standard deviation of 10.9. At the Tangalooma conference, Spurling argued that because of the high standard deviation for the CNRD banknotes the difference between the banknotes was not statistically significant. History shows that his concern was unfounded. The Turbula test proved to be a remarkably accurate predictor of the life of banknotes and was part of the valuable intellectual property of the project.

The other simulated wear test was the Hamann-pocket test. In this test Hamann took a banknote, sometimes a paper banknote and sometimes a CNRD banknote, and placed it in the pocket of his trousers for a period along with his keys, coins and other personal items. He claimed that the paper banknotes performed better in this test than the CNRD banknotes. It is clear that no significance should have been placed on the results of this test but when he unexpectedly presented his results to CNRD Committee meetings and at meetings between the Governor and the Chairman they were not dismissed out of hand. In retrospect, it is hard to understand why one of the nation's top physical scientists would seriously report the results of such a test. We should report that many other members of the team, including the present authors, also carried samples in their wallets or pockets to get a sense of substrate longevity. Very little deterioration was observed, but these tests were never reported formally to the CNRD Committee.

At a meeting of the CNRD Committee in May 1978, Hamann commented that the Bank's Assessment Panel had failed to take into account the results of his pocket test in its evaluation of the relative durability of paper and plastic banknotes. He volunteered to provide a supplement to the report. He did so, and submitted it to the Bank without any discussion with Solomon. His summary said:

> The security features of the CNRD banknotes have passed the pocket test satisfactorily. But the fragmentation of banknote b and the development of tears in banknotes c, g and h are causes of concern. On the basis of the present small sample, it seems that the substrate tested would be unlikely to outlive bank-note paper in rough-and-tumble handling.

Such a report, if believed by the Bank, should have been enough to end the project. The minutes of the 12 June CNRD Committee meeting noted that Hamann had circulated the paper but have no reference to any further discussion of the issue. The Governor clearly was sceptical of Hamann's results.

Optically variable devices

There was a lot of discussion about security devices at Tangalooma. Hamann led the discussion on moiré patterns and diffraction gratings. The Bank had accepted a tessellated pattern moiré but he wanted new designs to be simple, more recognisable and with numerals incorporated. The problem with a moiré pattern as a security device in a banknote was two-fold. First, it would be difficult to print the patterns on the banknote with line spacing fine enough to obtain the optical effect and second, if printed it would not be difficult for a forger to copy the pattern.

Hamann reported on a recent meeting between himself, Lee, Quint, Spurling and Wilson concerning the design of the diffraction grating. That meeting had come up with three possibilities.

1 A grating based on the Bank's medallion was suggested but dismissed because it would be essentially a straight line plot. The Tangalooma meeting decided to reconsider ways of doing this since it would be very acceptable to the Bank.
2 The second suggestion was a profile, but this was discarded.
3 The most favoured grating was a tessellated portrait. The meeting assigned Hamann, Lee, Quint, Spurling and Wilson to continue to generate such designs.

Graham Quint's intervention

Quint made an important intervention during the discussion of Hamann's paper.

Quint had joined CSIRO in 1947 as a clerk, straight from school. After some years the person in charge of administration at Fishermens Bend decided that Quint was not suited to clerical work but that he was intelligent and had a practical bent, and recommended that he enrol in a computing course at RMIT. When the workshop at Fishermens Bend purchased a CNC milling machine Quint was put in charge of programing it. He excelled at this task and soon became an accomplished computer programmer. He worked with Wilson to develop the computer programs needed to drive the electron microscope as an electron writing machine. After the end of the Bank project he worked in the division's drug design project and eventually obtained a Master of Pharmacy degree from the Victorian College of Pharmacy. His career is a very good example of the opportunities that the Bank project offered to those prepared to grasp them.

At Tangalooma he suggested that the final design of the diffraction grating should incorporate three elements:

1 a 'secure' or 'exotic' design with a unique and recognisable pattern;
2 an 'efficient' design with maximum brightness even after crumpling;
3 artistic designs (portraits and the like).

These three requirements occupied the minds of the CSIRO and Bank groups working on diffraction gratings for the next decade. The second requirement was the most difficult and was never fully met. As discussed earlier, to be effective, a primary security device needs to be easily recognised by the general public but difficult for a forger to simulate or reproduce. A portrait, especially of the Queen (see Plate 13), is easily recognised but unless the diffraction pattern is distinctive then it could be easily simulated by a forger. An alternative to a portrait would be a distinctive symbol or motif. The Wandjina figures of Aboriginal mythology were incorporated in some designs. They were distinctive figures but not necessarily uniquely recognisable to the general public.

Other security devices

The bank was always keen for the banknote to include more than one OVD and at Tangalooma three more were discussed in detail.

Girolamo led the discussion on birefringence and polarising film. The polypropylene substrate exhibited birefringence and could be used as a security device. It would be a secondary device because it needed to be viewed with a polariser and analyser. A polarising film can be used as a security device either on its own or in combination with birefringence. The meeting concluded that incorporating polarising films into banknotes would pose large production problems and so was not thought to be a high priority for further work.

Loder presented the work on the use of photochromic compounds and spectroscopic labels. Photochromic compounds are ones that change colour when exposed to light of a certain wavelength but revert to the original colour when the light source is removed. Most photochromic compounds are not reversible for many cycles and therefore not useful as a security device. However, a spiropyran compound which changes colour in sunlight was found to last up to 4000 cycles. Given that banknotes spend much of their life in the dark, this number of cycles would probably be adequate. However, there were two problems. The first was that since it was obvious where the compound was in the banknote it would be possible for a forger to discover what it was and include it in a forged banknote. The second problem was that the compound may not react quickly enough for its absence in a forged banknote to be noted. Primary security devices need to be recognised instantly by the general public.

Spectroscopic labels are compounds that absorb particular wavelengths of light and can be detected by an instrument. They are by nature secondary devices. The CSIRO team had devised many such compounds and one had been included in the design freeze banknote, but these devices were not pursued since the Bank was mainly interested in primary security devices.

Final discussion

The final session of the conference was a wide-ranging discussion on the diffraction grating. Solomon led this discussion. Hamann had already returned to the mainland.

Solomon noted that an ideal security device would outlast the carrier and that any device that failed well before the carrier warranted a very low rating. Note that the clear area is an acceptable device since it lasts as long as the carrier. The diffraction gratings that were included in the design freeze banknote had a short mean life because of its rapid change of appearance from new to crumpled condition. A rigid carrier would be crumple-free but obviously that is not acceptable for a banknote. The problem with the polypropylene carrier was that, when crumpled, it remained in a crumpled form. This destroys a macro pattern, such as a portrait, but not necessarily all the tessellations or (in later banknotes) the pixels. The meeting came up with some suggestions for overcoming this problem, all of which involved improving the substrate.

Endnotes

1 D.H. Solomon, personal communication.
2 NAA: B5609, 3/11.

Chapter 10
The Forward Planning Group (Fink Committee)

Forward planning at last

At the meeting with the Chief Executives on 23 June 1978, Governor Knight floated the idea of a high-level evaluation of the project.[1] He had previously rejected the CSIRO offer of an individual, Dr Jan Kolm of ICI, and preferred a committee. 'To assist the Bank in evaluating the project's prospects and possibly advancing production, the Bank had thought of seeking counsel of outsiders experienced in assessing innovation and development in production. The Bank was, however, inclined to hold back from this at present.' The Chairman of CSIRO 'hoped at the appropriate time he would pursue the concept of an industrial reference group. He thought the Bank would benefit from opinion in addition to that which CSIRO could offer.'

Following a further meeting with the Chief Executives on 26 February 1979, the Bank began to form what was to become known as the Forward Planning Group.[2] As will be noted later, this committee did not have its first meeting until June 1979, nearly a year after the idea was first floated. It was a long time for CSIRO to have to cocoon the project.

From an impressive list of possible members, the following committee was chosen: Professor P.T. Fink, CBE (Chairman; Professor of Mechanical Engineering, University of New South Wales; currently serving as Chief Defence Scientist, Department of Defence); H.M. Morgan (Executive Director, Western Mining Corporation and part-time Member of CSIRO Executive); E.E. Peacock (Chairman and Managing Director, Crooks, Michell, Peacock, Stewart, Consulting Engineers); Ralph Tobias (First Assistant Secretary, Productivity Development Division, Department of Productivity); H.W. Worner (Director, Institute of Industrial Technology, CSIRO); D.R. Parr (Adviser and Chief Manager, Accounting, Operations and Services, Reserve Bank); J.S. Pearson (Manager, Currency and Banking Operations Department, Reserve Bank, Secretary to the Group).

There was a range of experience on the committee.

Professor Peter Thomas (Tom) Fink AO was born in Germany in 1922.[3] His parents sent him to England for his secondary schooling and to the University of Sydney to study aeronautical engineering. He returned to the UK where he worked at the Royal Aircraft Establishment at Farnborough and at Boscombe Down and was a part-time Lecturer at University College, London. He returned to the University of Sydney in

1957 as a Reader in Aerodynamics and was appointed Peter Nicol Russell Professor of Mechanical Engineering in 1960. He became Professor of Mechanical Engineering at the University of New South Wales in 1968 and was Dean of Engineering there from 1969 to 1978. In 1978 he was appointed as Chief Defence Scientist and Head of the Defence Science and Technology Organisation. He held that position until 1986 when he returned to UNSW for a final year. His research expertise was in the dynamics of fluids and the study of vortices. His appointment as Chairman of the Forward Planning Group was because of his general engineering and management expertise rather than any knowledge of banknote printing or the plastics industry.

Dr Hill Worner was born in Kerang, Victoria in 1917 and was a metallurgist educated at the Bendigo School of Mines (Diploma Applied Chemistry, 1934) and the University of Melbourne (BSc 1936, MSc 1938, DSc 1953).[4] He worked for the Broken Hill Association of Smelters (1939), the University of Melbourne (1940), CSIR (1941–53), the Mines Board of Canada (1954–55) before his appointment as Professor of Metallurgy at the University of Melbourne in 1956. He remained at the University until 1975 when he was appointed a Member of the CSIRO Executive. After the restructure of CSIRO in 1978 he was appointed Director of the Institute of Industrial Technology. It was in that capacity that he was a member of the Forward Planning Group.

Hugh Morgan AC is an Australian businessman, born in 1940.[5] He has both Law and Commerce degrees from the University of Melbourne. He commenced his career as a Judge's Associate at the Commonwealth Industrial Court (1958–62) before joining the law firm, Arthur Robinson & Co. (1963–64). In 1965 he embarked on his career in the mining industry, becoming a solicitor at North Broken Hill Ltd. He worked for various mining companies in Australia and was Chief Executive of the Western Mining Corporation from 1986 to 2003. He was a part-time Member of the CSIRO Executive from 1978 to 1983 and it was in that capacity that he was a member of the Forward Planning Group.

Ted Peacock was the Chairman and Managing Director of Crooks, Michell, Peacock, Stewart Pty Ltd, a firm of consulting engineers.[6] It covered civil, structural, electrical, maritime, industrial, mining and pipeline engineering. The firm commenced in 1971 and was responsible for the design of the Ore Handling Plant No 2 at Mt Newman. Peacock was nominated to the Forward Planning Group because of his engineering and project management skills.

Ralph Tobias AM was First Assistant Secretary of the Commonwealth Department of Productivity.[7] He was an engineer and joined the Commonwealth Public Service in 1952 in the Department of Civil Aviation. He worked in the Department of Supply where he was involved in the commercialisation of a sonobuoy system to detect submarines. When the Fraser government was elected in 1975 he was part of the new

Department of Productivity led by Minister Ian Macphee. He took a great interest in policies to assist commercialising the products of Australian publicly funded research and in 1976 was involved in the commercialisation of the bionic ear. After he left the public service he was President of the Australian Inventors' Association and an Adjunct Professor at RMIT. He was made a Member of the Order of Australia in 2013.

This committee was known as the Forward Planning Group but usually referred to as the Fink Committee in recognition of Fink's role as Chairman.

The Group was asked to:[8]

- assess the progress and potential of the CNRD product, securing any technical or other advice considered necessary;
- consider possible courses and arrangements for the future carriage of the project and advise on the most suitable.

The Group first met on 1 June 1979 and submitted its unanimous report in August.

There are two points to note about this Group. The first is that it was asked to report on both the technical aspects of the project and the business model that the Bank should adopt to carry on the project. The second is that the Group had members with skills in physics, engineering and business related to those areas but no one with insights into the plastics industry. The senior management of the Bank, and to some extent of CSIRO, always had the view that the inclusion of optically variable devices in a banknote was the main innovation of the project and that the introduction of a plastic substrate was simply to facilitate the inclusion of the OVDs. However, the CSIRO team thought that both were key innovations, and that a plastic banknote with a clear area offered greater security than a paper banknote. As later events attest, this was the case. The plastic substrate was the key innovation and the one that is still the basis of the Bank's note printing business.

CSIRO input

It was nevertheless an important review of the project and CSIRO approached its submissions with even more vigour than normal. David Solomon, as Chief of the Division of Applied Organic Chemistry, was concerned that the large investment that CSIRO had made in the project was in danger of being lost through the indecision of the respective senior managements. Solomon needed a committed Bank with a clearly defined business model before he could commit his division to further work on the project. He realised that it was not possible to put the development on hold and maintain the enthusiasm and commitment of his staff – five years had passed since the Governor had informed his Minister that 'the burden of effort should be progressively shifted to the Bank' and that the project would reach the stage where commercial production could be contemplated in two years.[9] But in 1979 most of the effort was still focused at CSIRO.

We quote extensively from the Fink report because it was a significant milestone in the tortuous path from invention to issue of the plastic banknotes. Essentially it endorsed the position that Solomon and other officers of CSIRO had been putting to the Bank for years. The report reinstated a sense of optimism at CSIRO. Not only did it provide independent assessment of the value of the project but, with great future vision, it recognised that the existing Bank structure and staff would not accommodate the major changes necessary for the CNRD project to succeed.

The Fink report

> **Overview**
>
> The Group considers that the Currency Notes Research and Development Project has been suitably conceived and should be carried forward to the production of issuable currency notes. We assume that the Bank would wish to move to production of one complete denomination at the earliest possible time consistent with achieving a significant enhancement of security against counterfeiting and suitable performance in use; we believe that such an objective should be attainable within 3 to 4 years and we have outlined a programme to that end.
>
> It was not within our charter to consider wider commercial exploitation of the fruits of the project's research arising from the joint venture between the Bank and CSIRO. However we suggest that, in the national interest and subject only to maintenance of prime concern for the security of the note issue, potential for commercial exploitation should be explored.
>
> **CNRD Product**
>
> The Group has concluded that the CNRD concept for a currency note would, without undue increase in the cost of notes, meet the objective of significantly increasing the security of currency notes against counterfeiting. We are satisfied that, although no new technology could be retained for any substantial period as the absolute preserve of note producers, the range of complex processes involved would imply a high cost of assembly of necessary skills and equipment and would thus represent a significant widening of the technological gap between official note producers and potential counterfeiters.

We consider also that provided the Bank maintains an appropriate effort of research and development, as well as surveillance of technological developments and accessibility of relevant equipment and resources in the community generally, the CNRD concept also offers suitable potential for future development to maintain the desired technological gap.

Before arriving at these general conclusions, the Group gave particular attention to those aspects of the CNRD note about which the Chief Executives of the collaborating organisations had entertained some uncertainties. Our studies and enquiries have led us to conclude with high confidence that solutions are available. In particular we are satisfied that prime security devices in the forms of diffraction gratings and moiré interference devices are capable of being designed and produced to meet the requirements of uniqueness, recognisability and durability. We of course see need for achieving appropriate balance between scientific, artistic, production and security requirements; although not seen as a real constraint, greater emphasis may need to be given in the early stages to technical rather than artistic needs.

Like the recent CNRD Committee, we see need for the proposed note to be subjected to increasingly wide testing before issue but we do not see need for this to extend into the public arena. We do not doubt that with suitable promotion such notes would gain public acceptance but we would doubt the wisdom of issuing a prototype note before all developmental problems had been overcome and the Bank was ready at least to issue a complete denomination in the new form.

Future Carriage of the Project

The Group has concluded that it could express confidence in the feasibility of the production arrangements proposed for the CNRD note. There are still design and commissioning problems to be solved, but they are only of a nature that should be expected in passing from the development stage to the production stage for a project involving sophisticated technology. Our proposals for the future carriage of the project follow.

Recommendations

1. The Bank should decide to proceed with the CNRD project and should set in motion as soon as possible a programme for the

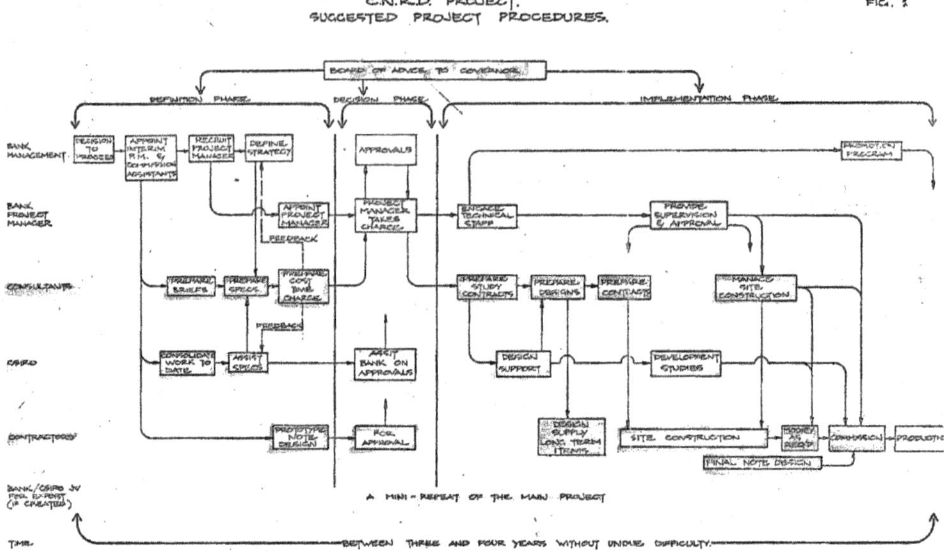

Fig. 10.1: Figure 1 in the Fink report.

recruitment of personnel and procurement of equipment to achieve production of an issuable note at the earliest practicable time.

2. To that end the Bank should:
   (i) Appoint an <u>Interim Polymer Note Project Manager</u> with a brief to –
   - commence the definitional phase indicated in the attached broad outline for an overall project plan – Figure 1 [Fig. 10.1];
   - identify the outstanding developmental tasks that will need to be completed and commission continuing work to resolve these at the earliest time.

   So that the necessary skills will be available promptly for this preliminary stage, the Interim Manager, who would be from the Bank, would appropriately obtain the assistance of a firm of project consultants and managers.

   (ii) Set in motion arrangements to recruit an individual with established technological and management skills for employment by the Bank as <u>Polymer Note Project Manager</u>. This appointee would have responsibility for:
   - completion of the work of the definitional phase including development of the Project Plan and specification of

management and operational decisions required for their timing;
- preparation of related budgetary proposals;
- securing suitable personnel resources for the project team, both by recruiting those to be employed by the Bank and procuring the services of consultants as required;
- completion of specifications and negotiations for procuring equipment and management of its installation and commissioning;
- arranging with CSIRO, and other bodies as required, provision of further scientific and technical assistance;
- arranging with the Bank's Note Issue Department for suitable accommodation of the envisaged production development both for the initial phase and in due course at the new note printing works at Craigieburn.

3. To maintain the advantage of enhanced security offered by the CNRD product, the Bank should:
    - provide for continuing research and development of the various security features of the note, and
    - establish a continuing surveillance group to monitor technological developments and accessibility of skills and equipment that could work to reduce the desired technological gap.
4. To provide for continuing research and development, the Bank in consultation with the Polymer Note Project Manager should in due course set in motion arrangements for recruitment of a Manager Strategic Research and Development.
    The project will of course require continuing support from CSIRO at least until the Bank's Strategic Research and Development Unit is fully staffed and functional.
5. While recommending carriage of the project to the stage of producing an issuable note, we consider that strategies for introduction of the CNRD concepts are for the Bank to decide. We do however recommend:
    - against issue to the public of a composite polymer note that did not incorporate the intended range of enhanced security features;
    - that the Bank should endeavour to avoid the product being described as a 'plastic note'.

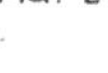

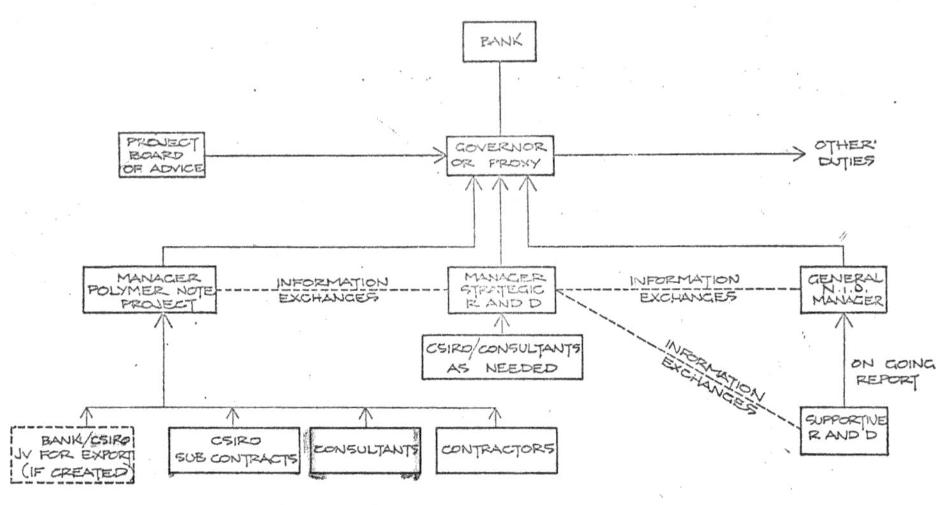

SUGGESTED MANAGEMENT STRUCTURE. DURING PROJECT IMPLEMENTATION.

Fig. 10.2: Figure 2 in the Fink report.

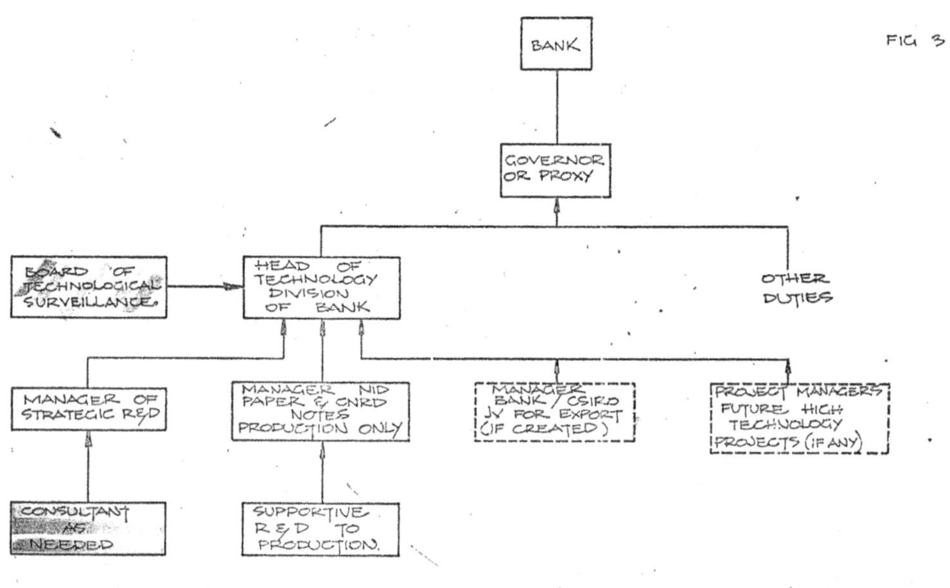

SUGGESTED MANAGEMENT STRUCTURE. FOLLOWING PROJECT IMPLEMENTATION.

Fig. 10.3: Figure 3 in the Fink report.

6. While the production facilities should be accommodated at the new printing works at Craigieburn when the major items of equipment were available, we recommend that responsibility for the project should be independent of production of conventional notes until the stage of production for issue has been reached. The Project Manager should derive his authority directly from the Governor and report directly to the Governor (or his proxy).
7. We propose that the Governor (or his proxy), to whom the Project Manager would report, should have access to a Board of Advice. Such recourse and use of the Board's advice would be completely within the discretion of the Governor (or his proxy). The Board would include a nominee of the Chairman of CSIRO, and the General Manager of the Bank's Note Issue Department or his nominee. The Board would also desirably include members experienced in commerce, industry and scientific development.

The attached schematic diagrams (Figures 1, 2 and 3 [Figs 10.1–10.3]) outline the programme that we propose for the future carriage of the project and the organisational arrangements that we envisage for the stages before and after issue of the CNRD note. They should not be regarded as rigid but as indicative of the thinking of the Group. The subsequent attachments discuss points touching our conclusions in respect of the CNRD product and the foregoing recommendations.

The report recommended structures for the completion of the CNRD notes (Figs 10.1–10.3). The organisation chart recommended by the Fink Committee is Fig. 10.1. Note the proposed CNRD project is not under the control of the General Manager, Note Issue Department.

No one from the Note Issue Department was in the Forward Planning Group. This was entirely proper since it was their project that was being reviewed. Similarly, the only CSIRO representative was Solomon's manager, Worner. The Bank representative was Parr, who was then an adviser to the Governor and the Chief Manager, Accounting, Operations and Services. So it probably made sense for him to be part of the unanimous recommendation to establish a new research and development infrastructure independent of the Note Issue Department, and reporting directly to the Governor. However, it was unlikely to be well accepted by the Note Issue Department, which had been involved with the project from the beginning and controlled all the technical resources of the Bank.

The importance of banknote design

Andrews' submissions to the Fink Committee were noteworthy! He now embraced the technology and his tentative designs for the way in which moiré interference patterns

Fig. 10.4: Gordon Andrew's diffraction pattern in the Fink report.

and diffraction gratings were to be incorporated fully included the technical advantages CSIRO had outlined to him (see Fig. 10.4 and compare to Plate 6). For example, he made excellent use of the variable line spacing and what was termed a patchwork grating, in which there were gaps between the various grating segments and which CSIRO had strongly recommended because it enhanced the value of the transfer foil technology. In developing a technology to combat forgery, it is necessary to remember that the forger does not have to reproduce accurately the banknote, only to simulate it: we were often subjected to the question 'What if they used something like a simple transfer foil or aluminium foil instead of diffraction grating?' This would have to be done by hand incorporation, whereas the transfer foil technology easily allowed for a gap within the grating as shown in Fig. 10.4. It was very satisfying for CSIRO to see Andrews incorporate this technology into his design.

Plastic or polymer?

The Fink Committee further raised the issue of using the word 'plastic' (discussed in other chapters). The Forward Planning Group also agreed that the new banknotes would be more difficult to counterfeit, that there were still development problems to be solved but that they were satisfied that the work carried out to date was fast approaching the development phase of the project. They also noted that problems regarding ink technology had been addressed by the Note Issue Department in printing small samples as sheets and they accepted the Note Issue Department's confidence that printing issues could be readily resolved. They accepted the proposal that CSIRO had been advocating, that ongoing research and development was needed to maintain the advantage of enhanced security offered by the CNRD product.

Testing and public release

The Fink Committee accepted the laboratory tests that CSIRO had developed and, while they supported further internal testing within the Bank, were sufficiently confident that it was not necessary to extend to public-arena testing. Solomon was very happy with the general summary.

The report strongly endorsed the idea that the first banknote released should contain all the available optically variable devices. This was the approach that had been adopted by the project since the design freeze had been adopted. At the Mornington meeting Solomon had proposed that the Bank issue a small-denomination banknote, using a plastic substrate but with no optically variable device, in order to familiarise the public with plastic banknotes. The Fink Committee was not in favour of that approach. The committee, like all its contemporary commentators, grossly underestimated the security value of the clear area. The recommendation to include an optically variable device in the first banknote put pressure on the Bank to purchase the EBX machine.

Endnotes

1 NAA: B5609, 1/5.
2 NAA: B5609, 6/25.
3 *The Australian*, 8 March 1994, p. 12.
4 <http://www.eoas.info/biogs/P001848b.htm>.
5 <http://www.cbcglobal.org/about/board-of-directors/mr-hugh-morgan-ac>.
6 NAA: B5609, 1/12.
7 NAA: B5609, 1/12.
8 This report is not in the Australian Archives collection but in the personal possession of D.H. Solomon.
9 NAA: B5609, 1/12.

Chapter 11
Response to the Fink report

Challenges all round

The Fink report posed challenges for both the Bank and CSIRO.[1]

The Bank had before it a report from a committee that included one of its senior officials, Parr, and its hand-picked consulting engineer, Peacock, which recommended, without reservation, that it would be possible to produce one complete denomination of the new banknotes within three to four years. The report outlined a detailed program to achieve that end. It recommended a management arrangement which would separate the development of the new notes from the existing note printing management and therefore from all the Bank's current technical expertise.

At CSIRO, the report was very well received. It contained a very strong endorsement of the CNRD concepts and a confident prediction that all technical problems still associated with the optically variable devices could be solved. However, despite this endorsement the report had three challenges for CSIRO. The first was that while CSIRO was confident that they could produce optically variable devices that met the requirements of uniqueness, recognisability and durability, it was still a research project and not ready to hand over for development. The second challenge was that CSIRO knew that almost all the expertise associated with the project resided within the organisation and transferring it successfully would probably require the transfer of some of the people involved. The report was silent on how this might be accomplished. The third challenge for CSIRO was the commercial use of the technology beyond merely producing Australian banknotes. The report suggested 'that, in the national interest and subject only to maintenance of prime concern for the security of the note issue, potential for commercial exploitation should be explored.'[2] No mention of the latter was made in any of the recommendations.

Both the Fink Committee and the CNRD Committee were right to consider that the security of the Australian currency was their prime concern. What is surprising, given the commercial experience of some of the members of the Fink committee, is that they did not recognise that the economic case for introducing the more secure banknote to Australia would be greatly enhanced if there was a market for the banknotes and their components greater than just the Australian market.

Given the favourable and detailed report by the Forward Planning Group, which included a senior Bank official, Parr, the project should have proceeded rapidly and smoothly. However, for this to happen the Governor, and particularly middle management of the Bank who were advising the Governor, needed to embrace the CSIRO vision, i.e. the Bank as a world leader in banknote research and development and an exporter of products and technology. It took a further three years and a change in senior management at Bank for this to occur. There was considerable evidence of the 'Australian cringe' in the Bank!

The Governor and the Chairman met on 24 September and agreed that CSIRO would assist the Bank in implementing the recommendations of the Fink report.

The Governor appointed Parr as Interim Project Manager, giving continuity to the Bank involvement. Parr had been associated with the project from 1974, had chaired the CNRD Committee and had been a member of the Fink Committee. Parr worked with a managing consulting company, PA Consultants, throughout the Fink Committee – it provided advice to the Committee – and continued to do so even when his path was at variance with the recommendations of the Fink report. In correspondence Parr used his substantive title of Chief Manager, Accounting, Policy and Services rather than his Project Manager title.[3]

It was during this period that Solomon came to the view that the project was stalling. No technical people were being recruited and Parr did not seem to be driving the project forward. In one informal technical meeting about ink formulation, Solomon indicated to Parr that the Bank should be fully responsible for ink selection and needed to recruit suitable staff to carry out the Bank's role in running the pilot plant. Parr replied that he was considering contracting out the building of the pilot line to PA Consultants. Solomon strongly disagreed. This would not build up the skill base in the Bank. Even more importantly, it was another indicator that Parr saw the project as having an end in a short time and it avoided the necessity to recruit tenured staff. It was an indication that the Bank had not moved from its 1968 business model.

In an attempt to progress the project, Worner and Solomon met with Parr on 13 November to discuss how CSIRO could assist the Bank in the next phase of the project. They all agreed that CSIRO would deal with the Bank only through Parr as Interim Project Manager 'in the light of the Forward Planning Group's Report of August 1979'.[4]

Solomon was therefore surprised when on 23 November he received from Sceats what seemed to be an alternative plan to progress the project.[5] It was entitled 'Thoughts on progressing the CNRD project'. In the accompanying letter Sceats said 'However, as will be noted, there is a fair degree of co-operation required with your people and it seems desirable for a quick meeting to discuss the proposals both for their feasibility and to establish just how far you feel you can assist in the exercise.' The Note Issue Department was unhappy with the Fink report recommendation that the CNRD notes development be under the control of a Project Manager reporting to the Governor in Sydney not under the control of the General Manager of the Note Issue Department. Solomon reported the new proposal to Worner.

Worner informed the Chairman of this development and informed him that 'As the NID proposal is essentially an alternative to the plan of action recommended by the Forward Planning Group, and because it would involve our Division of Applied Organic Chemistry in committing resources outside the ambit of our understanding with Mr Parr, I have requested Dave Solomon not to accede to Mr Sceats' wishes.'[6]

The agreed CNRD note at this time had Strand 78 as the substrate, all web manufacture and no intaglio printing. This originated in 1973 and had been supported in 1974 and at the 1978 review. It was the basis of submissions to the Fink review.

Sceats' 23 November document proposed two changes to the CNRD note, one to do with the printing on the note and the other to do with the production process. The change in printing was to use intaglio printing. The absence of intaglio printing on the CNRD note was entirely due to Brown's insistence that it would not be possible to do it on plastic and, anyway, there were sufficient security devices on the CNRD note without the need for intaglio printing. In a later telephone discussion with Solomon, Sceats admitted that on that point he had been misled by Brown who had always disagreed with the CSIRO view that intaglio printing would work as well on plastic as on paper. CSIRO had shown that intaglio printing on plastic was sharper than on paper. In the proposal, Sceats argued that the inclusion of intaglio printing would be a security device that the public already accepted, that it would eliminate the need for embossing and that it could be done on the new printing equipment being installed at Craigieburn. However, in earlier prototypes CSIRO had already eliminated the need for embossing by the use of a varnish to control 'feel'.

From the 1970s the Note Issue Department had been planning and building a new production facility at Craigieburn, a northern suburb of Melbourne. The old factory at Fitzroy was to be sold; it is now a campus of the Australian Catholic University. As part of the move, the latest equipment was purchased and installed. A consequence was that some of the old intaglio machines were now free and available for experimentation in the CNRD project.

The change in the production process was more of a concern to CSIRO. One of the features of the CNRD process was the increased efficiency of using a continuous web process rather than a sheet feed process. Sceats argued that making this change would speed up the introduction of the new banknotes because they could use the new equipment being installed at Craigieburn. Sceats informed Solomon that he thought that with these changes the new banknotes could be released within two years.[7] This process was very similar to that already being used in the pilot plant (see Fig. 8.3).

The document noted that 'The broad approach as outlined above carries *the enthusiastic support of the NID staff concerned so far in this work. In CSIRO's eyes this is no doubt a welcome change* but it does have a major bearing on how the project should be handled from here [our emphasis].' Namely, that the control should be handed back to the Note Issue Department!

Following these interactions with CSIRO there must have been discussions within the Bank because on 14 December, Parr wrote to Solomon attaching some of the technical details that had been contained in the Sceats document saying that he had cleared the release of the information and hoped that it would help 'us to press on with all speed along the path indicated in the agreement between the Governor and the Chairman.'[8]

At this point Solomon decided to ignore Worner's instructions and work directly with Sceats on developing a plan acceptable to both CSIRO and the Bank. He understood that Sceats was now keen to get on with the job and that since he was in charge of all the Bank's technical resources this provided the best chance of success. Solomon was also encouraged by the appendix to Sceats' document that clearly assigned research and development tasks to the Bank. This was an indication that the Bank was at last taking ownership of the project.

There were many meetings and discussions in the first months of 1980, building up to the meeting with the Chief Executives on 22 April 1980. There was an informal meeting between the Governor and the Chairman on 10 March at which they requested their respective organisations to prepare proposals on the management of the project for the April meeting and to prepare draft proposals for a formal agreement.

Within CSIRO there was general acceptance of the proposed technical direction of the project although CSIRO was keen to have an understanding that the sheet fed process would be superseded by a web system at some stage. Most of the informal meetings were about devising an appropriate way of managing the interaction between CSIRO and the Bank. During the course of these informal discussions Sceats produced a detailed chart of the 'Interim plan for the production of CNRD in sheet form' which allocated responsibility for each step under three headings, 'RBA activity', 'Joint CSIRO/RBA' and 'Contract' (see Fig. 11.1).[5] Solomon was very pleased with this chart as it clearly indicated the Bank was accepting responsibility for the project.

The Bank provided very detailed minutes of the 22 April meeting.[9] The discussion centred on whether CSIRO and the Bank could be involved in joint management of the project. The Governor started the discussion by advocating a 'high-powered consultant' role for Solomon. Both the Chairman and Worner ventured the notion that, on the contrary, 'it was vital for R&D people to be intimately involved in a managerial capacity in getting a new-technology product into commercial production'. The Deputy Governor made an important intervention. He said 'the Bank would be crazy if it came out of this exercise without somebody having a detailed knowledge of the processes.' He felt that if Solomon was too close to the project, Bank people might never get the experience necessary.

The Governor stated 'his immense respect for Dr Solomon and his innovative work and accepted that Dr Solomon had at times been frustrated by the Bank machine.' The minutes recorded that, after full discussion, the Governor said he could sense a consensus forming and put forward the following as a basis for agreement:

> The Group agrees that the conduct of the Project can best proceed if Dr Solomon takes charge, within the Bank structure and with an appropriate Bank designation, of a unit at Bayfords.
>
> The Bank is grateful for having Dr Solomon available for this role and understands that he would need to draw on other CSIRO facilities and staff. The Bank would wish to meet the costs involved.
>
> For general administrative purposes it will be necessary for Dr Solomon to report to Mr Sceats. He would frame a suitable budget and seek Bank approval.
>
> A Deputy to Dr Solomon should be appointed to whom transfer of responsibility for project management should be made as early as practicable,
>
> This Group should continue to meet periodically to review progress and to resolve any problems of an administrative or policy nature which may arise from time to time. The Governor may commission an independent monitoring of project progress by a consultant reporting directly to him.

In relation to the last point, in July 1980 the Governor retained Peacock, a member of the Fink Committee, as his independent consultant. His task was to 'monitor progress of the project in sufficient detail to be assured that it is progressing in an efficient and workmanlike manner and give advice on any aspect where the Bank so requests or where it is agreed that project performance so warrants.'

The Chief Executives' request for a draft agreement took longer to negotiate. The first draft circulated by the Bank divided the technology into two categories: that determined by the Bank to be available for commercial exploitation and that not so determined. With respect to the second category the Bank wanted:

> (i) RBA to have free use for its own purposes, including use in producing notes or components of notes for other note issuing authorities;
> (ii) RBA to determine any charges to other note issuing authorities for use of know-how, patent rights, etc;

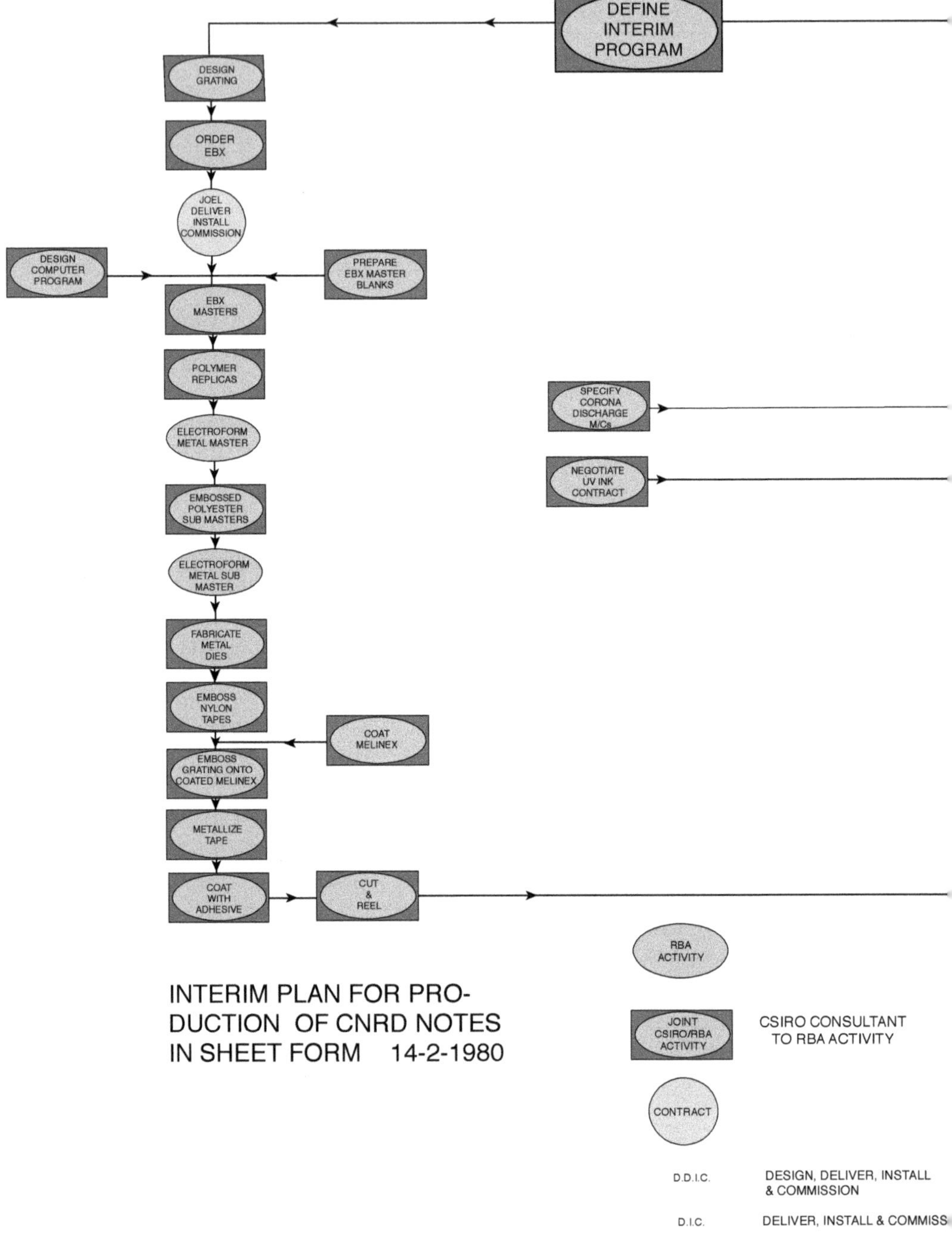

Fig. 11.1: Sceats' flowchart showing an interim plan for production of the polymer note.[5]

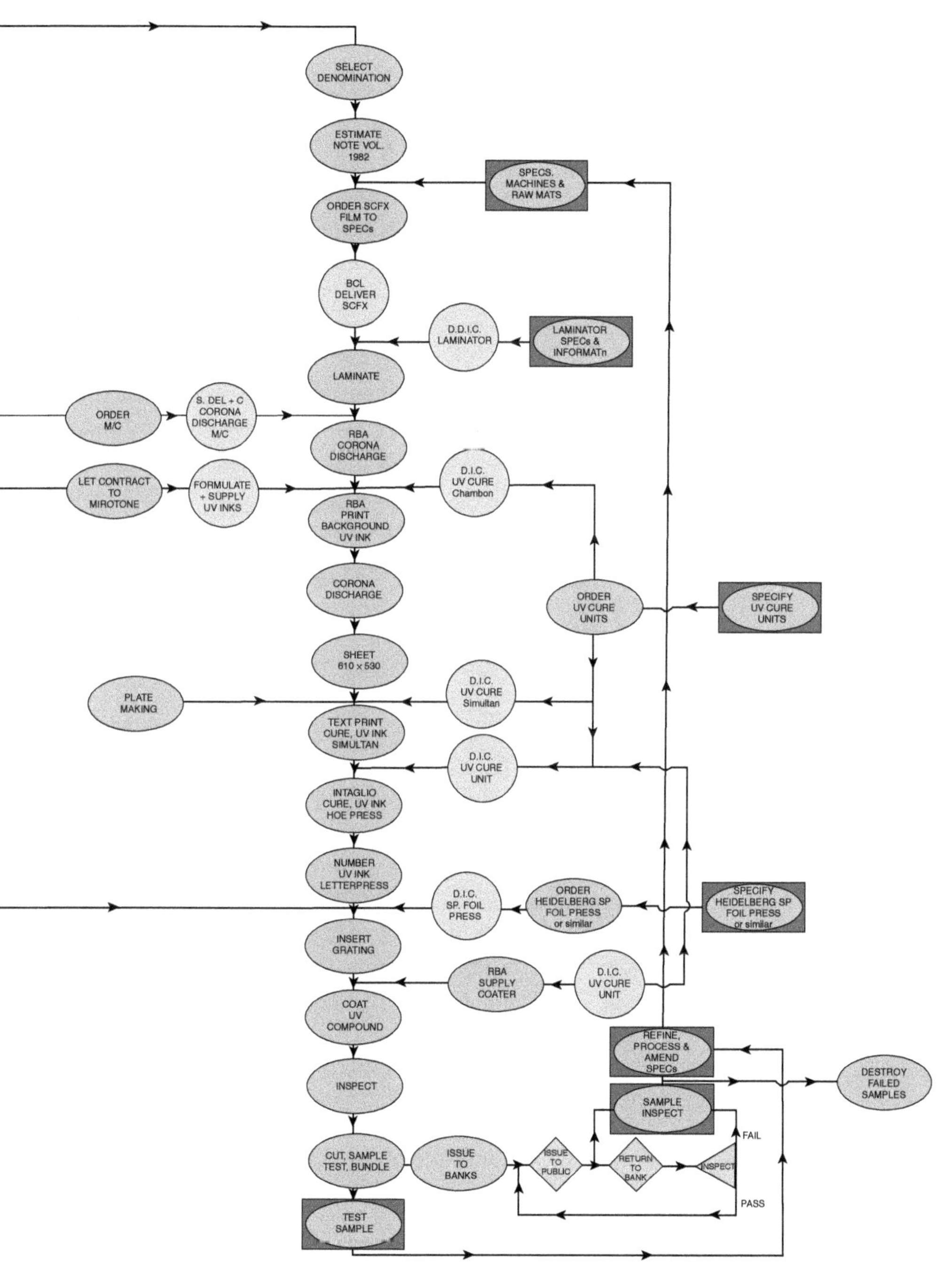
SELECT DENOMINATION
ESTIMATE NOTE VOL. 1982
SPECS. MACHINES & RAW MATS
ORDER SCFX FILM TO SPECs
BCL DELIVER SCFX
D.D.I.C. LAMINATOR
LAMINATOR SPECs & INFORMATn
LAMINATE
ORDER M/C
S. DEL + C CORONA DISCHARGE M/C
RBA CORONA DISCHARGE
LET CONTRACT TO MIROTONE
FORMULATE + SUPPLY UV INKS
D.I.C. UV CURE Chambon
RBA PRINT BACKGROUND UV INK
CORONA DISCHARGE
ORDER UV CURE UNITS
SPECIFY UV CURE UNITS
SHEET 610 x 530
PLATE MAKING
D.I.C. UV CURE Simultan
TEXT PRINT CURE, UV INK SIMULTAN
D.I.C. UV CURE UNIT
INTAGLIO CURE, UV INK HOE PRESS
NUMBER UV INK LETTERPRESS
D.I.C. SP. FOIL PRESS
ORDER HEIDELBERG SP FOIL PRESS or similar
SPECIFY HEIDELBERG SP FOIL PRESS or similar
INSERT GRATING
RBA SUPPLY COATER
D.I.C. UV CURE UNIT
COAT UV COMPOUND
REFINE, PROCESS & AMEND SPECs
INSPECT
DESTROY FAILED SAMPLES
SAMPLE INSPECT
FAIL
CUT, SAMPLE TEST, BUNDLE
ISSUE TO BANKS
ISSUE TO PUBLIC
RETURN TO BANK
INSPECT
PASS
TEST SAMPLE

(iii) CSIRO to be consulted in advance of completion of arrangements with other note printing authorities and RBA to take their views into account; and

(iv) CSIRO not to open negotiations with any organisation other than RBA with a view to licensing use in production of currency (notes and coin).

None of these clauses were acceptable to CSIRO and the document sparked some acrimonious discussions. They reflected the Bankers' Club mentality discussed earlier: the Bank was prepared to give away the technology to its club members. At the 22 April meeting the Chairman stated that 'the circulated documents had helped to focus on the problems' and asked Grant and Parr to prepare a further paper for the next meeting.

It was at the April meeting that the Governor floated an idea that would be the eventual outcome. The minutes recorded, 'The Governor mentioned as one thought – which he did not embrace, mainly because it implied a non-continuance of a hitherto fruitful partnership – which was the possibility that the Bank might at some stage buy out CSIRO interest in the CNRD processes. The CSIRO representatives expressed interest in this.' The Governor's 'thought' was pursued vigorously by Grant in the agreement negotiations but the idea was not supported by the Bank. It would be six years before this 'thought' was revived.

The further paper on the agreement was presented to the next meeting of the Chief Executives, which was held on 22 May.[10] Parr and Morriss were overseas at a meeting of the Four-Nation Group. The Governor circulated a telex message from Parr 'outlining North American and British interest in polymeric substrates for currency notes'. CSIRO was privately fearful that the Bank had disclosed more than was necessary to its colleagues.

The next meeting of the Four-Nation Group was to be in Melbourne in November 1980 and the Bank was keen to showcase the CNRD project. This gave it a great incentive to conclude an agreement with CSIRO since Solomon would need to be the main presenter at the meeting.

Grant and Parr worked on the agreement and the paper to be presented to the Chief Executives at their August meeting. Most of the differences between CSIRO and the Bank had been resolved. In particular, the clause relating to negotiations with overseas issue authorities now read:

> RBA will be free to negotiate and conclude arrangements with overseas issue authorities for production in Australia of non-Australian currency notes in whole or in part on terms whereunder CSIRO will receive a just share of the benefits accruing to the RBA from the use in such production of the CNRD technology.

The problem for CSIRO was another clause in the section clarifying who could negotiate with whom. It read:

> The party so charged with the carriage of any particular negotiation shall, subject to such consultations, have the final decision as to the consideration for which the CNRD technology shall in that particular case be disposed of.

In CSIRO's view, that was shorthand for the Bank giving the technology away to its Four-Nation colleagues.

Grant reported CSIRO's problems to the 18 August meeting.[11] The Governor then outlined the Bank's general philosophy including the 'need for it to maintain a close relationship with other note issuing and printing authorities'. Grant raised the sell-out option again but this was quickly dismissed by both the Governor and the Chairman.

After some discussion the Bank agreed to drop the offending clause; the agreement was signed on 18 September 1980. It included a termination clause:

> If RBA has not adopted and used a substantial part of the CNRD technology in Australia within four years from the date thereof or such later date as may be agreed then:
> (i) CSIRO shall have the sole right to the CNRD technology and to its marketing and to its disclosure to others; and
> (ii) CSIRO shall from the proceeds of such marketing reimburse RBA for its costs incurred in developing the CNRD technology.

The implied date of 1984 proved to be optimistic. It was not the first optimistic forecast. In 1974 CSIRO and the Bank predicted that a decision to release could be made in 1976, and in 1979 Sceats predicted to Solomon that his suggested changes would result in a release in two years. The Fink report had suggested a release by 1982.

The EBX story

An example of how Solomon 'had at times been frustrated by the Bank machine' was the process for deciding on the purchase of the EBX machine. Parr asked PA Consultants to advise on the diffraction grating production and recommendation for the purchase of the EBX machine. The consultant was to review the CNRD technical work and method of making the diffraction grating and to report on the CSIRO (CNRD) recommendation to purchase an EBX machine from JEOL, the Japanese scientific instrument company. The CSIRO team was not impressed. They had produced diffraction gratings which were unique, had surveyed the instruments available and submitted reports to the Bank. CSIRO had actually made prototype diffraction gratings on the selected machine in Japan. That the consultant's report agreed with the CSIRO viewpoint and method of manufacture was of small consequence. CSIRO considered the exercise a waste of money and time and, even worse, it gave little confidence in the chance of the project being completed in a reasonable time.

Staff recruitment: Bank uncertain

The Fink report and the paper on organisation and administration required the appointment of a Deputy Project Director. Solomon was to train this person and hand-over as soon as possible. It was explicit in the Fink report that this appointment be for a career in the Bank and part of a planned build-up of technical personnel. Thus CSIRO was amazed that Parr (a member of the Fink Committee) aimed to make a limited-tenure (e.g. three years) appointment. Curiously, he was supported in this approach by Sceats whose long-term interest would have been better served by a career appointment. Of course, CSIRO strongly opposed this approach and was surprised that PA Consultants, retained by Parr, did not counsel Parr that this did not fit with the long-term plans for the project and the ongoing research. Solomon recalls a question from the Governor, 'What will we do with the technical staff when the project is over?' to which he replied 'It will never be over; we are going to get out in front and stay there.' It was to take three years and a change of Governor to make the career appointment. Without properly qualified senior staff the Bank could not possibly fulfil its part of the collaboration.

Perceived 'competitive' Four-Nation technology: better than CSIRO!

Through the Four-Nation Group, the Bank had the option (or commitment) to join in funding Four-Nation Group research proposals. One of these was a $US900 000 proposal from RCA, the large US media company, for work on diffraction gratings. The Bank was always very open with CSIRO about these proposals although it was galling that the immediate assumption was that the proposals were superior to, or even superseded, the CSIRO work.

Knight indicated that he intended to join the Four-Nation funding of the alternative proposal which, in financial terms, was not an onerous burden on the RBA; it paid on the basis of a pro rata formula.[12] What was of great significance was that, without knowing the details, the Bank concluded that the RCA proposal made the CNRD work obsolete. Knight visited the CSIRO Chairman, Wild, and informed him that the RCA grating work had 'superior optics' to the CNRD work and got Wild's agreement to again postpone purchase of the EBX machine. The Bank did enable Hamann and Solomon to have access, on a need-to-know basis, to the RCA proposal. Solomon presented an analysis of the proposal at the Four-Nation meeting in November 1980: RCA was proceeding along a path CSIRO had investigated and rejected because those gratings were easily forged. The Canadians were also following work on thin metal films and both Worner and Solomon had met the inventor of this technology in Canada.

CSIRO's assessment of both the RCA and the Canadian work was:

1 neither had any thoughts on using plastic film substrates so as a minimum they were complementary to not competitive with CSIRO work;
2 the optical physics did not supersede the CSIRO work.

However, the alternative proposals essentially put on hold the CSIRO program and resulted in yet another period of little progress.

Solomon had a vigorous discussion with Wild over the decision to defer purchase of the EBX because he saw it as much more than refusal of funds. He asked Wild to consider how Knight knew the RCA proposal had 'superior optics' and that the RCA proposal was for work to be done, i.e. it was speculative. The answer to the first point is obvious; Knight had accepted a statement by a proponent of the work. Quite a contrast to how the CNRD work was reviewed.

The Four-Nation visit

Parr had visited overseas banks during 1979–80 and reported that there was great interest in the CNRD work, particularly the new plastic substrate. The Four-Nation Steering Committee was to meet in Melbourne during the week of 24 November 1980. This visit was a dilemma for the Bank; on the one hand it wanted to honour its commitment to the Four-Nation Group and, on the other, to respect CSIRO's position on the non-disclosure of the technology. Knight was quite open about this issue and very professional. He even suggested that a possible solution would be for the Bank to buy out CSIRO's interest, which it eventually did. The Chief Executives' meeting on 18 August 1980 noted that:[13]

> The commitment for a presentation on the substrate to be made to the Four-Nation Group when they visited Melbourne in November 1980 was reviewed. It was also noted that scope for discussion over a wider range could develop. Presentations generally should be directed to showing enough of the CNRD technology to arouse interest, but not sufficient to reveal all details of manufacture, etc.
>
> A firm proposal for presentation of a package of CNRD technology covering substrate, laminating procedure, ink systems and testing procedures should be developed. Estimates of the value of the package should also be prepared; this value may not equate with the cost of development to CSIRO and RBA but could be related to the estimated

> cost to the Four-Nation Group to develop technology of the same level. Dr Solomon and Mr Sceats were charged with developing plans for a suitable presentation.

Sceats and Solomon spent considerable time planning for this meeting. Sceats was now sympathetic to the CSIRO position that it would expect a commercial return and he accepted and reported that CSIRO would have the support of the Minister for that position. CSIRO was pleased that Sceats saw its attitude as strengthening the Bank's hand in dealing with the Four-Nation Group.

Sceats and Solomon explored various options from a 'sufficient to arouse interest' through to complete disclosure and to the safeguards CSIRO required. There was contact between Morriss of the Note Issue Department and a Mr Bennett, who was coordinating the arrangements for the Four-Nation Group.[14] Bennett had indicated that the Group wished to spend two days with CSIRO and that he expected the presentation should cover the whole of the technology 'at least substrate *and* diffraction grating.' He also wanted to visit the pilot plant at Fishermens Bend.

CSIRO was concerned that it might well receive nothing for its 10 years' work. It was a year since the Fink report and, of the two senior staff at the Note Issue Department involved in the project, Brown had retired and Sceats was to retire the following year. The search for a project manager was not going well; both Parr and Sceats were in favour of a limited-term contract, at variance with the Fink report. Solomon had opposed this, but the Bank's middle management had yet to be convinced of the need for a career appointment. CSIRO thought that this meant that the Bank's senior management did not understand the ongoing nature of the CNRD project. Within CSIRO, the Commercial Group was concerned that it was fast approaching the position where there would be nothing left to sell, because of the real or perceived disclosures to other banks and the overall slow pace of the project. Solomon agreed with Sceats that he would make a detailed presentation but did not agree to show the Four-Nation Group delegation the CNRD equipment, as that would have disclosed too many details. CSIRO did not show the tumble or Turbula test and its correlation with field performance. As part of the agreed presentation, Solomon was to comment on the relative merits and problems of the RCA thin film proposals. The Bank and CSIRO agreed on a confidentiality agreement to be signed by all attending. This proved invaluable later when the US threatened to develop its own plastic substrate.

Sceats recognised that the CNRD technology should be costed on the value to the purchaser, not the cost of the R&D, and a figure of $15 million was mentioned. Solomon made it clear that CSIRO was not interested in any trade-off of its proven technology for shared access to R&D overseas.

CSIRO and the Bank agreed on a format for the presentation of the CNRD technology to the Four-Nation Group. There were some technical issues to be dealt with. The Note Issue Department had contracted Wrightcel to carry out printing trials and there were minor problems. However, it was agreed to show the plastic film, after opacification, being printed on a Simultan® and intaglio machine at the Note Issue Department; Sceats was most anxious to show this as expected of a production manager.

Previously all printing trials had been carried out at the Bank by passing single sheets of plastic film through the printing press either carried on a paper background or fed manually by hand. CSIRO did not have access to the machine nor the time or materials to carry out trials of a stack. Solomon pointed out to Sceats that it was not normal scientific methodology to demonstrate a first trial to an outside audience, but Sceats prevailed. At Bayfords the team added silica to the ink to make the surface rougher (easier to pick up).

Parr (not as Project Manager!) wrote on 3 October 1980 to the Chair of the Four-Nation Group Steering Committee, William H. Wallace, at that time Staff Director for Federal Reserve Bank Activities, Board of Governors of the Federal Reserve System, outlining the decisions that had been taken and what was intended for the meeting in Melbourne in November. This memo was a significant document.[15] Parr indicated:

1. Subject to a production trial, about which we (RBA) have a high degree of confidence, we have an effective alternative substrate for banknotes. Samples have stood up well to exhaustive testing.
2. With OVDs we had a method of incorporating these in notes and this was at an advanced stage but further work on design was required. The transfer technology may be adaptable to paper substrates.
3. The savings in time and confidence by going with proven technology thus avoiding the 'frustration of research and development by the Four-Nation Group.

Parr indicated the 'delicacies in how far we can go in disclosing technology and results for appraisal without producing potential for commercial exploitation which our associate, CSIRO, is statutorily committed to pursue.'

The presentation to the Four-Nation Group

The technical disclosure was presented to the Four-Nation Anti-Counterfeiting Group at the Note Issue Department premises, then located in Victoria Parade, Melbourne. There were 18 people present at the meeting: a Steering Committee of 10 and an eight-member Working Party. The US had four representatives on the Steering Committee representing the four different agencies involved in the production and distribution of banknotes in the US. As noted above, the Chair was Wallace representing the Board of Governors of the Federal Reserve System, Harry R. Clements was Director of and representing the Bureau of Engraving and Printing, Department of the Treasury, H.

Stuart Knight was Director of the US Secret Service and Robert P. Forrestal was representing the Federal Reserve Bank of Atlanta, one of the 12 Federal Reserve banks in the Federal Reserve System. The UK was represented by Michael J.S. Cubbage and Geoff L. Wheatley, both from the Bank of England Printing Works. Canada was represented by Sterling V. Suggett and Don G.M. Bennett, both from the Bank of Canada Department of Administrative Operations. Australia was represented by Parr, Chief Manager, Accounting, Operations and Services of the Reserve Bank of Australia and Sceats, General Manager of the Note Issue Department. The Working Party of eight had five members from the US including Joseph R. Carlon, Special Agent in Charge, Counterfeit Division of the US Secret Service. CSIRO had spent considerable effort in preparing posters to complement Solomon's oral presentation. There were also extensive exhibits of the components of the note, and the test results. The design freeze note (birds in flight) was shown, and the existing paper $1 and $2 notes had been printed on plastic.[16] Every issue of importance to the decision-making group was addressed. Photographs of the presentation room are shown in Plate 14.

In summary, the team had presented a convincing story and demonstration that the CNRD process was not a laboratory curiosity but a feasible production process for a technically superior banknote. But all was not well. An event occurred which had serious and significant consequences for the project and for CSIRO's position.

The stolen note

After Solomon's presentation in the morning Sceats gave the delegates 111 samples of plastic notes so that the handling properties could be judged by each person. One hundred of these were in a bundle ready for the counting machine, five were marked with fluorescent dye to check the rejection by the sorting machine, and six were available for scrunch tests. These notes were tabled before inspecting the printing operations on both the Simultan® and intaglio printing presses. Just before lunch, the sample notes were collected; *there was one missing*. During the lunch break Sceats, Solomon and Parr had a most acrimonious discussion. One delegate had left for the airport and Solomon wanted him stopped as he suspected that the person may have the missing note. He also wanted to halt any further demonstrations or disclosure until the note was found. Solomon remembers Sceats saying 'These are all honourable people', to which Solomon replied that 'At least one of them is not!'

Parr and Sceats insisted that the presentation had to continue and Solomon reluctantly agreed. After lunch Sceats asked the delegates to check their seats and pockets for the note – they all knew what had happened. Solomon wrote a file note and copied it to Wild, the CSIRO Chairman.[17] Wild was appalled. CSIRO does not know if Sceats wrote a file note but years later Governor Johnston indicated that he was unaware of the stolen note incident.

During the visit Solomon was surprised when some of the delegates told him that the Bank had been keeping them informed of the CNRD work. But as the purpose of the Four-Nation Group was for banknote authorities to keep each other informed of anti-counterfeiting developments, Solomon probably should not have been too surprised that they knew some details of the project. Given the lack of technical expertise of most of the delegates, it was unlikely that the exchange of information would have resulted in new products in the other three countries. Solomon was surprised that at the end of the visit Parr claimed that all the exhibits and lecture slides belonged to the Bank and could not be taken to Fishermens Bend. It was an indication to Solomon that the Bank treated CSIRO as contractors rather than as collaborators.

Outcomes of the Four-Nation meeting

The reports back to CSIRO following the presentation and the meeting of the Four-Nation Committee were very positive. Knights was enthusiastic about the US interest and communicated this to Wild, commenting on:

1 the positive written submission to the Four-Nation Group on the CNRD by Parr;
2 the excellent reception the presentations had received;
3 the excellent production demonstration.

Solomon had expected the CNRD project would proceed rapidly with the transfer of technology from CSIRO to appropriately qualified staff at the Bank. Such was not to be and there was even a suggestion from Parr that the US, with its network of contractors, could produce the first notes.

Evaluation of the CNRD technology

Following the meeting with the Four-Nation Group, it was necessary to prepare a submission for discussion with the appropriate authorities in the US, the UK and Canada regarding the sale of the CNRD technology. Parr requested PA Consultants to do a world survey for a person suitable to assess the technology. Early on this search focused on the US. The CSIRO Commercial Group was unhappy with this process, first because it had been initiated by the Bank without consulting CSIRO and they were concerned that the Bank's position (free use of technology to other banks) would be put more clearly than CSIRO's, and second because they felt there were Australian consultants who would be appropriate. There was unease within CSIRO that an American was to be recruited to sell to the US. There was a terse interchange of letters between Wild and Knight about this exercise. Both Knight and Parr reassured CSIRO:

1 that the appointment was to be considered a joint one and that the Bank would not hold separate discussions with the consultant;

2 that they would consider and add to their list the Australians suggested by CSIRO, but they saw no issues with using an American to sell to the US.

Following a worldwide search, Dr Mike Smith of the PA Centre recommended Kenneth E. Payne as an appropriate person.[18] He was known to CSIRO through his participation in the worldwide Patent Attorneys Association. Payne turned out to be an excellent choice. He was easy to get along with, readily understood the technology and quickly developed an excellent working relationship with Solomon. The Bank left all the technical briefings to Solomon, who frequently talked to Payne without the presence of any Bank officials. In this, the Bank was treating CSIRO as a trusted collaborator rather than as an external contractor. Parr allowed CSIRO to talk independently about their estimate of the value of the technology. When Parr eventually heard of the value being discussed he thought that it was too low.

Payne's report to the Bank stated 'We estimate a current value of the technology in the range of $24–27 million.'[19] Payne also recommended a payment procedure. His report assessed the technology under four headings:

1 polymer substrate;
2 transfer technique for thin foils;
3 optically variable device design;
4 testing procedures and equipment.

The Payne report assessed the cost of the US attempting to develop its own technology as about $US6 million: $2 million for the substrate, $3 million for thin film transfer technology and $1 million for the diffraction grating and moiré technology. However, such an approach would take time and was uncertain of success. All these aspects were considered in detail by Payne and costs allocated.

Payne saw great value in the test procedures that had been developed (but did not allocate a dollar value), particularly for anyone trying to reverse engineer the banknotes – exactly the point that CSIRO had been trying to impress upon the Bank by urging it to restrict the distribution of the test methods. The recommendation was that the technology be offered first to the US and then to the other two members of the Four-Nation Group.

Payne's report explored the virtues of buying the CNRD technology as distinct from each nation developing its own, the removal of risk by doing so, the cost savings in time by having the technology available sooner rather than later, and the general security and economic advantages of a new technology. He discussed various possibilities for the financial returns and addressed issues such as the flow-back of technology, which had long been an issue for Solomon personally with the licensing of technology into and out of Australia. The close collaboration between the banking fraternity of the world would be best served by flow-back of technology and by a financial arrangement which recognised it as part of the total financial package. Payne requested that if there were to be a presentation to the US then both Parr and Solomon accompany him and that the Bank proceed rapidly in preparing for such a presentation.

The US to produce first plastic notes with 'our' technology?

Following the presentation to the Four-Nation Group in 1980 there was renewed interest in the CNRD project. Knight enthusiastically reported that other banks, particularly the US ones, were very interested in the technology. On the commercial side, the value and selling strategy was progressed by retaining Payne. On the technical side the project was reactivated, but with the locus of activity at the Bank. CSIRO staff were seconded to work at Fitzroy and/or Craigieburn. However, the project was grossly understaffed in numbers and experience. Even as late as 1981, the Bank staff at Bayfords (the experimental production facility) comprised only an Administrative Officer, a Technical Officer on contract and one unskilled labourer. A junior graduate in ink technology was to be transferred to the project.

Solomon found this contradictory. On the one hand, the Bank had consistently avoided any major commitment in the way of appropriate tenured staff or of building up in-house skills. Yet obviously the Bank had confidence in the project as long as someone else did the work. Reluctantly, CSIRO had to commit to this course of action as it appeared to be the only avenue to get commercialisation of the CNRD technology. Even more difficult to understand was that the Note Issue Department claimed a note could be prepared in-house in two years. Why dilute the financial return by involving the Four-Nation Group before there was a turn-key operation?

The policy of trying to get the US to commercialise the technology meant a greatly reduced financial return: a non-integrated pilot plant does not equate to a turn-key process. Furthermore, the change from a web to a sheet process meant the CNRD team had not even developed pilot equipment for some aspects of the web/sheet process. For example, the transfer foil needed for a sheet is different from that for a web and no equipment had been developed to apply the outer varnish to a sheet. Importantly, the ink system needed extensive and detailed work. The use of intaglio in the web/sheet process subjected the opacifying layer to great stress, not experienced in the all-web process.

Presentation to US authorities

Following Payne's report, the next step was to present the proposal to the other parties in the Four-Nation Group. The first presentation was to be to the US Federal Reserve and then to Bank of Canada and Bank of England. Payne was retained to prepare the presentation and he requested that both Parr and Solomon take part.

The presentation to the US authorities took place on 11 May 1981 at the Federal Reserve Bank of Dallas in Dallas.[20] There were six US representatives at this meeting.

Wallace had transferred from his position at the Board of Governors of the Federal Reserve System to be the First Vice President of the Federal Reserve Bank of Dallas; he hosted the meeting. His successor in Washington, Theodore Allison, was present, as was Robert Forrestal from the Federal Reserve Board Bank of Atlanta, Charles Bennett from the Board of Governors of the Federal Reserve System, Harry Clements from the Bureau of Engraving and Printing and Stuart Knight from the US Secret Service.[21] All but Allison had been at the November 1980 presentation in Melbourne. The general reaction was that the sums of money being suggested were such that the US would seek similar technology locally. Payne's presentation was frequently interrupted by technical questions which either Parr or Solomon answered. The Reserve Bank's commitment to purchase the EBX and other major equipment was alluded to but which EBX being purchased was not revealed.

Whether or not a clear area in a note was a security device was always a matter of debate between Parr and Solomon. It was Parr's view that the plastic note required a diffraction grating or other optically variable device to be as secure as the metal thread in the paper note. Solomon argued that the clear area in a plastic note provided more security than the metal thread. The metal thread could be easily simulated, as was demonstrated by the 1966 forgeries, whereas a clear area was very difficult to include in a paper forgery. Solomon was pleased when one of the US delegates at the meeting noted that a clear area would be 'a marginal improvement over the current U.S. notes'. The clear area is a major security device on all current Australian banknotes. Parr acknowledged this acceptance gracefully.

Rejection by the US

The US had mentioned its aversion to royalties early in the meeting. The Chairman indicated in his report of the meeting that the sums of money requested left the US with 'no alternative but to seek some Research Funding Proposals (RFPs) from American industry.' Delegates felt they needed to do this before even considering the Australian proposal further. So much for the Bankers' Clubs!

Worse was to come. The Chairman of the Steering Committee, Wallace, indicated that unless some agreement was reached on the Bank/CSIRO technology he was proposing 'contractual arrangements for research and development should be pursued covering *alternative substrates* and adhesion systems for incorporating OVDs on the surface of current substrates and in *alternative substrates*' [emphasis added]. He did not dismiss outright the Australian offer.

Parr responded[22] firmly that in effect the RFPs for alternative substrates should not draw on the 'information provided to the group in Australia'. Solomon strongly supported Parr and indicated that no other proposals had mentioned plastic film, hence the idea had been generated by the disclosures in Melbourne in November 1980.

The possibility of the CNRD team submitting an RFP and the 'likely attitude of Australia to participating in financing such RFPs' was raised. Parr and Solomon reserved their position. The suggestion was bizarre. The Bank project had a substrate and was willing to share it, at a price, with the US. Why would Australia pay to develop what it already had?

The Australian delegation was asked whether they wished to meet again the following day. They did not, but accepted an invitation to a social event in the evening where important information came to light. In summary, the points noted were that:

- recent events may have somewhat dampened earlier enthusiasm for 'going plastic' and increased support for more conventional multicolour/watermarks/threads;
- some individuals had made 'fairly hairy estimates' of the sums likely to be involved in the proposed Australian royalty arrangements;
- the front-end payments indicated by Australia had been much larger than the US had hoped for as the price of obtaining access to the technology for evaluation;
- the Bureau of Engraving and Printing had apparently argued strongly that there were good prospects of generating research and development proposals for plastic substrates from local sources, possibly more cheaply.

Overshadowing all these aspects was the point that Wallace had highlighted, i.e. that the sums involved in the Australian proposals were of a magnitude that required approaches to the local market for comparison quotes.

In the light of these points, Parr phoned Wallace and acknowledged the US had problems with the up-front payment and some dubious calculations on royalties. Parr confirmed the Australian calculation of $9 million up-front and royalties of $25 million gave a figure of about $35 million for the package. Both sides wanted to keep the possibilities open and Parr certainly pursued this on his return to Australia. He also realised the importance of patent protection and asked Payne to advise the Bank on future actions. Payne agreed with the CSIRO view that it was important to seek patent protection where appropriate.

Testing by other banks

By 1981–82 the project was clearly focused at the Note Issue Department, located at Craigieburn. Sceats and Brown had retired, but there were still no senior tenured technical staff. CSIRO was deeply concerned that there was a risk of seeing no result from their decade of research. Virtually all the project was in the hands of the Note Issue Department but CSIRO staff, including Solomon, were always available to assist. Within the Note Issue Department a committee, named the Senior Technical

Committee, was controlling the project. The Bank had agreed to supply samples of notes for testing to the other Four-Nation partners and entered into arrangements to provide samples to Canada, the UK and the US. Clearly its strategy was to have the other banks at least as partners, not to go it alone. The intention expressed to Solomon by Parr was that the US would build the first production line, using contractors.

CSIRO was certainly still committed to the project but the focus of the work had moved to the Note Issue Department. CSIRO seconded Dr Jonathon Hodgkin and Jack Ross to the Bank and Solomon visited whenever required.

Staff transfers

In general the CSIRO scientists who worked on the CNRD project were, even with the long gestation period, still highly motivated and committed to the project. They would have been prepared to transfer to the Bank if career appointments had been offered or if satisfactory contracts could be negotiated. However, for several reasons this did not eventuate. The Bank had extremely generous fringe benefits (health scheme, low-interest housing loans) and the CSIRO staff, if they were to be on equivalent total packages for contract appointments, were expecting higher salaries.

Only one CSIRO staff member transferred. Alan Wilson, an excellent experimental scientist and operator of the EBX, accepted a contract through to retirement.

The lull before the storm

The period between the excitement and controversy of the Four-Nation Group visit and the appointment of Governor Johnston was frustrating for all players.

Sceats retired in 1981 and Parr was appointed General Manager of the Note Printing Branch. Peter Morriss was his Deputy. Both had excellent understanding of the Bank's business and priorities but neither had the technical knowledge and vision to drive the CNRD project. They knew and accepted the Bank's 1968 business model and expected that CSIRO would deliver a turn-key operation.

One of the first actions of the new management was to complete the transfer of all the equipment to Craigieburn. Parr asked for a list of every piece of equipment that CSIRO had purchased with Bank funds and expected all items on the list to be sent to Craigieburn, regardless of whether they were of any use there or whether CSIRO might need them for any further research to assist the Bank. This was consistent with the view that CSIRO was transferring a completed technology, but was at odds with reality. CSIRO had completed the research and pilot plant stage but not the full production phase. A rule of thumb is that, for any new process, if the research phase costs \$1, the development phase costs \$10 and the full production phase will cost \$100. CSIRO and the Bank had spent the \$11 and the Bank was going, without fully understanding it, to the \$100 phase.

Consistent with the view that CSIRO was transferring a fully completed process the Bank asked for complete documentation on the use of all the equipment returned and on all the processes developed during the project. This was provided and it is an excellent account of the technical aspects of the project. Whether it was much use to the Bank in going to the next phase is arguable. Complete technology packages can be codified and transferred by means of written manuals and reports, but much of the knowledge important to the Bank project was tacit knowledge which is best transferred by people talking to each other and by practical demonstrations. The Bank wanted codified technology transfer when tacit transfer would have been more appropriate. This did happen to some extent with the secondment of CSIRO officers to the Bank and with Solomon's frequent visits to the Bank.

But none of this activity helped solve the real problem. The Bank had not made the decision to go to the full production phase of the project and therefore had not allocated the resources needed. That would have to wait until the appointment of Johnston as Governor.

Endnotes

1 Report in the personal collection of D.H. Solomon.
2 Report in the personal collection of D.H. Solomon, p. 1.
3 NAA: B5609, 5/17.
5 NAA: B5609, 5/15.
6 NAA: B5609, 5/18.
7 NAA: B5609, 5/15.
8 NAA: B5609, 5/15.
9 NAA: B5609, 1/1.
10 NAA: B5609, 1/2.
11 NAA: B5609, 1/3.
12 NAA: B5609, 1/3.
13 NAA: B5609, 1/3.
14 Assistant Director, Division of Bank Operations, Board of Governors of the Federal Reserve System, US.
15 NAA: B5609, 11/2.
16 In 1980 Australia was still using paper notes for $1 and $2. The change to coins occurred later.
17 NAA: B5609, 11/4.
18 NAA: B5609, 5/18.
19 NAA: B5609, 6/28.
20 NAA: B5609, 6/11.
21 The US Secret Service is a US law agency with the dual role of protecting national and visiting foreign leaders and protecting the US financial system. Solomon and Parr were met at Los Angeles airport by US Secret Service Special Agents, who accompanied them throughout their visit there.
22 NAA: B5609, 6/11.

Chapter 12
The $10 commemorative banknote

Governor Bob Johnston: a critical appointment

Robert (Bob) Alan Johnston was appointed Governor of the Bank in August 1982 and remained in that position until his retirement in 1989. The Bank Board and the Treasurer both commented on his contribution to Australia. Neither mentioned his role in the Bank project (see Fig. 12.1). However, he played a critical role in the Bank project and it was his decision, a momentous one in banking circles, to release the world's first plastic banknote.

RETIREMENT OF R.A. JOHNSTON, A.C.

R.A. Johnston, A.C., retired on 18 July 1989 as Governor of the Bank and Chairman of the Board.

The Board, at a meeting on 4 July 1989, passed the following resolution:

> "That this Board record its recognition of Mr R.A. Johnston's long and dedicated service to the Bank, over almost 49 years. His term of office as Chairman has seen a transformation of Australia's financial system. Mr Johnston provided outstanding leadership and drive both in initiating many changes and in ensuring their smooth implementation. This contribution was the greater as his term coincided with an unsettled period in economic conditions with consequent major demands on the Board's responsibilities for monetary policy.
>
> Throughout his term, Mr Johnston's commitment to the highest professional standards in the conduct of the Bank's work, and in communicating the Bank's activities to the widest audience, has enhanced the status of the Bank both within the financial sector and also in the wider community. He has earned the highest respect of his colleagues and the staff of the Bank."

In a public statement on 5 July 1989, the Treasurer, the Hon. P.J. Keating, M.P., in expressing on behalf of all Australians the Government's great gratitude to Mr Johnston, said:

> "During Mr Johnston's period as Governor, Australia has been through a transformation in banking and financial markets the like of which we have never seen before. These changes, stemming from internationalisation, innovation and deregulatory reform, have required the Reserve Bank itself to undergo major changes in operations and structure. In its relations with financial markets and with the business community generally, the Bank has earned a well deserved reputation for the conduct of its market operations, for fair and open dealing and for professional thoroughness."

Fig. 12.1: Comments on the retirement of Johnston.[1]

Unlike all his predecessors, Johnston came to the position without having previously served as Deputy Governor. His first senior management position in the Bank was in 1967 when he took over from Knight as Manager of the Investment Department. In 1969, he was appointed Chief Manager of the International Department and remained in that position until 1976, when he was seconded to the International Bank for Reconstruction and Development (part of the World Bank in Washington, DC). He returned to Australia in 1980 to be Secretary of the Bank.

Johnston had attended Dr Coombs' Thredbo meeting but had no further contact with the project until 1981, when he accompanied the Governor to the meeting of the Chief Executives with Payne in March and in June to discuss the disappointing outcomes of the US meetings.[2] His Deputy Governor, Don Saunders, had been Deputy Governor under Governor Knight, and had been closely involved with the project since 1975.

In 1982, the Bank project was not top of the priority list of the new Governor, monetary policy was. As Secretary, Bob Johnston had been in charge of the Bank's input and dealing with the Committee of Inquiry into the Australian Financial System, chaired by J.K. Campbell; this included Bob Hawke. The committee reported to government in 1981 and recommended deregulation of the financial system.[3] Johnston clearly understood the arguments in favour of floating the exchange rate. At that time Australia had a fixed exchange rate which was adjusted from time to time by the government on the advice of the Treasury and the Bank. According to P.D. Jonson, there was wide agreement among economists in the Bank, the Treasury and academia that floating the exchange would help make Australia a more successful nation.[4] From Johnston's appointment in 1982, in the last few months of the Fraser government, through the election of the Hawke government in March 1983 and to the decision to float the Australian dollar in December 1983, these matters were at the centre of his attention.

The Bank takes over

The first indication to the CSIRO group that the new Governor was taking an interest in the project was in November 1982, when the Bank took an unusually long time to approve the project budget for 1983.[5] Solomon sent his request for \$100 000 to Parr on 11 November 1982 and on 15 November had a reply stating that 'I shall be seeking the Governor's formal concurrence. I would not expect any problems'. He asked that all meetings proceed as usual. But it wasn't until 14 December that Solomon heard from Morriss that the Governor's approval had been obtained.[6]

The Governor came to Craigieburn in March 1983 to review the project and decided that some change in its management was needed.[7] In informal discussions with one of the authors, Johnston indicated that his Deputy, Saunders, had recommended that change was needed.[8] It was at a routine CSIRO/Bank technical meeting on 9 June 1983 that Morriss[9] announced details of the new Research Manager, Dr Bruce Hardwick, who was to commence 'next week'. Hardwick's first title was in fact Manager, Project Engineering and Development. His title was changed to Manager, Research and Development in the 1984/85 Annual Report of the Bank.

Not quite!

A curious incident occurred in August 1983.[10] The Bank had clearly decided to recruit suitably qualified staff for the project and consulted Solomon on the wording of an advertisement for a Research and Development Chemist. As well as requesting this assistance, Morriss asked Solomon if CSIRO would consider jointly funding the position for two years. Solomon replied that the only way CSIRO could do so was by applying to Head Office for funds from the Development Fund, but before doing so he would need a letter from the Bank indicating why CSIRO should do this. The Bank did not pursue the matter further but it was an indication that even in 1983 not all in the Bank had accepted full ownership of the project.

The appointment of Don Addison

During this period the Bank was recruiting a new General Manager of the Note Printing Branch from outside the Bank, who had experience in manufacturing and project management rather than in banking. The new recruit was Don Addison, an engineer with considerable experience in the steel fabrication industry in Australia and the US.[11] He immediately took ownership of the project.

Addison was appointed General Manager of the Note Printing Branch in October 1983, at the age of 53. He completed his matriculation St Peter's College in Adelaide, after which he did a four-year trade indenture at British Tube Mills in Adelaide. He then completed a Mechanical Engineering degree at Adelaide University and the South Australian School of Mines. He worked for British Tube Mills and Page Hersey Tubes until 1975, when he joined Doehler Australia as General Manager and Director. Doehler was a manufacture of aluminium/zinc castings.

The change in attitude and the interaction with the CSIRO staff, particularly Solomon, was dramatic. Whereas Parr expected CSIRO to fix any technical problems, Addison knew that it was his project and that he had to meet all technical challenges from within the Bank but with help where necessary from CSIRO. Solomon enjoyed a good working relationship with Addison, who had no 'baggage' from the 10-year struggle that had gone on before his appointment. Addison considered most of what was done in 1982–88 as belonging solely to the Note Printing Branch! He instilled an attitude that his team had invented the banknote. Solomon could live with that if it meant getting the plastic banknote onto the market. To Addison and Hardwick, the history of plastic banknotes started in 1982.

Governor's reviews

Addison's first CNRD review with the Governor was in December 1983.[12] It was clear from the document that he had taken complete responsibility for the project. Solomon was invited to attend this and subsequent meetings and his contributions were valued by the Governor. At the December 1983 meeting Addison set out two objectives: the first was to 'Perfect a new-generation banknote' and the second was to 'Produce an initial quantity on an as-for-issue basis (100 million pieces).

The first objective had four elements:

- a polymer-based substrate (laminated film and coatings);
- imaging with intaglio, tints and numbering;
- primary security, i.e. an optically variable device (OVD), recognisable by the 'person in the street';
- tertiary security, i.e. a machine-readable feature, for authentication in high-speed sorting.

The document claimed that this was consistent with both the Thredbo think-in (1968), where the aim was to 'produce a more secure form of banknote', and the Forward Planning Group recommendations of August 1979 (the Fink report). Addison was able to report considerable progress since the Governor's previous, lower-key review in March 1983.

There were three issues of interest to Solomon. The first was that they could produce patterns from the EBX machine and that they had defined and ordered the equipment needed to replicate and incorporate them. There was no mention of any difficulties with scrunching. The second point of interest was that a trial design had been completed and a printing plate was being engraved. This was a good sign; the Bank was taking the project seriously when it had involved a designer and an engraver. The third was that the Bank had done trials with the Xerox® (Four-Nation) machine-readable feature. This was an area of research discussed at the Mornington conference but not one into which CSIRO had put much effort. No workable system had been transferred to the Bank.

The Bank was considering a new banknote series to replace the 1966 decimal banknotes. The December 1983 review noted that 'The CNRD banknote design and the New Banknote series are to be complimentary [sic] in view of the closely related timetables.'

At the review in 1983, Addison reported 'it is considered the project is viable provided the total security package is improved'. He also reported that printing intaglio on plastic gave a better quality than paper. Thus Addison had embraced what CSIRO had been arguing for the last 10 years. There was no 'memory' in the Bank of the technical issues; Brown and Sceats had retired and that memory had gone with them.

Addison's reports to the Governor represented a quantum shift in the transfer of responsibilities. For example, when Addison reported problems he also stated, in optimistic terms, that he and his team could solve them.

The machine-readable feature

The second Governor's review under the new management at the Note Printing Branch was in July 1984.[13] It showed details of the security features of the various CNRD notes. The 1981 CNRD banknote had no machine-readable feature; the 1984 banknote, designated the CNRD '98' banknote, incorporated the Xerox® machine-readable feature, and while the 1984 trial CNRD note did not have a machine-readable feature there was no work scheduled to develop it. Remembering all his previous interventions on this topic, Solomon asked for an explanation of this omission and was informed that the Bank had encountered some problems with the Xerox® system. Solomon offered to seek new ideas from within his CSIRO division and report back to the Bank. The next day he introduced two excellent chemists from the Division of Applied Organic Chemistry, Dr W.H.F. Sasse and Dr A.W.-H. Mau, to the team at Craigieburn and the pair soon came up with an idea that all agreed should work. Hardwick and CSIRO agreed on a research project on the machine-readable feature.[14] Since then, Sasse, Mau and their successors have had a continual involvement with the Bank. By the August 1985 Governor's review the Bank was able to report that 'a machine readable feature (MRF), under development by the CSIRO, is showing promise.'[15]

Note that machine-readable features were considered by CSIRO early in the project. At the Mornington meeting it was noted that 'several possible counting methods for bundles of old banknotes were discussed without arriving at a satisfactory solution. These included radioactive counters, conductivity and weighing methods. The problem is to be pursued further and the Bank invited to redefine the problem.'

In the eight projects outlined at Mornington, 'Section 1 Design of Grating, moiré and other OVDs' included the duty 'To devise counting techniques for new and used banknotes.'[16] This was a late addition to the official proceedings since it is hand-written.

In its January 1975 response to the Mornington meeting, the Bank produced a document entitled *Desirable Features in Notes*,[17] which included as an essential feature a 'secret device for laboratory test of genuineness' and as a highly desirable feature a 'device to enable automated count in bundle or greater lots'. As a result of these two documents the CNRD Committee requested on 24 April 1975 that CSIRO produce a forward plan for the project, which it did by 6 May.[18] The plan did not mention either counting or authentication devices, CSIRO did not report any work in that area in the following years and the Bank did not seem anxious to pursue it.

The earliest plastic banknotes (e.g. Design Freeze 1976) included a CSIRO machine-readable feature, a chemical compound with known spectral characteristics.

CSIRO aimed to use the specific adsorption and the concentration to denominate and to authenticate banknotes by a machine. The CNRD note, unlike paper banknotes, allowed the protection of the compound either within the laminate or by the outer varnish.

By 1985 the work was showing sufficient promise for the Bank to request a detailed quotation for a one-year project to develop the ideas. Solomon wrote to Hardwick on 14 October 1985 saying that the cost of the minimum effort in the division to achieve the agreed goal would be $285 000. He noted that this new technology would become part of the overall CNRD technology package and therefore CSIRO would fund half the cost, and that because the payment was in excess of $100 000 he would need to obtain the approval of his Director and the Minister for Science. He was confident that the Director would approve but less confident that the Minister would agree. However, the Minister did approve and the project proceeded.

It soon became clear to both CSIRO and the Bank that while CSIRO had the capability to do the chemical research necessary for the success of the project, neither organisation had the skills to design and construct the machine needed to process the banknotes that contained the invention. The Bank contracted Vigilante Systems Pty Ltd to do the work and this proved to be a very successful three-way collaboration.

Optically variable devices

Both the December 1983 and July 1984 reviews were confident about progress with the OVD. In 1983 it was reported that they could produce any pattern on the EBX with confidence and in July 1984 that they were working on all the design elements. At that time they 'were still to produce a satisfactory design integrated with banknote design'. Neither review mentioned anything about the problem of scrunching that was well known to CSIRO although the diffraction grating passed the tests specified by the Bank. A change came in the July 1985 review, which noted that the Bank and CSIRO were working on developing a more scrunch-proof diffraction grating. This came about because of an unrelated contact between Bob Lee and Alan Wilson.

Lee had been recruited to the project in 1975 to assist on the problem of predicting the diffraction pattern that would be observed from a generalised grating from the form of the line pattern. His work was reported to the Bank in a series of internal papers from 1976 to 1979 and published in 1983 in a series of five papers in *Optica Acta*, 'Generalized curvilinear diffraction gratings'.[19] The fifth paper in the series had the subtitle 'Diffraction catastrophes' and showed how to construct the grating functions appropriate for gratings with the potential for very bright predictable diffraction patterns, from geometrically small diffraction gratings. His work enabled a systematic design procedure to be devised to take into account the effects of scrunching and light source variation.

Lee left the project in 1980, when it was in the doldrums, and was transferred to the CSIRO Division of Chemical Physics where he worked on the channelling of subatomic particles in crystals and the propagation of light in optical fibres. In searching for ways to test his new theory connecting the particle properties of a microscopic system to its interfering wave properties, he realised that the situation occurred at the macroscopic level in optical systems that generate special types of diffraction patterns called diffraction catastrophes. As a result he returned to work on applying the generalised grating theory to the design of catastrophe gratings. This was why in 1984 he contacted Wilson,[20] the former CSIRO scientist now working for the Bank at Craigieburn, to see if he would be willing to fabricate any catastrophe grating designs on the Bank's EBX machine. Wilson was willing to do so if the instrument was not being otherwise used for Bank work. Lee designed two catastrophe gratings and sent the specifications to Craigieburn. Wilson did the work in 1985 and invited Lee to visit Craigieburn on 23 April 1985. During that visit Lee was made aware that the Bank was having difficulties in designing a grating that passed its new scrunching test. He offered to help and suggested that a design based on the diffraction catastrophes might work because of their structural stability.

It was at this point that the internal structure of CSIRO, with its Chiefs of Divisions sometimes acting independently, went against a sensible commercial outcome. Importantly, the agreements between the Bank and CSIRO were actually all initiated by CSIRO so the move to bring in another independent Chief was confusing, at least to the Bank. Lee, aware that collaborative arrangements with entities external to the organisation were the responsibility of the Chief, suggested that a meeting between his Chief, Dr Lewis T. Chadderton, and the General Manager of the Note Printing Branch be arranged as soon as possible. This meeting took place on 16 May and was attended by Addison, Chadderton, Dr John Willis (Assistant Chief of the Division of Chemical Physics), Alan Perryman (Divisional Secretary), Barry Mahoney (the Bank scientist working on the diffraction gratings) and Lee. The result was a verbal agreement that if the test grating Lee designed proved resistant to scrunching, a more formal agreement between the two organisations would be drawn up to enable the design and fabrication of a diffraction grating suitable for inclusion in a banknote. Lee completed the design studies by the second week of June 1985 but it took several months to complete the fabrication of the complicated structure. The observed diffraction pattern agreed perfectly with that predicted by the theory. The Division of Chemical Physics worked with Sirotech to apply for a patent covering this class of gratings, which were called catastrophe pixel (Catpix) gratings. Lee continued to work on the theory. He invented a new class of diffraction grating known as Catpix II, which was a special class of generalised curvilinear diffraction gratings based on the idea of representing a given portrait in terms of an array of interconnected Catpix gratings. It was as if the artist could use a palette of diffraction gratings to 'paint' the portrait.

The testing of the first Catpix gratings, which are referred to as Catpix I, took place from April 1985 to January 1986. During this period Solomon and various CSIRO executives were involved in discussions with the Bank on how to progress any future arrangements with the Bank.[21] Solomon and Jack Coombe (Deputy Executive Secretary of CSIRO) were both invited guests at the Governor's reviews of the project. At the 1983 review the Note Printing Department management told the Governor 'It is considered that the project is viable provided the total security package is improved', which they were confident of doing. By July 1984 the Governor was told, 'Work on the design of our OVD, the diffraction grating, has concentrated on the development of design elements suitable for integration into an overall design. While integrated designs have been produced, it still remains to produce a satisfactory OVD design integrated with the banknote design as a whole.' The impression given to the Governor was that there was a design problem not a technical one. The August 1985 review did mention some problems with the OVD. It reported that 'it has been determined that the breakdown of the OVD during crumpling is mainly a function of the brittleness of the coating'. It was also reported that 'a CSIRO scientist and the NPD physicists are working on the development of a "catastrophy" [sic] diffraction grating OVD which is theoretically more capable of resisting crumpling than our current faceted grating'. In this presentation to the Governor the Note Printing Department mentioned only 'CSIRO', not any specific Division.

In the course of testing the catastrophe grating, Lee observed that the groove depths of the diffraction gratings were considerably less than what had been specified by CSIRO to obtain the maximum optical brightness.

Lee prepared a report about the issues in January 1986 'because recent telephone calls from the Note Issue Branch [sic] of the Reserve Bank to the Acting Chief of the Division and myself requesting me to keep in contact with the project suggests that the bank has found some value in my advice over the past eight months.'[22] The report was critical of the Bank's approach to OVD development. It said, 'The consequences of the Reserve Bank not supporting the development of the project with an adequate number of scientific staff, especially in the area of diffraction grating design, should now be apparent to the Bank'.

Lee made a list of people who he thought should read his report. The suggested recipients were the Chairman of CSIRO, Governor of the Bank, Director of the Institute of Physical Sciences, General Manager Note Issue Branch [sic], Chief of the Division of Chemical Physics, Chief of the Division of Applied Organic Chemistry, and Managing Director of Sirotech. It is not clear who received a copy of Lee's report but it was widely circulated within both CSIRO and the Bank.

Before discussing the CSIRO and Bank reaction to the technical issues raised by Lee in his report, it is important to understand the internal process that led to its circulation. Solomon had been the principal CSIRO contact person for the Bank since the first meeting of the Technical Committee in 1972 yet he was not consulted by the Division of Chemical Physics about the content of the report, whether it should be sent to the Bank in its present form and, if it was sent, who it should be sent to. He had not been informed that staff from the Division of Chemical Physics had been to the Bank or that the Bank was having problems with the diffraction grating. Indeed, the review meetings that he attended as the senior CSIRO technical person gave the impression that all was going well with the OVD work. Even though the Bank project was highly confidential, Chadderton would certainly have known that Solomon was the principal CSIRO person involved. So Solomon was surprised and angered that such a sensitive report went to the Bank from within CSIRO without him knowing anything about it.

Solomon quickly sent a briefing paper to his manager at that time, Dr W.I. Whitton (who was not on Lee's suggested circulation list).[23] William I. (Bill) Whitton was Director of the CSIRO Institute of Industrial Technology from 1983 to 1988.[24] He was born in 1924 and graduated in Chemistry from the University of Melbourne (BSc Hons 1944, MSc 1948) and the University of St Andrews (PhD 1951). He enlisted in the Australian Army in February 1945 and served as a lieutenant in the Royal Australian Engineers until November 1945. He joined ICI in England in 1951 and returned to Australia in 1953 to the ICIANZ Research Laboratories. From 1960 to 1963 he was Technical Manager and Director of ICI (NZ) Ltd, returning to Australia in 1963 as Research Manager of ICIANZ Ltd. He was an Executive Director of ICI Australia from 1970 to 1983, when he joined CSIRO as Director of the Institute of Industrial Technology. Whitton was a Foundation Fellow of the Australian Academy of Technological Sciences.

In his briefing to Whitton, Solomon made two important introductory comments:

1 he conceded that Dr Lee's report will have served a useful purpose if it results in the successful resolution of the problems facing the project;
2 he noted that while the Note Printing Branch had been in effective control of the project since 1979/80, the failure of the project would be a severe blow to the reputation of CSIRO in general and the Division of Applied Organic Chemistry in particular.

He then went into more detail about the diffraction grating problems, all of which he maintained could be solved using scientific principles.

On grating design he noted, 'To be an effective security device in a banknote, a diffraction grating must be able to withstand "scrunching", be not easily simulated by holographic or other techniques, be difficult to contact print and be recognisable to the ordinary person. A great deal of the conflict which has arisen between CSIRO and the Bank over the years has been connected with the meeting of these objectives.' He noted that the Bank had argued that the recognisability criterion should be considered first and that artists be closely involved in the design of the grating, whereas CSIRO had always maintained that while recognisability was important, it could be taught whereas the other features were intrinsic to the grating. Solomon was confident that the application of Lee's theories would overcome the scrunching problem.

His briefing note pointed out that 'Effective cooperation between the two organisations has been hampered by the failure to negotiate an agreement since the previous one expired in 1984. CSIRO should as a first priority seek to enter into an Agreement with the Bank before commencing work on the grating design.' CSIRO did not take Solomon's advice.

The Bank requested a meeting with CSIRO to discuss ways of resolving the issues raised by Lee. It was held on 4 April 1986 at Whitton's office in Melbourne.[25] The Bank circulated a list of nine questions it wanted to discuss; all were technical questions relating to the fabrication and copying of diffraction gratings.

Representing the Bank at the meeting were: D. Addison (part of the time), B. Hardwick, B. Mahoney and A. Maker (all from the Note Printing Branch), M. Diamond (from Head Office) and A. Page (a consultant). Representing CSIRO were: W.I. Whitton (part of the time), D.H. Solomon, W.H.F. Sasse, A.W.-H. Mau and T.H. Spurling (all from the Division of Applied Organic Chemistry), L. Chadderton, R.A. Lee and I. Wilson (all from the Division of Chemical Physics).

The meeting was chaired by Hardwick and the file note indicates that the Bank's questions were answered. The fact that the $10 banknote was issued on schedule with a recognisable grating shows that to be the case.

The CSIRO participants at this meeting detected a great sense of urgency among the Bank participants. This was because of an unusual intervention by the Governor. Early in 1986, Johnston had decided that it was time to decide whether the aim of the project was to produce 'an initial quantity on an as-for-issue basis', as stated in the August 1985 review document, or whether the aim was to produce banknotes to issue. His view was that if he kept the former objective the scientists at the Note Printing Branch would never complete the project. In a unique approach to forming an opinion on whether to proceed, Johnston called a meeting of the Note Printing Branch team and asked each member individually whether there was any reason why the Bank should not go ahead with the new banknote. One by one they agreed, and he made the decision to issue the bicentennial banknote.[26] The stated objectives of the CNRD project were changed in June 1986 to:

- Produce an initial quantity on an as-for-issue basis (105 million pieces – $10 Commemorative design)

- Produce the entire new note series on the polymer substrate (incorporating an OVD).

Johnston took the actions necessary to issue a commemorative banknote. In Australia, such a decision is the Governor's alone and he simply informs the government of the decision. Johnston was not convinced that the CSIRO staff involved with the project understood the enormity of his decision. If it went wrong it could severely undermine the financial system.

A curious event in August 1986 illustrated the weakness in the way CSIRO then approached its major commercial collaborators.[27] On 10 July 1986 Chadderton sent the following telex to Addison:

> Dr R A Lee is planning to attend a centenary conference of Schrödinger and wave particle duality in early 1987. He will also be taking advantage of the opportunity to visit experts in Zürich, the UK and the USA for extensive discussions with corresponding experts on problems associated with devices similar to Catpix – to be held of course in the utmost discretion, having full regard for the confidentiality of our joint effort.
>
> Financial support for Bob Lee for this overseas trip might be one way in which you could tangibly recompense the Division of Chemical Physics for his efforts.
>
> Just a suggestion.

Addison waited a month then wrote a terse response to Whitton: 'This visit should not occur – I would like to discuss, at your convenience.'

Whitton phoned Addison and Chadderton and by the afternoon Chadderton sent a fax to Whitton 'that Bob Lee's forthcoming travel overseas is primarily to present a paper on Mathematical Physics at the Schrödinger Centenary Conference in Bristol. He will not be planning to visit banks where there might be a conflict of interest with the discoveries he has made and which are incorporated in our Catpix elements.'

Agreements

The first agreement with the Bank concerning the polymer note project was an exchange of letters in 1968 in which CSIRO's main concern was to ensure that it had the right to publish its research results. Despite many attempts by CSIRO to enter into a commercially oriented agreement, that letter remained the basis of the relationship until 1980.

The 1980 agreement was signed on behalf of the Bank by Johnston, then Secretary of the Bank.[28] It acknowledged that the Bank and CSIRO had been collaborating 'for a period of years' in a currency note research and development project which had reached an advanced stage and commercial exploitation was under consideration. It defined the 'CNRD' technology to include 'the body of information generated by CSIRO and the RBA either jointly or separately in the course of, or in relation to, the joint research program established in 1968.' That included 'the concept of the all plastic banknote, the choice of materials, fabrication techniques, optically variable devices (OVD's) [sic], methods of OVD incorporation, and evaluation methods and techniques.'

It specified that neither side would disclose the technology except by agreement, that the Bank would have free use of the technology for the production of Australian currency notes, that the Bank would be free to negotiate with overseas issue authorities on terms where CSIRO would receive a just share and that any overseas deals would be on a fully commercial basis. The agreement gave the Bank the right to negotiate with note issue authorities and CSIRO the right to negotiate with other potential users. The agreement was between the Bank and CSIRO, not a specified division of CSIRO.

The Bank also agreed that if it had 'not adopted and used a substantial part of the CNRD technology in Australia within four years from the date hereof or such later date as may be agreed' then CSIRO would have the sole right to the technology.

As noted earlier, Solomon had been invited to the Governor's reviews of the CNRD project in December 1983 and July 1984 and had reported progress to Whitton and Wild. Coombe from the CSIRO Head Office was also present at those reviews and had presumably reported back to his boss, L.G. (Gratton) Wilson, the CSIRO Executive Secretary. It was around this time that CSIRO had decided to establish the commercialisation company, Sirotech, and had appointed its first Managing Director, Julian Doyle, who established the company in Melbourne. CSIRO still retained the Commercial Group in Canberra; Paul Grant was Officer-in-Charge of that group. One of the first matters referred to Doyle by Wilson was the status of the agreement with the Bank. Doyle discussed the matter with Coombe and noted in a letter to Wilson: 'The agreement was for a period of four years and I will be asking Paul to let me have his comments on whether it has to be renewed and on what sort of basis. It certainly seems on the face of it to have several important commercial implications and we would need to discuss these fully with Dave Solomon of AOC.'[29]

There were discussions with Solomon and the two of them met with Addison on 21 August 1984. Doyle 'felt that it was a very useful and almost optimistic meeting and there certainly seems to be an attitude of mind on his part which would be conducive to our getting a more vigorous commercial approach than the Bank has previously appeared to favour.'[30]

Internal discussions continued and by early September a letter was sent from the Chairman to the Governor.[31] In that letter the Chairman stated that 'we are likely to see the fruits of CSIRO/RBA labour not later than some time in 1988.' In light of this, the Chairman said that 'CSIRO will be happy to adopt a generous view in respect of the words "adopted and used a substantial part of the CNRD technology in Australia"'. The letter informed the Governor that CSIRO had established Sirotech to assist with the commercialisation of its intellectual property and that he wanted to involve Sirotech in any further discussions. He wrote that CSIRO had no intention of foreclosing at the conclusion of the 1980 agreement, asked the Governor to inform him with whom Doyle should begin discussions and noted that Solomon and Coombe would be part of the CSIRO negotiation group. The letter was sent on 14 September 1984.

The Governor replied on 5 October.[32] He said that he was pleased that CSIRO had no intention of foreclosing at the end of the four-year period but, while optimistic, he couldn't guarantee an issue date. He was not at all enthusiastic about proceeding with commercialisation or about the involvement of Sirotech:

> You will recall that the Bank has always held strongly to the view that the first priority is that the technology must be applied and proven in the Australian currency note issue. Accordingly, although we may be satisfied that some formidable barriers have been identified and passed in the refinement of the CNRD technology, I think it would be decidedly premature at the moment to proceed in any material way towards releasing any of the technology to others – either to overseas issue authorities or to the commercial (non-currency note) sector.
>
> While, therefore, I do not see immediate scope to advance plans for commercialisation, if you would wish people associated with Sirotech to have fuller understanding of the project and where we have got to, we would be very happy to receive them.

The Governor's insistence that it would be decidedly premature to release the technology to anyone is odd as the Bank, without informing CSIRO, had already told the Four-Nation Anti-Counterfeiting Group considerable detail of the work in September 1983.[33] This was contrary to the 1980 agreement which clearly stated that 'CNRD technology will not be disclosed to or made available to others except by agreement between the parties.'

CSIRO was expecting a more positive response from the Governor. In a letter to Solomon, Doyle, Coombe, Whitton and Taylor, Wilson reported that since the Governor's letter 'required translation or interpretation' he had dispatched Coombe to find out what should happen next.[34]

Coombe spoke with Morriss (in the absence of Addison who was overseas) and reported to CSIRO that the Bank appreciated that:

1 CSIRO was not seeking immediate commercialisation;
2 there was a need to discuss and update the agreement;
3 the Governor had no worries in general about interaction.

Coombe recommended that someone (probably Doyle) should arrange a meeting at the Note Printing Branch and that Solomon and he should be invited. He said it would be prudent to describe the purpose of the meeting as primarily to fix up the agreement.

Wilson agreed with Coombe's recommendation and said to Solomon that 'It seems to me that we should regard the matter from that point on as being handled by Sirotech on CSIRO's behalf. I take it from our earlier conversations that you agree?' This letter was dated 8 November 1984.[35]

In December 1984 Solomon and Coombe but not Doyle were invited to the Governor's review of the project. In his report of the meeting to the Chairman Solomon commented that the project was proceeding very smoothly and that it was a pity that Addison had not been at the Bank some years ago. He made no mention of commercialisation or agreements.

The Bank moved slowly on the agreement. The proposed meeting between Sirotech, CSIRO and the Bank did not take place. However, in May 1985 there was a meeting between Sirotech, Solomon and Chadderton, where the parties agreed that Sirotech would negotiate with the Bank on behalf of CSIRO as a whole with the aim of maximising the proportion of overseas earnings returned to CSIRO.

Solomon reflected on the outcomes of that meeting in a letter to Doyle on 30 May 1985.[36] He suggested that it was important that CSIRO/Sirotech settle on the philosophy they would follow:

> For reasons associated with the long history of this project the CSIRO position is now weak. Because the major revenue will come from Banknote applications I have been seeking to use our current work on machine readable identification features (MRFs) to strengthen CSIRO's position in the revenue sharing. Naturally I think that we would be better off if Chemical Physics-improved OVD and any other CSIRO work were similarly used, i.e. we ask only for reimbursement of direct costs for these new projects.

He warned against the tactic of asking the Bank to pay the whole cost of Lee's five years of research, predicting that the Bank would reject the approach and not use either the new OVD or machine-readable feature.

One side issue concerning the nature of the relationship between CSIRO and Sirotech is documented in a note filed by Solomon in early June 1985. Solomon had phoned regarding his concern that Sirotech would be charging the Division of Applied

Organic Chemistry for work on the CNRD project. Doyle reassured him that there would be no charge to the division, that he would be arranging the split in royalty income between CSIRO and the Bank, and that the Bank paid the Sirotech fee in exchange for a higher percentage of the income.[37] There is no record of Sirotech receiving any income from the eventual settlement.

Sirotech continued discussions with the Bank without involving the Division of Applied Organic Chemistry or taking any notice of Solomon's advice. The issue came to the surface in July 1985 when Hardwick invited Solomon to the July Governor's review. In the course of conversation he referred to two documents that he had received from Sirotech, namely, a market proposal and the draft agreement, expecting Solomon to know what he was talking about. Solomon was highly embarrassed because he had seen neither. He was also angry because his prediction that arguing for greater equity for the machine-readable feature and grating projects would only lead to the Bank expecting CSIRO to pay for the projects was evident in the phone call with Hardwick. Solomon solved this problem for the Division of Applied Organic Chemistry by insisting that the project was within the complete CSIRO package and not part of any new arrangements with Sirotech.

Both Solomon and Coombe went to the 2 August Governor's review and were encouraged by the progress. In his report to the Chairman, Coombe reported that the Governor 'requested that the timescale be shortened' but also indicated his embarrassment. He told the Chairman that Addison had said that Sirotech had a proposal before the Governor which he had not seen.

The Bank must have been bemused by all this. Since 1968 it had presented a uniform face to CSIRO. It clearly had internal arguments but these were always resolved before meetings with CSIRO. It was used to CSIRO scientists having different points of view at meetings, but to have senior executives acting in complete isolation from each other took the problem to a new level.

In early September the Bank told Doyle that a Deputy Governor was having difficulty with the Sirotech proposal. Doyle rang Solomon and proposed a high-level meeting with the Governor to resolve the issues. All these discussions were delayed by the reaction to Lee's report, discussed above.

In August 1986, nearly two years after Wilson's letter suggesting the involvement of Sirotech, Dr Geoff Taylor, a member of the CSIRO Executive, decided to intervene.[38] He suggested that the most productive form of meeting would involve him, Whitton, Fletcher and a note-taker on the CSIRO side and a corresponding group from the Bank. His main departure from the usual CSIRO practice was his insistence that the CSIRO/Bank meeting be preceded by an in-house CSIRO meeting to which all the above would come, and possibly Doyle. He set out the purpose of the CSIRO/Bank meeting:

1. To negotiate a new agreement between CSIRO and the Bank to replace the one which has now lapsed.
2. To arrange for future liaison between CSIRO and the Bank at both formal and informal levels.
3. To agree on attitudes to commercialisation of the various technologies of relevance to the project.
4. To arrange for CSIRO–Bank working parties to progress matters of detail, eg commercialization.

Both meetings took place but there are no notes of the internal CSIRO meeting. The CSIRO/Bank meeting took place on 7 October 1986. The Bank had only one representative, Jim Mallyon, and CSIRO had three, Taylor, Fletcher and Solomon.[39] Whitton was on extended sick leave and Solomon was there as Acting Institute Director. Mallyon was Head, Central Bank Services Group.

The participants had a general discussion about all the issues raised by Taylor and made a crucial decision – that Solomon would be the main CSIRO contact and that Mallyon would be the Bank contact. Solomon was to prepare the file note for the meeting and a draft new agreement. In addition CSIRO would submit a formal proposal covering the Catpix grating work. Solomon acted quickly and by 26 November 1986 submitted the draft proposal to Mallyon.

Solomon's draft agreement was an updated version of the 1980 agreement. It would prove to be nothing like the final agreement, but by acting swiftly Solomon had set in motion the basis of that final agreement.

CSIRO sells the technology

In the first months of 1987 the Bank and CSIRO were taken up with technical issues concerning the OVD and the machine-readable feature along with issues concerning the leaking of information about the design of the $10 banknote. The Bank made no formal response to Solomon's draft agreement but there were many informal discussions between the two organisations. It became clear to Solomon in 1987 that the Bank would never agree to share the commercialisation of any technology that was critical to the security of its currency notes. The 1980 agreement already gave the Bank considerable control over the technology. Under that agreement CSIRO had given the Bank free use of the technology in Australia and the right to veto any overseas sale if the Bank thought that it could adversely affect the security of the Australian currency. From informal discussions with Mallyon, Solomon knew that the Bank would be open to the suggestion that it buy out CSIRO's interest in the technology. His first task was to determine a reasonable asking price then sell the notion within CSIRO. He assembled a small team at Fishermens Bend to work on the proposal. The team comprised Max Jordan, the Division of Applied Organic Chemistry's Business Manager (who had extensive experience in the plastics industry), Bryan Loft, an intellectual property specialist, and Tom Spurling. They worked out that in 1987 dollars the project had cost CSIRO $7 million more than the Bank had contributed to the project. The calculation was based on a multiplier of 2.5 on the actual cost to CSIRO.

On 6 August 1987 Solomon wrote to the CSIRO Chairman, Dr Keith Boardman, outlining his arguments.[40] He said that he had had informal discussions with the Bank about it purchasing CSIRO's share of the technology and he would like Boardman to formally authorise him to negotiate a price. He gave the basis of the estimated $7 million cost to CSIRO and presented his argument for the sale:

> The CNRD project had as its principal aim the development of advanced technology to protect the security of the Australian currency. The agreement between the RBA and CSIRO provided for no financial return to CSIRO for the use of the technology by the Bank in Australia, but states that the return from the sale of the technology to overseas users and for non-currency users in Australia will be shared equitably between the two parties. If the basis for this equitable sharing is the relative investment of the two groups in the technology, then CSIRO should receive between 5% and 10%. We have previously estimated the technology to be worth around $50 000 000 in the American market, making our share around $5 000 000. It should be noted that both establishing an Australian industry and selling the technology abroad were secondary aims of the project. During the first decade of the project, the Bank's attitude was such that there would have been little possibility of any commercialisation of the technology. We in CSIRO recognised this and therefore had little expectation of gaining revenue for CSIRO. Recently, however, the attitude of the Bank has changed and they now look to commercialize their technology where this is consistent with their primary aim of producing a secure currency. The Bank have now some incentive to try to obtain some return from their investment and possibly believe that this would be easier for them to do, especially to overseas central banks, if they did not need to consult us.

Solomon suggested that he open negotiations with the Bank at $8 million.

Boardman agreed, and authorised Solomon to commence formal negotiations. Events moved quickly from that point. Boardman and Solomon were both invited to a function at the Bank's Sydney office on 21 August where the Governor announced that he had decided to go ahead with production of the polymer-based banknote. In a letter to Boardman he described this as an 'almost historic decision'. In the same letter, dated 14 September, he reported that the Deputy Governor, John Phillips, had told him of the brief discussions between himself and Boardman about the buyout and confirmed that the Bank was interested in pursuing the transaction. He attached a list of CNRD technologies 'to which sole rights might be vested in the Bank'. The Bank was 'happy to agree on a price based on the direct costs to CSIRO (adjusted to present day values) plus something recognising your broader but unquantifiable contribution to the project'. CSIRO's starting price was $8 million but in a reversal of the usual course of a negotiation, the final price was $9 million ($19.5 million in 2012 dollars). Solomon argued that CSIRO should receive a $1 million bonus for success!

In the negotiations the Bank made the following offer:

A. To buy out the CSIRO interest in the CNRD technology for $9 million, or
B. To buy out CSIRO's interest in that part of the technology in current use for a lesser amount and allow CSIRO free use of the remainder.
C. To consider a proposal for the development of the Catpix II gratings on the basis of a fully funded research contract. The RBA will undertake to exploit this technology for non-currency use and CSIRO will earn a royalty for such uses. If the RBA does not wish to proceed with the development of Catpix II, then CSIRO will be free to do so.

In his briefing to the CSIRO Board, Solomon recommended accepting options A and C. He explained that option B was not attractive to CSIRO since:

i. We now have no active research program in this area.
ii. The main patents expire in 1990 and 1992.
iii. We can see no use for the residual technology other than for banknotes.

Part C is attractive to CSIRO because, while there are clearly non-currency note applications of the Catpix II technology, the RBA is the only organisation in Australia with the equipment needed to develop the idea.

The CSIRO Board accepted the advice; $9 million was paid to CSIRO on 31 December 1987.

The Bank was given a proposal to develop Catpix II but decided not to proceed. While it was true that in 1987 the Bank was the only organisation in Australia with the equipment needed to develop Catpix II, it was also clear that CSIRO could purchase such equipment and develop Catpix II itself.

The approach of CSIRO and the Bank to Catpix II is quite instructive.[41] All organisations, but especially publicly funded research organisations, that do research and development have to decide when to stop spending money on a particular project in order to spend it on a project with higher priority. Solomon, in rejecting the Bank's option B, had clearly decided that CSIRO had spent enough on this project and that if CSIRO was to continue its research in polymer science it should be in more prospective areas. The Bank, in rejecting the offer to develop Catpix II, decided that the technology it had bought was sufficient for its purposes and it did not need to develop Catpix II. In hindsight, this was a good decision since none of the Australian banknotes now in circulation include a diffraction grating of any sort. The clear area proved to be a very satisfactory security device. CSIRO chose to invest in the equipment needed to develop Catpix II. Whether that money would have better invested in other projects is beyond the scope of this book.

Using a diffraction grating as a security device was an enduring aim of the project. It was mentioned at the Thredbo meeting, thought about by Solomon and Hamann before 1972, suggested independently by Bowen and included in the 1972 Brown banknote. The team had four problems to solve:

- fabricating the grating;
- incorporating it into the banknote;
- designing a diffraction grating that would be recognised by the public;
- ensuring that the grating would not deteriorate faster than other features of the banknote.

Solomon and his team had the first two problems well and truly solved before the important 1974 meeting with the Governor. The last two problems were more difficult to solve. The difficulty was to some extent masked by the Bank's reluctance to purchase the EBX machine. In 1974, the team knew that they could use an EBX machine to fabricate any diffraction pattern that could be represented mathematically but, because they did not have access to an EBX machine, they could only include inferior gratings in the prototype banknotes. They had identified very early in the project that pixelating the grating provided a way to 'paint' portrait as well as minimising scrunching.

The plastic banknote is released!

The Bank released the polymer $10 banknote on 26 January 1988. In its Annual Report for 1988/89 the Bank reported that 17 million $10 commemorative banknotes had been put into general circulation by 30 June 1989, along with 380 million other banknotes. It also reported that some 850 000 of the banknotes were issued in souvenir form. These cost the collector $14, grossing the Bank $11.9 million. The Bank easily recovered its $9 million! The Bank conducted a study around Newcastle, NSW, where a higher proportion of commemorative $10 banknotes were issued. The study found that the new banknotes were more robust than paper banknotes and were generally well received by the public.

Secrecy and the press

Both CSIRO and the Bank had kept the existence of the Bank project and therefore any technical details remarkably secret since the first meeting in 1968. The project was first made public in 1980 in the context of negotiations between the Bank and the Commonwealth Bank Officers Association over the move of the Note Printing Branch from Fitzroy to Craigieburn. There was a hint of the project in an article by Julianne Schultz in the 10 June 1980 edition of the *Journalists' Clarion*, the strike newspaper of the Australian Journalists' Association, Victorian Branch. The article noted:

> In addition, the CBOA is demanding that the Reserve Bank establish a joint union–management committee to discuss the terms of introducing the new technology in the banking and printing industries.[42]

Another hint was in *The Sun* on Friday 13 June 1980, which reported that:

> The Reserve Bank of Australia is trying something most of us find almost impossible – to make money last longer. The bank is considering coating bank notes with plastic, making the notes from stronger materials and the use of different inks and papers.[43]

The Sun had contacted Sceats who commented that 'the search for a better banknote was still in its early stages'.

More details were revealed in an article in the *Sunday Press* on 15 June 1980.[44] '"Funny money" gets a frown' reported that men who work at the note printing branch 'claim to have learnt of a secret project to replace paper notes with long lasting plastic legal tender'. The work 'is being done by the CSIRO. And it could pose a risk to their jobs'.

The next disclosure was on 14 September 1983, when *The Age* science reporter, Peter Roberts, published a detailed account of the project based on the published patents.[45] He reported details revealed in the international patent application lodged in March 1983 by CSIRO and the Bank, which described the use of polymers for substrates and the incorporation of various OVDs. Roberts reported that:

> While some CSIRO researchers say privately that it is inevitable that Australia will use the new technologies, Mr Parr yesterday played down suggestions that plastic notes were only a few years away. 'We are working on it, yes, but we don't have in prospect the issuing of plastic banknotes,' Mr Parr said.

The Bank itself told the *Canberra Times* on 25 August 1984 that:

> In conjunction with the CSIRO it had been working to develop a more secure and durable polymer-based form of note. Equipment had been installed during the year to produce experimental batches but it was likely to be some time before the feasibility of this development could be assessed.[46]

Jim Kouts, in *The Australian* of 23 December 1985, wrote that CSIRO scientists 'who have been working on perfecting the counter-proof notes for more than 15 years say they could be introduced in the next few years, probably before 1990.'[47]

The first time the project was mentioned in the Bank's Annual Report was in its 1985/86 report, tabled in federal parliament in August 1986: 'The Note Printing Branch itself is working on the development of a polymer-based form of note which it is hoped will improve the security and durability of the currency.'[48]

Bob Beale, in the *Sydney Morning Herald* of 14 March 1987, wrote an article about the introduction of new technologies into the banking industry: 'The Reserve Bank has sworn the CSIRO to secrecy, and will say very little about its for new banknotes beyond confirming that it is working on "polymer based materials"'.[49]

So there was consternation in both the Bank and CSIRO when on Saturday 25 April 1987 the *Canberra Times* featured an article, '"Super" money on issue soon', containing details not previously released and of value to forgers.[50] The article revealed that the Bank was to issue a bicentennial $10 banknote using a polymer-based substrate and incorporating 'an image or a number of images within thin, laminated layers of plastic which will be infinitely more spectacular and colourful than the holograms presently used on Visa and Mastercard'. It also revealed that the banknote would include a picture of Captain Cook's head incorporating one of the spectacular images. The article claimed that 'Discovery of the "unforgeable image" was made during research into theoretical physics in the division of chemical physics, and several scientific sources have described it as a major breakthrough for Australia', the author's source completely misrepresenting the long history of interaction between the Bank and CSIRO.

The *Canberra Times* journalist, Keith Scott, had spoken with Solomon and Dr Neville Fletcher, Director of the CSIRO Institute of Physical Sciences, neither of whom revealed any information that was not already on the public record. Solomon had immediately telephoned Johnston alerting him to the journalist's inquiries. After the article appeared Johnston wrote to Solomon thanking him for the phone call and saying:[51]

> I am sure you will not be surprised that I am incensed about the release of supposed details of our proposal to issue a special currency note for the

> Bicentenary. I am not so much concerned about the CNRD technicalities but about the 'administrative' aspects, namely what note, when to be issued, what detail depicted etc. At a later stage, when we are set to go, we will, of course, want to flood the media with the right information. In the meantime, naturally, we do not want creative competitors pre-empting us.

He assured Solomon that 'this will not cause any problem in the traffic between CSIRO and the Bank – it is certainly not intended to do so.' Addison wasn't as conciliatory. In a phone conversation with Solomon on 6 May he questioned whether it was possible for the Bank to work with CSIRO at all and pointed out that no commercial entity would have been guilty of the disclosures in the *Canberra Times* article. Solomon defended CSIRO, making the point that CSIRO and the Bank had worked together for 20 years without any breach of security and there was no proof that the leak had come from CSIRO.

The Bank itself recorded in its 1986/87 report that:[52]

> The Bank plans to issue a special commemorative note in 1988. It is possible that this note will be printed on a polymer-based substrate developed in Australia jointly by the CSIRO and the Bank, and will incorporate several technological advances in note printing, designed to enhance the security of the currency. A series of notes based on the new technology is also under consideration.

The Bank invited Solomon and the CSIRO Chairman, Boardman, to the announcement on 21 August 1987 that it was going to release the commemorative banknote on 26 January 1988. As the Governor had promised in his 4 May letter to Solomon, there was a press function in Sydney on 15 December 1987 where technical details of the new banknotes were released.

Chadderton, by then a Visiting Fellow, Research School of Physical Sciences, Australian National University, took the opportunity of the release to comment on the origin of the technology embodied in the new banknotes. In a letter to the *Canberra Times* published on 18 December 1987, he said that 'It would be churlish to try to apportion success in effort to either the CSIRO or the Reserve Bank' – then proceeded to be churlish by claiming that 'a brilliant young theoretical physicist – Dr Robert A Lee – working in the conducive fundamental research atmosphere of CSIRO's Division of Chemical Physics (now sadly demised) was virtually entirely responsible for inventing, developing and applying the optically variable device technology.'[53] He 'noted that this highly relevant and applied device came directly from the much-despised "'curiosity-motivated research"'.

Lee responded in a letter published in the *Canberra Times* on 24 December 1987, saying that the claim that he was 'virtually entirely responsible' was 'totally false'.[54] He gave credit to Hamann, Quint, Wilson and Solomon from CSIRO and to the development work of the Note Printing Branch led by Addison. He also commented on the motivation behind the work, saying that his work 'formed a very small part of the whole project, which was initiated by the Reserve Bank of Australia and is a successful example of "market-led research", not "curiosity-motivated research" as suggested by your correspondent'.

The $10 commemorative banknote was a handsome banknote and was well received by the public.

Souvenir notes for CSIRO staff

The Bank readily agreed with Solomon's request for a specimen commemorative banknote to be given to each CSIRO staff member who had contributed to the project. All the notes had the same serial number – AA 00 000 000 – but a unique specimen number. They were not legal tender and are now collectors' items. Plate 15 shows both sides of these notes. Those who received the notes are listed in the order of specimen numbers: D.H. Solomon, M. Girolamo, S.D. Hamann, D.G. Hawthorne, J.H. Hodgkin, L. Julius, R.A. Lee, M. Linton, J. Loder, B.C. Loft, A.W.-H. Mau, G.L. Quint, J.B. Ross (widow of), W.H.F. Sasse, M. Seuret, E.G. Bowen, T.H. Spurling, J.D. Swift, R. Brett, A. Chapman, A. Desira, R. Eibl, I. Marwick, G. Rolstone, I.C. Thomas, J. Wardrop, B. Williams, J.A. Allen, K. Boardman, V.D. Burgmann, P.A. Grant, J.R. Price, J.P. Wild, H.W. Worner, N. Wran and W.I. Whitton.

Endnotes

1 RBA press release.
2 NAA: B5609, 5/20.
3 *Committee of Inquiry into the Australian Financial System*. Australian Government Publishing Service, Canberra, 1981.
4 <http://www.quadrant.org.au/magazine/issue/2012/4/the-mysteries-of-the-floating-dollar>.
5 NAA: B5609, 5/13.
6 NAA: B5609, 5/13.
7 NAA: B5609, 3/24.
8 T.H. Spurling, Notes on meeting with R.A. Johnston, Union Club, Sydney, 13 June 2009.
9 NAA: B5609, 8/292.
10 NAA: B5609, 6/31.
11 Details summarised from an excerpt from a Bank staff bulletin issued in October 1983 and in the possession of the authors.
12 NAA: B5609, 3/25.
13 The July 1984 review document is not in the Australian Archive collection but is in the possession of the authors.

14 NAA: B5609, 6/15.
15 The August 1985 review document is not in the Australian Archive collection but is in the possession of the authors.
16 NAA: B5609, 3/9.
17 NAA: B5609, 1/13.
18 NAA: B5609, 1/15.
19 R.A. Lee (1983) *Optic Acta* **30**, paper 1, p. 267, paper 2, p. 291, paper 3, p. 431, paper 4, p. 441 and paper 5, p. 449.
20 NAA: B5609, 8/304.
21 NAA, B5609, 6/13.
22 NAA: B5609, 8/304.
23 NAA: B5609, 6/32.
24 <http://www.eoas.info/biogs/P004063b.htm>.
25 NAA: B5609, 6/32.
26 T.H. Spurling, Notes on meeting with R.A. Johnston, Union Club, Sydney, 13 June 2009.
27 NAA: B5609, 6/32.
28 NAA: B5609, 8/320.
29 NAA: B5609, 6/13.
30 NAA: B5609, 6/13.
31 NAA: B5609, 3/5.
32 NAA: B5609, 3/5.
33 NAA: B5609, 11/5.
34 NAA: B5609, 3/5.
35 NAA: B5609, 3/5.
36 NAA: B5609, 6/13.
37 NAA: B5609, 6/13.
38 NAA: B5609, 6/28.
39 NAA: B5609, 6/28.
40 NAA: B5609, 6/28.
41 NAA: B5609, 6/32.
42 *The Clarion*, 10 June 1980, p. 5.
43 *The Sun*, 13 June 1980, p. 6.
44 *Sunday Press*,15 June 1980, p. 3.
45 *The Age*, 14 September 1983, p. 1.
46 *Canberra Times*, 25 August 1984, p. 30.
47 *The Australian*, 23 December 1985.
48 RBA Annual Report 1985/86, p. 41.
49 *Sydney Morning Herald*, 14 March 1987, p. 1.
50 *Canberra Times*, 25 April 1987, p. 1.
51 NAA: B5609, 6/32.
52 RBA Annual Report 1986/87, p. 42.
53 *Canberra Times*, 18 December 1987, p. 2.
54 *Canberra Times*, 24 December 1987, p. 2.

Chapter 13
The legacy

Despite the robust argument and debate during the course of the project, or possibly because of it, the Bank project was a great success. Australia has a more secure and durable currency, a thriving export industry has been established, and CSIRO has greatly improved its processes for commercialising its intellectual property.

A more secure and durable currency

In its Annual Report the Bank provides the public with a great deal of information about the state of Australian currency.

In 2011/12, only 7781 counterfeits were detected compared to the estimated 20 000 high-quality banknotes and a possible 60 000 lower-quality banknotes produced by the 1967 forgers.[1] As shown in Fig. 13.1 this equates to 6.9 counterfeits detected per million genuine banknotes, which the Bank comments is low by international standards. There are occasional spikes in the detection level, as in 2010/11, but is usually around 6 ppm. The $50 is the most counterfeited denomination, usually accounting for more than 90% of the counterfeits detected. The Bank reported

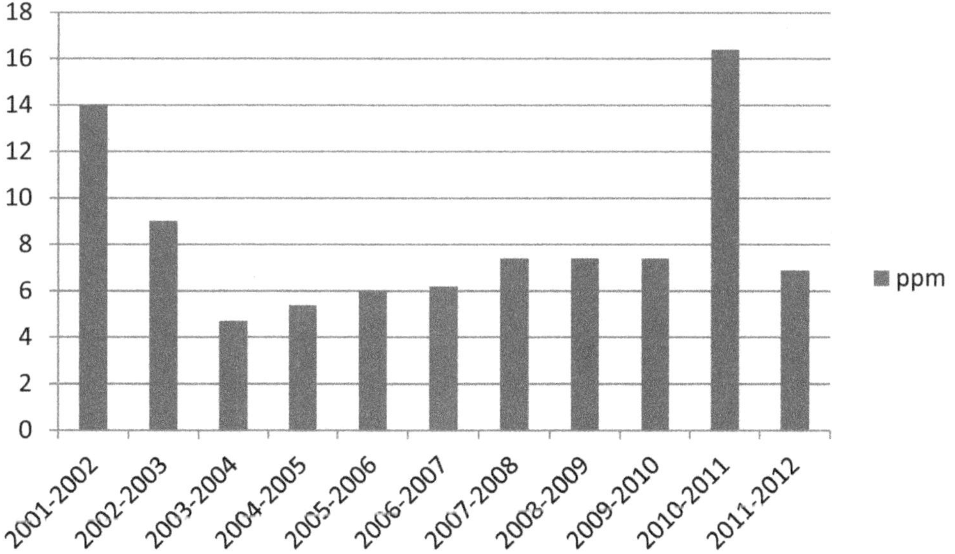

Fig. 13.1: Australian counterfeits detected.[2]

Table 13.1: Australian banknotes on issue and purchased 2011/12[3]

	Number in circulation	Number purchased	
Denomination	Million banknotes		%
$5	147.4	29	19.7
$10	105.9	29	27.4
$20	149	0	0
$50	513.3	40	7.8
$100	231.56	31	13.3
Total	1147.2	129	11.2

in 2008/09 that 'there is no evidence of "professional" counterfeiting in Australia, with most counterfeits being printed on paper and only a crude attempt made to simulate the clear window and its printed image. These counterfeits are easily detected by visual inspection and feel.'

Australian currency is very durable. Table 13.1 shows that the Bank purchased ~11% of the total number of banknotes in circulation in 2011/12. The number of banknotes in circulation in Australia increases by nearly 6% a year so the number being replaced averages ~5% a year. The first two digits on the number on Australian banknotes refer to the year that it was printed. Readers with access to Australian currency will find that most banknotes in their wallets were printed more than five years ago.

A thriving export industry

As at March 2012, 34 countries had adopted the polymer substrate technology. One path to adoption, which Australia used, is to issue a commemorative banknote and then issue banknotes in general circulation. 19 countries have issued commemorative banknotes; 12 went on to issue banknotes for general circulation. 15 countries have issued banknotes for general circulation without first issuing a commemorative banknote, making a total of 27 countries with plastic banknotes in general circulation.

Of the countries that have adopted plastic banknotes, six are members of the Group of 20 major economies. These are Australia, Brazil (commemorative only), Canada, China (commemorative only), Indonesia and Mexico. Only Canada is a member of the Group of Eight major economies. On 18 December 2013 the Bank of England announced that it would be converting to polymer banknotes, commencing with the release of a £5 banknote in 2016.

Securency has established a plant in Mexico and seven of the other adopting countries are in Central or South America. These countries are Costa Rica, Chile, Dominican Republic, Guatemala, Honduras, Nicaragua and Paraguay.

Countries in Asia and the South Pacific account for 14 of the other adopting countries. These countries are Bangladesh, Brunei, Hong Kong (commemorative only), Malaysia, Nepal, New Zealand, Papua New Guinea, Singapore, Solomon Islands, Sri Lanka (commemorative only), Taiwan (commemorative only), Thailand, Vanuatu, Vietnam and Western Samoa.

Of the other five countries, two are in Europe, i.e. Northern Ireland (commemorative only) and Romania, two in Africa, i.e. Nigeria and Zambia, and the last is Kuwait (commemorative only) in the Middle East.

But paper banknote suppliers won't give up easily

Many countries with a long tradition of producing paper banknotes stayed with their tradition despite the plastic banknote offering longer life and greater security. This is not surprising, given the conservative nature of central banks and the dominance of a few companies in the industry. For example, in the US, Crane & Co. in Dalton, Massachusetts has been producing cotton paper for banknotes since 1801 and won a contract to supply the US Bureau of Engraving and Printing in 1879. It is still the major supplier of paper for US banknotes.

In the face of competition from plastic banknotes, the traditional suppliers did not stand still. The largest commercial printer of banknotes is De La Rue plc, which was founded in 1830 as Thomas de la Rue, to print playing cards. In 1855 it began printing British postage stamps and in 1860 printed banknotes for Mauritius, an island nation in the Indian Ocean. The UK took over the island from the French in 1810 during the Napoleonic wars and it gained independence in 1968. Its official currency between 1820 and 1877 was the Mauritian dollar and it was this currency with which de la Rue commenced its long history of banknote printing. In the late 19th century the company became internationally prominent in printing postage stamps and banknotes.

The company's fortunes ebbed and flowed in the 20th century. It went public in 1921 and was nearly ruined due to its failure to invest in new technologies and processes. It revived in the 1930s mainly due to its entry into the Chinese market. It had a factory in the Shanghai French Concession and a back-up factory in Rangoon, Burma. It moved its operations to Rangoon after the defeat of France and then to Bombay after the Japanese invaded Burma. The De La Rue factory in London was destroyed in the World War II Blitz but it was able to fulfil all its commitments by adopting offset lithography.

After World War II the company embarked on a series of mergers, acquisitions and demergers to emerge in the 21st century as the world's largest commercial banknote printer and banknote paper manufacturer. It acquired a rival printing firm, Waterlow & Sons, in 1961 and formed a joint venture with Organisation Giori in 1965. That company had been formed in 1952 by Gualtiero Giori with the aim of supplying printing equipment to central banks to enable every country to produce its own banknotes. The company's speciality was the production of multicolour intaglio printing presses. The joint venture with De La Rue ended in 2001, when Giori was acquired by the German printing machine manufacturer Koenig and Bauer, with which it had had a cooperation agreement since 1952. De La Rue acquired the banknote paper manufacturer, the Portals Group in 1995, and the Bank of England's printing works in 2003. It is a leader in payment systems producing cash handling equipment, cash dispensing systems, sorting machines and cash processing software systems. It can therefore offer its customers complete systems.

One of De La Rue's competitors is the German private company Giesecke and Devrient GmbH, located in Munich. This company was founded in 1852, specialising in high-quality printing of currency and security documents. It supplied currency during the period of hyperinflation in Germany in the 1920s. Like De La Rue, in the 21st century it still produces banknotes and security printing, but also supplies complete security systems to governments, banks and transit authorities. Of particular interest is its subsidiary, Louisenthal, a manufacturer of banknote paper, security paper and security features. In 2009 Louisenthal released a new banknote substrate, Hybrid, remarkably similar to the CNRD Strand 75. It has a paper core enclosed with a thin polymer film. The company brochure claims that 'the core is as secure as any paper banknote, and the outer layers make the banknote as strong as a polymer film'. Note that the Louisenthal product has all the disadvantages of Strand 75 – no clear area without punching a hole in the inner paper inner core and a multistep production process.

The final business model

The business model that was finally adopted to commercialise the technology is slightly different from the arrangements for paper notes but exactly as proposed by CSIRO early in the project. Innovia Films (Asia Pacific) Pty Ltd produces the biaxially oriented polypropylene film at a purpose-built plant in Craigieburn. That film is supplied to Securency International Pty Ltd, a joint venture between the Reserve Bank of Australia and Innovia Films, which applies its unique coatings and security features. Securency then sells its product to Note Printing Australia and to overseas-based banknote printers who produce the final printed product. Securency International and Banco de México entered a joint venture agreement in 2007 to establish a polymer security substrate manufacturing plant in Querétaro, Mexico. The joint venture is known as Securency México, and services the region. In November 2010, the Bank and Innovia Films announced their intention to undertake a joint sale of Securency. Innovia Films acquired the Bank's 50% share of Securency in February 2013 and the company now trades as Innovia Security.

It should be noted that in July and August 2011, charges were laid against Note Printing Australia and Securency alleging that between 1999 and 2005 the two companies and several individuals had engaged in a conspiracy to bribe public officials in Indonesia, Malaysia and Vietnam. Both Innovia Films and the Bank have taken steps to tighten controls and strengthen governance arrangements. Certain of these matters are still being considered by the courts and will not be discussed further here.

CSIRO, the Bank project and the Australian innovation system

In 1968 when the Governor called his meeting of the top scientists in Australia, the majority were from CSIRO. When the banknotes were released in 1988, an equivalent meeting would have had a much higher proportion from the expanding university research sector. In 1968, CSIRO's main concern was to retain its right to publish the scientific results from the project. It had no concern for the commercial potential of the work and was prepared to leave that entirely to the Bank. While this project is correctly described as a market-pull project, it is also true that within CSIRO in the early days there was a certain amount of 'science push' at work.

By the decision in 1974 to move to pilot production, the view within CSIRO was quite different. Dr Solomon was now in control and he had developed a vision for the project which included the development of an export-oriented banknote production and security document industry in Australia. This vision was enthusiastically supported by the team at Fishermens Bend but was not necessarily the vision of the CSIRO Executive or the Bank.

The 1980 agreement between CSIRO and the Bank showed that both organisations had gone some but not all the way towards adopting Solomon's vision. The Bank was given free use of the CNRD technology for the production of Australian currency banknotes but would have to share with CSIRO any benefits from use of the technology for production of non-Australian currency banknotes. CSIRO would have the right to negotiate with non-currency users and share any benefits with the Bank. When negotiating that agreement, the two organisations had not yet thought about how they were going to involve the supply chain of companies that would be needed to actually print banknotes both for Australia and for overseas banknote issuing authorities.

Within CSIRO, the agreement was well known to Solomon and his staff at the Division of Applied Organic Chemistry and to the Commercial Group in Canberra. It is not clear how well it was known outside that group. For example, in 1984 Dr Bob Lee had arranged to visit Europe to discuss his Catpix technology with various banks and credit card companies, a clear breach of Clauses 2(a), 2(c), 3(a) and 3(b) of the agreement. No one outside his then Division of Chemical Physics would have known about this if Dr Chadderton had not written to Mr Addison asking for some financial assistance for Lee's travels (see Ch. 11).

By 1987, CSIRO had considerably more interest and experience in commercial dealings. It had a more commercially oriented Board established by the 1986 changes to the *Science and Industry Research Act* and had some years' experience in commercialising research through Sirotech. It also had a budget requirement to raise some of its revenue from external sources. So selling the technology to the Bank was an attractive proposition.

In 1968, when the Governor of the Bank had been surprised by how easily and well his new banknotes had been forged, he had called a meeting of some leading scientists to think about technologies to thwart forgers. It is clear that he had no plan of how those ideas would be followed up or developed. The Bank quickly accepted the idea that if it funded any research, CSIRO could publish it and the Bank would have free use of any results in the production of banknotes. The Bank had no scientific research capacity of its own but had an efficient banknote production plant.

When presented with a complete proof of concept in 1974, the Bank did not know what to do. It still had no full-time research capability and still thought that it could purchase a turnkey operation from a research organisation. It did not have an immediate problem with forgeries but was reluctant to drop the project in case a problem emerged in the future. So it went ahead with the project but did not employ any permanent staff and did not build up any internal research capability. It actively discouraged CSIRO from discussing the project with supplier companies and therefore did nothing to build up a supply chain in Australia. This approach was formalised in the 1980 agreement. Despite the Fink report and the advice of consultants, the Bank maintained the group in Melbourne as a production facility.

Governor Johnston was the first to change the approach of the Bank. He started to build up a research capability at Craigieburn with the appointment of Dr Bruce Hardwick and commenced the transformation of the Note Production Branch by appointing a non-banker, Don Addison, as its General Manager. With these developments it made no sense to have CSIRO and the Bank still jointly developing and marketing the technology. The 1987 agreement was the only option for the Bank. But it still saw itself as having bought a completed technology rather than having commenced the long journey of developing a completely new way of producing banknotes.

After the success of the 1988 commemorative banknote, the Bank had to decide whether to convert the whole series to plastic. It decided to do so but soon found that it needed to build up the supply chain to ensure continuity of material. This led to the decision by the Belgian chemical company, UCB, to establish a polypropylene plant in Craigieburn and the decision by the Bank and UCB to establish the joint venture, Securency, to manufacture and market the substrate. This all took some time and it was not until 1993 that the $5 polymer banknote was introduced. Solomon's vision was achieved at last.

Endnotes

1 Reserve Bank of Australia Annual Report, 2011/12.
2 Reserve Bank of Australia Annual Report, 2011/12.
3 Reserve Bank of Australia Annual Report, 2011/12.

Index

Figures in **bold** refer to illustrations

www.ingramcontent.com/pod-product-compliance
Lightning Source LLC
LaVergne TN
LVHW052351100826
845147LV00013B/814

* 9 7 8 0 6 4 3 0 9 4 2 7 7 *